NEW YORK REVIEW BOOKS

POETS

ARTHUR RIMBAUD (1854–1891) was born and educated in Charleville, in the Ardennes region of northeastern France. When he was sixteen, he wrote an ambitious letter to Paul Verlaine, who so admired the younger man's poems that he bought him a one-way ticket to Paris. The pair soon began a tumultuous affair, which ended two years later, in July 1873, with Verlaine shooting Rimbaud in a Brussels hotel room. Soon after this, Rimbaud finished *A Season in Hell* while visiting his family's farm near Charleville; the next year, in London, he composed many of the prose poems included in *Illuminations*, the last work he completed before abandoning literature at the age of twenty. In his final decade, he struggled to find success as a trader and gunrunner in Africa. Rimbaud died of cancer at thirty-seven, having seen almost none of his writing in print.

MARK POLIZZOTTI has translated more than fifty books from the French, including works by Gustave Flaubert, Patrick Modiano, Marguerite Duras, André Breton, and Raymond Roussel. He is the recipient of numerous prizes and the author of eleven books, including *Revolution of the Mind: The Life of André Breton*, *Highway 61 Revisited*, and *Sympathy for the Traitor: A Translation Manifesto*. His essays and reviews have appeared in *The New York Times*, *The New Republic*, *The Wall Street Journal*, *ARTnews*, *The Nation*, *Parnassus*, *Bookforum*, and elsewhere. He lives in New York.

Arthur Rimbaud

The Drunken Boat
Selected Writings

EDITED, TRANSLATED, AND WITH
AN INTRODUCTION AND NOTES
BY MARK POLIZZOTTI

NYRB/POETS

 NEW YORK REVIEW BOOKS *New York*

THIS IS A NEW YORK REVIEW BOOK
PUBLISHED BY THE NEW YORK REVIEW OF BOOKS
435 Hudson Street, New York, NY 10014
www.nyrb.com

Portions of the introduction previously appeared, in substantially different
form, in *The New Republic*.

Library of Congress Cataloging-in-Publication Data
Names: Rimbaud, Arthur, 1854–1891, author. | Polizzotti, Mark, translator,
    editor. | Rimbaud, Arthur, 1854–1891. Œuvres complètes. Selections.
    English. | Rimbaud, Arthur, 1854–1891. Illuminations. Selections. English.
    | Rimbaud, Arthur, 1854–1891. Saison en enfer. English. | Rimbaud,
    Arthur, 1854–1891. Correspondence. Selections. English.
Title: The drunken boat: selected writings / by Arthur Rimbaud; edited,
    translated, and with an introduction and notes by Mark Polizzotti.
Description: New York: New York Review Books, [2022] | Series: New York
    Review Books poets | Identifiers: LCCN 2021050600 (print) |
    LCCN 2021050601 (ebook) | ISBN 9781681376509 (paperback) |
    ISBN 9781681376516 (ebook)
Subjects: LCSH: Rimbaud, Arthur, 1854–1891—Translations into English. |
    LCGFT: Poetry. | Personal correspondence.
Classification: LCC PQ2387.R5 D7813 2022 (print) | LCC PQ2387.R5 (ebook)
    | DDC 841/.8—dc23
LC record available at https://lccn.loc.gov/2021050600
LC ebook record available at https://lccn.loc.gov/2021050601

ISBN 978-1-68137-650-9
Available as an electronic book; ISBN 978-1-68137-651-6

Cover and book design by Emily Singer

Printed in the United States of America on acid-free paper.
10 9 8 7 6 5 4 3 2 1

Contents

SELECTED LETTERS, 1870–1875

Heart of a Clown and Soles of Wind

RIMBAUD'S LIFE AND POETRY have become so freighted with legend that it's difficult to take them on their own terms. There's the precocious child rebel, eluding the confines of school for the adventurous highway. There's the young messiah (or "Satan in the midst of the doctors," as one observer put it), shaking up the stultified world of Parisian letters, then saying goodbye to all that with a one-finger salute. There's the poster child for the "drug culture," whose experiments with hashish as a creative spur prefigure those of the Beats, the sixties generation, and countless musicians. There's the avatar of nonbinary sexuality and gender fluidity, practicing his own dictum that "love has to be reinvented." And finally, there's the ascetic in the desert, purging himself in the unforgiving climate and rigors of the African marketplace. While such legends have helped perpetuate Rimbaud's fame and nurtured our lasting fascination with him, the image they send back is seldom without distortions and often beside the point.

Once we clear away the bracken, however, we find compelling reasons for appreciating Rimbaud's works and days in and of themselves. A century and a half later, his writings remain thrillingly fresh, whether the dynamic early sonnets, the tortuously self-reflective *A Season in Hell*, the mathematically rigorous *Illuminations*, or even his cheeky letters to friends and mentors. The freewheeling liberties Rimbaud took with language, his startling imagery and frequent borrowings from the writings of others—what today would be called "sampling"—make him a precursor of surrealism, the Beats, and hip-hop, while his use of sonority as a textual generator (in poems such as "Memory" or "Metropolitan") prefigure Dada sound poems. His interest in scientific principles as a basis for literature foreshadows the work of Oulipo writers like Raymond Queneau, Georges Perec, and Harry Mathews. His experiments with verse that eliminated rhyme and meter, and the irreverent spirit that drove these explorations, would become hallmarks of the century to come.

"Before Rimbaud," said Paul Valéry, "all literature was written in the language of common sense." Other poets, like Paul Verlaine and Charles Baudelaire, were opening the door to new forms and subjects for poetry, but Rimbaud kicked out the jambs. He was perhaps the first to intuit that poetry didn't need to be coherent in the traditional acceptance of the term, that images and rhythms could be their own justification, that poetry could be less about *sense* than *sensation*. But while the meaning of Rimbaud's poems can be hermetic, this doesn't mean they have none. Though famous for his "disordering of *all the senses*," Rimbaud shows great control in his work, whether in the strict adherence to formal rules in his early poems or in the seemingly looser but no less regulated prose of *Illuminations*. Much of his writing, like his life, revolves around the conflict between cold-eyed rationality and the seductions of folly, both thematically and in their tightrope walk between scrupulous metrics and exhilarating freedom.

One reason for the perceived obscurity of Rimbaud's poems is that they are so intimately intertwined with his biography; and while that claim can be made for many writers, the difference is that Rimbaud frequently derives phrasings and imagery from personal associations for which he doesn't bother to provide the key. The critic and ethnographer Victor Segalen, in an otherwise sympathetic study (*Le Double Rimbaud*, 1906), threw up his hands and confessed that many of Rimbaud's poems remained "inert" for him because they offered no foothold for his own memories and interpretations. And yet the genius of these poems, as with *some* surrealist poetry, *some* New York School poetry, is that even from the depths of their obscurity they speak to the reader, they resonate. My experience in preparing these translations (with the benefit of a century of research at my disposal) was that the deeper I ventured into the life and mind that engendered them, the less opaque they became and the more they pulled me in. The following synopsis and the notes at the end of this book, then, are meant to provide a backdrop against which the poetry can be better appreciated.

The "fabulous opera" of Jean-Nicolas-Arthur Rimbaud's life began on October 20, 1854, in the town of Charleville in the Ardennes, not far from the Belgian border. He was the second son of Frédéric Rimbaud, a career army officer, and Vitalie

Cuif, a farmer's daughter; his older brother, also named Frédéric, was born the previous year. By the time Arthur was six, his father had visited the family just often enough to sire three more children (all daughters, one of whom died in infancy) before disappearing with his regiment for good. From that point on, Vitalie Rimbaud—"proud, strict, rigid, with fierce if limited ambitions for her children," as the biographer Charles Nicholl writes—became Arthur's central authority figure and primary antagonist, the woman whom generations of Rimbaud scholars have loved to hate. Rimbaud himself disparaged her as "La Mother" and, copping from Victor Hugo, the "Mouth of Darkness." Henry Miller, with a fair dose of autobiographical bile, vilified her as "this witch, this harridan from whose loins he sprang... the very incarnation of stupidity, bigotry, pride, and stubbornness." Others have taken a more nuanced view, sympathizing with Vitalie as a single parent struggling to make ends meet, but none has entirely pardoned her.

In his childhood—a period acerbically memorialized in the poem "Seven-Year-Old Poets"—Rimbaud made his mother duly proud by winning all the school prizes, having his early verses printed in the local paper, and slicking his hair down for his first Communion (though his facial expression in the commemorative photograph foretells the bumpy ride ahead). Then came the season of adolescent rebellion, with which the post-surrealist, post-Beat, post-punk world is well acquainted, and which Rimbaud, who foreshadowed all of these, elevated to a fine art.

At age fifteen, he ran away from home for the first time, to Paris, but was detained on arrival for having insufficient train fare. He spent a week in jail, then went to stay in Belgium with his former teacher Georges Izambard, one of several older-brother/father/mentor figures who would punctuate the poet's life.* Barely a week after returning home he left again, this time on foot for Charleroi and Brussels, arriving dusty, disheveled, and unannounced on people's doorsteps, composing pages of sonnets as he went (a number of these early pieces, such as "At the Green Tavern," "Cunning," and "My Bohemia," chart his peregrinations practically in real time). Then again, and again, to a Paris in the throes of revolt, *perhaps* taking part in the Paris Commune of 1871, *perhaps* being gang-raped in a barracks. A poem from this time, which has often been read as evidence of the rape ("Tortured Heart," also known as "Heart of a Clown" or "Stolen Heart"), marks a turning point from the giddy freedom of the road songs to harsher, more doleful, more aggressive tonalities, illustrated by works like "Paris Repopulates" and "Jeanne-Marie's Hands."

During this period, Rimbaud also formulated the ars poetica that constitutes a fundamental part of his legacy, expressed in two letters from May 1871 known as the "Seer letters." These missives contain (with variants) the famous watchwords "I is an Other" and "The Poet makes himself a *seer* by a long, massive, and reasoned *disordering* of *all the senses*," and for 150 years they have been the road map of record for the aspirant visionary, a Baedeker of the mind that has inspired a seemingly infinite number of readings and misreadings.

---

*See the notes at the end of this volume for more details about individuals and events, as well as about specific publications.

By far the most titillating part of the Rimbaud legend centers on his two-year relationship with fellow poet Paul Verlaine, an intense, soul-draining interlude in which the protagonists were cast variously as Frankenstein and his monster, old letch and young prey, or, as Rimbaud sardonically styled it, the "Infernal Bridegroom" and the "Foolish Virgin." Though the age difference between them was only ten years, Verlaine's balding pate and pinched expression made it seem greater. As did their difference in literary standing, for by the time Rimbaud appeared at the other man's door in September 1871, Verlaine was well published and well connected, not to mention one of the few living poets to have earned Rimbaud's genuine respect—the ultimate brother/father.

Verlaine had earlier dabbled in same-sex experiences, but by now had settled into the life of a civil servant and poet on the rise. He was recently married, expecting his first child, and living with his uptight in-laws in their rigidly bourgeois Montmartre residence. It was into this setting that Rimbaud erupted that fall, stinky and lice-ridden and bearing as his calling card the manuscript of his verse masterpiece "The Drunken Boat." To the horror of both Mathilde Verlaine (barely more than a child herself) and her mother, Paul immediately began spending all his time with his new protégé, getting drunk in the local absinthe joints, introducing "Rimb" to his literary acquaintances, indulging in the Bohemian bad habits he'd so reluctantly left behind.

The protégé himself, a gangly bumpkin with ill-fitting clothes, hands "large and red and covered with chilblains" (said Edmund White), and penetrating blue eyes the color of "forget-me-nots and periwinkles," soon found that these city poets were easy to impress or to outrage; that simply by being his obnoxious, brilliant self he could outshine them all. The list of pranks is long: He openly maligned his elders and shouted out obscenities at their readings; he stole from his various hosts, stabbed one with a sword stick, masturbated into another's glass of milk behind his back. And yet throughout all of this he was tolerated, even grudgingly admired. "We are witnessing here the birth of a genius," one observer noted at the time. Barely seventeen, he was now fully the "Rimbaud" who defines our image of him, though this image actually applies to no more than three or four years of his life.

By the summer of 1872, off-color comedy had darkened into melodrama. Verlaine, having grown violently abusive at home, left Mathilde and his newborn son to follow his "great and radiant sin" to Brussels. Pursued by his wife and mother-in-law, he agreed to return to the conjugal fold, then at the last moment escaped again with Rimbaud, this time to London. There the two men lived on the cheap, exiles among other exiles who had fled France after the fall of the Paris Commune. Verlaine, guilt-ridden over abandoning his family, made and retracted several overtures of reconciliation with Mathilde. Rimbaud, annoyed, decamped in the spring of 1873 to his mother's farm in the village of Roche, where he began writing the hallucinatory autobiographical confession *A Season in Hell*.

Then from drama to burlesque: By midyear, both men were back in London, but at each other's throats. "My pitiful brother! How many awful nights he caused me!" Rimbaud wrote in the prose poem "Vagabonds." Verlaine huffed off to Belgium alone, then sent Rimbaud histrionic letters full of suicide threats. Rimbaud replied in calmer tones, urging reconciliation—"Only with me can you be free...The only true words are: come back, I want to be with you, I love you"—though his arguments suggest less genuine desire than a dread of abandonment, and no doubt of penury. Joining his lover in Brussels, where the latter had taken a hotel room with his mother, Rimbaud immediately resolved to leave again for Paris. Verlaine, drunk and desperate, bought a revolver, shot Rimbaud in the wrist, and was arrested. Though his victim declined to press charges, Verlaine was sentenced to two years of hard labor, during which time he found religion—much to the disgust of Rimbaud, who henceforth disparaged him as "Loyola."

Once recovered from his wound, Rimbaud returned to Roche and finished *A Season in Hell*, some of which satirizes his time with Verlaine. (Though this is less often noted, it also gives voice, however ambiguously, to Rimbaud's advocacy of feminism, inspired by social philosophers such as Flora Tristan and Jules Michelet, and perhaps even more so by the example of women who had fought as equals in the Paris Commune.) Privately printed, possibly with his mother's money, *A Season in Hell* was his only book to be published through his own efforts, and he set his hopes for it high. "My fate depends on this book," he told a friend. But when the volume came off the press that fall, Rimbaud found that the Parisian contacts to whom he sent it were less than welcoming: blaming him for Verlaine's misfortunes and still smarting from his insolent behavior, they shunned both *A Season in*

Hell and its author. Discouraged, Rimbaud returned to England in early 1874 with the young poet Germain Nouveau. During this period, he wrote many of the prose poems that make up *Illuminations*, envisioning himself "standing in the peppery plains," living in "a sumptuous dwelling surrounded by all the Orient."

If there is one book on which Rimbaud's current renown rests, it is *Illuminations*. Edmund White has noted that while *A Season in Hell* is "retrospective, post-Christian, and autobiographical," *Illuminations* is "often glacial, futuristic, and impersonal." The critic Félix Fénéon, who helped assemble the first publication, called it a work that "stands outside all literature and is probably superior to all." It contains the most forward-looking and disruptive (in the current sense) texts of Rimbaud's entire oeuvre, and it is hard to imagine much of the poetry that has defined our age had it not been for what amounts to a series of loose pages, which Rimbaud himself never organized into a volume. Moreover, while *A Season in Hell* is often described as Rimbaud's "farewell to literature," it is actually *Illuminations*—the composition of which continued for several years after *Season*—that stands as the culmination and summit of Rimbaud's literary career, in both chronology and achievement.

The five years following Rimbaud's return from England in late 1874 were a time of transition, when the already rootless poet gave way to, in Verlaine's wistful phrase, "the man with soles of wind." Between 1875 and 1880, his wanderings took him to Germany, Italy, and various parts of France; to Stockholm (where he reportedly worked for a circus) and Java as a mercenary in the Dutch army (from which he deserted after three months); as well as through a smorgasbord of occupations that included pianist (for which he had no talent) and scientist. Even Rimbaud's appearance changed, as his friend Ernest Delahaye related: "His cheeks, once so round, were now hollowed, quarried, hardened... His voice had lost the shrill and rather childish timbre which I had hitherto known, and had become grave, deep, and suffused with energy." Only the piercing blue eyes gave away his former identity. And along with the "fresh, rosy, English child's complexion" apparently vanished all desire to write: What is generally considered his last known poem, an offhand ditty about cheese and farting, was inserted into a letter of 1875; after that, when the subject came up, Rimbaud dismissively replied that he "didn't think about" literature anymore.

By the fall of 1880, having spent several months working in a quarry in Cyprus, Rimbaud was in Aden (in what is now Yemen), where he found work as a business agent for the Bardey exporting company, and was soon transferred across the Red Sea straits to Harar, in Abyssinia (now Ethiopia). Apart from a geographic report on one of his explorations—published in 1884 by the French Geological Society to professional acclaim—practically his only writings from these years are copious and detailed letters to his family in France, letters that have become as famous for their arid sobriety as his poetry was for its daredevil inventiveness. Still, behind the lengthy reports of money saved and money earned, one can yet see the love-starved child who perhaps left others behind out of fear that they might leave him. "What is happening at home? Would you prefer I come back?" he had written from Cyprus. And later: "Give me news of everything at home...Don't forget me."

As it happened, Rimbaud's abandonment of poetry marked not the end of his literary career but the beginning, for back home the gears of renown were clicking into place. Not long after he arrived in Africa, his early verses started appearing in French literary periodicals and gaining a small but dedicated following, though many believed their author had died. In 1884, Verlaine included a selection of Rimbaud's poems in a volume called *Les Poètes maudits*, for which he provided a biographical sketch, and he helped bring about the first publication of *Illuminations* in 1886. Rimbaud, who occasionally caught wind of these publications from French business contacts passing through Africa, and who once had put so much energy into obtaining such notice, now reacted with annoyance and embarrassment, and changed the subject.

Rimbaud's ten years in Africa are the last great element of his myth, powered by the fact that his frightening precociousness ended not, like a Mozart or a Keats, because death interrupted him at the height of his powers but because he willingly dismissed his literary talents to become an anonymous trader in a far-flung colony—to become "an Other." André Breton, who wasn't alone in this, later remarked that this period, which saw Rimbaud "turning his back on his life's work," accounted for "a large share of [the surrealists'] passionate interest in him." Scholars have long debated whether Rimbaud's swapping of his writer's notebook for a merchant's ledger constitutes an about-face or a continuation of the same quest by other means. Some, following the grand academic tradition in which literature is literature and all the rest is secondary, see the "African" half of Rimbaud's life as a tragic, unimportant, or mystifying coda, an incomprehensible rejection, not to mention a stupendous waste, of his gift.

But this begs the question of why the rupture should shock us in the first place. Rimbaud's lightning streak through written poetry is proof above all that the "man with soles of wind" couldn't sit still for long, whether in "sampling" poets he admired, striking out into his own violently disruptive verse, retooling the memoir genre, or virtually inventing the prose poem (and poetic language) as we know it today: having done all that, it was time to move on. One of Rimbaud's most important lessons, though not always heeded by even his most devoted readers, is that we should not fetishize the "writer's hand," that poetry is a trade like any other. It's also possible that Rimbaud stopped writing poetry not because he turned his back on it but because it turned its back on him. Perhaps, after the brief, brilliant gush of compositions from 1870 to 1875, the geyser simply ran dry.

It also bears remembering that at the time Rimbaud stopped writing, he looked upon his poetry as a resounding failure. His frenzied attempts to make himself a visionary had led to disorder without the expected enlightenment, and his hard work had produced nothing but poems that remained unpublished and a memoir that no one wanted. For all his rebelliousness, Arthur was still Vitalie's son, and even his early letters contain many references to the necessity of making a living, preferably with minimal effort. By 1875, the yield of his previous half decade must have suggested it was time to look to other outlets. In this light, the fact that he settled on a profession that finally brought him an appreciable measure of respect and profit (the complaints in his letters notwithstanding) is not so mystifying.

Having shed his literary persona, it's as if Rimbaud was now intent on escaping his European identity as well. He frequently dressed in Muslim fashion and adopted numerous local habits (apparently including that of squatting to defecate). He studied the Koran, which he discussed in Arabic, but in so unorthodox a fashion that he was beaten by local zealots. His employer, Alfred Bardey—one of many associates at the time who appreciated the young man's business acumen and sober lifestyle—recalled that Rimbaud "avidly absorbed the essential qualities of the regions in which he traveled and assimilated himself as much as possible to the manners and customs of the native people."

Which is not to imply happiness with his new surroundings, for stasis as ever bred contempt. In his letters home he lamented—a bid for La Mother's sympathy?—being "lost in the midst of these Negroes whose lot one would like to improve...Obliged to speak their gibberish, to eat their dirty food, to endure a thousand frustrations on account of their laziness, their treachery, and their stupidity."* Beneath these petulant outbursts there was nonetheless a deeper component to his self-transformation, a stoic acceptance of his lot that

---

*As repellent as these sentiments are, we might also keep in mind Edmund White's caution that Rimbaud "wasn't merely racist; his misanthropy was general. He despised everyone." For years, it was believed that Rimbaud had also participated in the African slave trade, which is false—though, like many, he profited from it indirectly.

contrasted sharply with his earlier recklessness. For if his time in Paris followed his famous prescription of disordering all the senses, his African years seem largely to fall under the watchword *Insh' Allah*. "It is more than probable that I will never find peace of mind; that I will neither live nor die at peace," he wrote to his family in 1884. "In the end, as the Muslims say: It is written! That's life: it's no laughing matter."

Nor were the vicissitudes of fate merely theoretical: In the spring of 1891, a persistent painful swelling in the knee forced Rimbaud to liquidate his assets and return to France. After a long and torturous journey, he arrived at Hôpital de la Conception in Marseille, where a malignant tumor was diagnosed and his leg amputated. He briefly returned to the family farm in Roche to recuperate, then departed again for Marseille with his sister Isabelle, intending to return to Africa. He made it no farther than the hospital from which he'd been discharged one month earlier: the cancer had spread, his condition rapidly deteriorated, and Rimbaud died on the morning of November 10, soon after his thirty-seventh birthday. His last writing, dictated to his sister the previous day and left unfinished, was a letter to the head of a shipping company, inquiring about the cost of passage to Suez.

—*Mark Polizzotti*
November 2021

A NOTE ON THE TRANSLATION

THE FOLLOWING SELECTION represents about half of the major verse poems, half of *Illuminations*, and the entirety of *A Season in Hell*, along with most of the known letters by Rimbaud up to 1875. I have tried to fit as complete a picture as possible into a relatively compact space, and to provide an approachable, and I hope enjoyable, introduction to Rimbaud's work. The fact that I haven't included his more casual writings, such as *Album zutique* or *A Heart Under a Cassock*, doesn't mean I don't consider them worth reading. At the same time, not everything the boy genius produced is of equal caliber, and I've preferred to showcase what he could do when he put his mind to it.

Every new translation of a canonic text is indebted to those who went before, and the present versions would not have been possible without the work of my many predecessors, too numerous to name here. The occasional overlaps between my versions and theirs are as accidental as they are inevitable. That said, one of my main reasons for undertaking this project is that I could never quite find in previous English versions of Rimbaud's work, however brilliant, a tone that seemed to echo his French voice. As I see it, to translate Rimbaud effectively, you have to both believe in the essential power of poetry and fundamentally not give a fuck, or at least put yourself in that mind-set. The durable effect and potency of his writing, at least the best of it, lies in the constant tension between a kind of persnickety meticulousness and a nonchalance and spontaneity so extreme that they bang shoulders with automatic writing (an aspect the surrealists didn't fail to notice). With all due acknowledgment of linguistic, cultural, and historical differences, I have tried to create English poems that sound to my inner ear like Rimbaud's French.

A virtual compendium of nineteenth-century literature, Rimbaud zipped through many different styles, voices, and tones in his rush across the literary landscape. Accordingly, rather than adopt a one-size-fits-all approach, I've employed different translation strategies for different works, ranging from strict rhythm and rhyme to free verse as the music and mood of each piece seemed to dictate, while also staying attentive to his use and abuse of traditional forms, as well as to the license he sometimes granted himself to take prosody and (as Verlaine put it) wring its neck. I've also tried to retain as much as possible of Rimbaud's idiosyncratic punctuations—the scattershot exclamations and slapdashes—that give so much of his writing its flavor. Rimbaud's poetry is above all a poetics of feeling, or, as he described it, of sensation. Henry Miller observed that he never properly appreciated the strength and beauty of Rimbaud's utterances until he tried to translate them. I couldn't agree more.

The primary text of reference is Antoine Adam's 1972

Pléiade edition of the complete works, supplemented by facsimiles of the original manuscripts when available. For their insights and comments, I'm indebted to Alex Andriesse, James Brook, Edwin Frank, Jacky Colliss Harvey, Charles Kaiser, and Christopher Sawyer-Lauçanno.

Poems

Les Étrennes des orphelins

I

La chambre est pleine d'ombre; on entend vaguement
De deux enfants le triste et doux chuchotement.
Leur front se penche, encore alourdi par le rêve,
Sous le long rideau blanc qui tremble et se soulève...
—Au dehors les oiseaux se rapprochent frileux;
Leur aile s'engourdit sous le ton gris des cieux;
Et la nouvelle Année, à la suite brumeuse,
Laissant traîner les plis de sa robe neigeuse,
Sourit avec des pleurs, et chante en grelottant...

II

Or les petits enfants, sous le rideau flottant,
Parlent bas comme on fait dans une nuit obscure.
Ils écoutent, pensifs, comme un lointain murmure...
Ils tressaillent souvent à la claire voix d'or
Du timbre matinal, qui frappe et frappe encor
Son refrain métallique en son globe de verre...
—Puis, la chambre est glacée... on voit traîner à terre,
Épars autour des lits, des vêtements de deuil:
L'âpre bise d'hiver qui se lamente au seuil
Souffle dans le logis son haleine morose!
On sent, dans tout cela, qu'il manque quelque chose...
—Il n'est donc point de mère à ces petits enfants,
De mère au frais sourire, aux regards triomphants?
Elle a donc oublié, le soir, seule et penchée,
D'exciter une flamme à la cendre arrachée,
D'amonceler sur eux la laine et l'édredon

The Orphans' Gifts

I

The room is in shadow; and softly we hear
The sad, quiet whispers of two little boys.
Their foreheads bent forward, still freighted with dreams,
Beneath white bed curtains that billow and rise...
—Outside the birds huddle to fend off the cold;
Their wings growing numb in the sky's grayish hues;
With its train of deep fog, the snowy New Year,
Dragging the pleats of its wintery robe,
Sings as it shivers, and smiles through its tears...

II

And the two little boys, 'neath the curtain afloat,
Murmur as if on a pitch-blackened night.
They listen, in thought, to a far-distant sound...
And often they jump at the clear golden ring
Of the morning bell striking again and again
In a bubble of glass its metallic refrain...
—But the room is ice-cold...we see dropped on the floor,
In heaps 'round the beds, the dark clothing of grief.
The harsh winter wind laments under the door
And into the household it blows its sad breath!
From all this, we worry that something is wrong...
—Is no mother present for these little boys,
A mother with elated eyes and bright smile?
It seems she's forgotten, last evening, alone,
To stoke up a flame from the ember outlived,
To pile some woolens and quilts on her sons

Avant de les quitter en leur criant: pardon.
Elle n'a point prévu la froideur matinale,
Ni bien fermé le seuil à la bise hivernale?...
—Le rêve maternel, c'est le tiède tapis,
C'est le nid cotonneux où les enfants tapis,
Comme de beaux oiseaux que balancent les branches,
Dorment leur doux sommeil plein de visions blanches!...
—Et là,—c'est comme un nid sans plumes, sans chaleur,
Où les petits ont froid, ne dorment pas, ont peur;
Un nid que doit avoir glacé la bise amère...

III

Votre cœur l'a compris:—ces enfants sont sans mère,
Plus de mère au logis!—et le père est bien loin!...
—Une vieille servante, alors, en a pris soin.
Les petits sont tout seuls en la maison glacée;
Orphelins de quatre ans, voilà qu'en leur pensée
S'éveille, par degrés, un souvenir riant...
C'est comme un chapelet qu'on égrène en priant:
—Ah! quel beau matin, que ce matin des étrennes!
Chacun, pendant la nuit, avait rêvé des siennes
Dans quelque songe étrange où l'on voyait joujoux,
Bonbons habillés d'or, étincelants bijoux,
Tourbillonner, danser une danse sonore,
Puis fuir sous les rideaux, puis reparaître encore!
On s'éveillait matin, on se levait joyeux,
La lèvre affriandée, en se frottant les yeux...
On allait, les cheveux emmêlés sur la tête,
Les yeux tout rayonnants, comme aux grands jours de fête,
Et les petits pieds nus effleurant le plancher,
Aux portes des parents tout doucement toucher...

4

Before leaving them there with a cry of: Forgive!
Did she not foresee the deep chill of the morn,
Or shut the door tight on the harsh winter winds?...
—The motherly dream is a carpet so warm,
A feathery nest where the children all nestled
Like adorable chicks gently swayed by the branch
Sleep soundly while visions of white fill their heads!...
—But here, it's a nest without padding or heat,
Where the children are cold, cannot sleep, are afraid;
A nest frozen hard by the fierce winter chill...

III

Your heart has caught on:—these are motherless boys.
No mother at home!—and the father long gone!...
—And so an old maid tends to them when she can.
The tots are alone in this house without warmth;
Four-year-old orphans, and now in their thoughts
Comes alive by degrees a loving memory...
Like counting in prayer on a sweet rosary:
—And oh, what a morning, this morning of gifts!
Each, during the night, had dreamed of his own
In strange dancing visions where fabulous toys,
Sweets covered in gold, and baubles that gleam,
Spun madly about, in capering noise,
Then hid behind curtains, then came back again!
They woke in the morning, got up feeling joyful,
Lips full of cravings, and rubbing their eyes...
On tiptoe they went, hair on their head tousled,
Eyes shining bright, as on great holidays,
And shoeless feet silently grazing the floor,
So softly to knock at the parental door...

On entrait!... Puis alors les souhaits... en chemise,
Les baisers répétés, et la gaîté permise!

IV

Ah! c'était si charmant, ces mots dits tant de fois!
—Mais comme il est changé, le logis d'autrefois:
Un grand feu pétillait, clair, dans la cheminée,
Toute la vieille chambre était illuminée;
Et les reflets vermeils, sortis du grand foyer,
Sur les meubles vernis aimaient à tournoyer...
—L'armoire était sans clefs!... sans clefs, la grande armoire!
On regardait souvent sa porte brune et noire...
Sans clefs!... c'était étrange!... on rêvait bien des fois
Aux mystères dormant entre ses flancs de bois,
Et l'on croyait ouïr, au fond de la serrure
Béante, un bruit lointain, vague et joyeux murmure...
—La chambre des parents est bien vide, aujourd'hui:
Aucun reflet vermeil sous la porte n'a lui;
Il n'est point de parents, de foyer, de clefs prises:
Partant, point de baisers, point de douces surprises!
Oh! que le jour de l'an sera triste pour eux!
—Et, tout pensifs, tandis que de leurs grands yeux bleus,
Silencieusement tombe une larme amère,
Ils murmurent: "Quand donc reviendra notre mère?"

. . . .

V

Maintenant, les petits sommeillent tristement:
Vous diriez, à les voir, qu'ils pleurent en dormant,
Tant leurs yeux sont gonflés et leur souffle pénible!

Les tout petits enfants ont le cœur si sensible!
—Mais l'ange des berceaux vient essuyer leurs yeux,
Et dans ce lourd sommeil met un rêve joyeux,
Un rêve si joyeux, que leur lèvre mi-close,
Souriante, semblait murmurer quelque chose...
—Ils rêvent que, penchés sur leur petit bras rond,
Doux geste du réveil, ils avancent le front,
Et leur vague regard tout autour d'eux se pose...
Ils se croient endormis dans un paradis rose...
Au foyer plein d'éclairs chante gaîment le feu...
Par la fenêtre on voit là-bas un beau ciel bleu;
La nature s'éveille et de rayons s'enivre...
La terre, demi-nue, heureuse de revivre,
A des frissons de joie aux baisers du soleil...
Et dans le vieux logis tout est tiède et vermeil:
Les sombres vêtements ne jonchent plus la terre,
La bise sous le seuil a fini par se taire...
On dirait qu'une fée a passé dans cela!...
—Les enfants, tout joyeux, ont jeté deux cris... Là,
Près du lit maternel, sous un beau rayon rose,
Là, sur le grand tapis, resplendit quelque chose...
Ce sont des médaillons argentés, noirs et blancs,
De la nacre et du jais aux reflets scintillants;
Des petits cadres noirs, des couronnes de verre,
Ayant trois mots gravés en or: À NOTRE MÈRE!

Small children have such very sensitive hearts!
—But a guardian angel will come dry their tears,
And in their deep sleep place a jubilant dream,
A dream of such joy that their half-open lips,
With a smile, seem to murmur a phrase of content...
—They're dreaming that, propped on their round little arms,
Gently on waking, they lift up their heads,
With hazy eyes staring around at the room...
They think they're asleep in a pink paradise...
In the brightly lit hearth a warm fire gaily sings...
Through the window outside they see crystal blue skies;
Nature wakes and grows giddy on warm morning rays...
The earth, semi-naked, so glad to revive,
Feels shivers of joy at the kiss of the sun...
And in the old household it's cozy and red,
The dark garments no longer litter the floor,
The wind has stopped howling under the door...
It's like a good fairy has swept through the place!...
—The children, in unison, give shouts of joy...
There, near Mother's bed, 'neath a lovely pink beam,
There, on the large rug, something glitters and gleams...
With medallions of silver, and ebony, and white,
Of jet and of pearl, dazzling to behold;
And borders in black, and wreaths made of glass,
With three words, FOR OUR MOTHER, written in gold!

Sensation

Par les soirs bleus d'été, j'irai dans les sentiers,
Picoté par les blés, fouler l'herbe menue:
Rêveur, j'en sentirai la fraîcheur à mes pieds.
Je laisserai le vent baigner ma tête nue.

Je ne parlerai pas, je ne penserai rien:
Mais l'amour infini me montera dans l'âme,
Et j'irai loin, bien loin, comme un bohémien,
Par la Nature,—heureux comme avec une femme.

Mars 1870

Sensation

On blue summer evenings, I'll wander the paths,
Pricked by the wheat, and I'll trample the grass:
Daydreaming, I'll feel it cool underfoot.
I'll let the wind wash my bare head as I pass.

I won't say a word, I won't have a thought:
But an infinite love will arise in my soul,
And like a bohemian I'll go far away,
Through Nature,—contented, as if with a girl.

March 1870

Ophélie

I

Sur l'onde calme et noire où dorment les étoiles,
La blanche Ophélia flotte comme un grand lys,
Flotte très lentement, couchée en ses longs voiles...
—On entend dans les bois lointains des hallalis.

Voici plus de mille ans que la triste Ophélie
Passe, fantôme blanc, sur le long fleuve noir;
Voici plus de mille ans que sa douce folie
Murmure sa romance à la brise du soir.

Le vent baise ses seins et déploie en corolle
Ses grands voiles bercés mollement par les eaux;
Les saules frissonnants pleurent sur son épaule,
Sur son grand front rêveur s'inclinent les roseaux.

Les nénuphars froissés soupirent autour d'elle;
Elle éveille parfois, dans un aune qui dort,
Quelque nid, d'où s'échappe un petit frisson d'aile:
—Un chant mystérieux tombe des astres d'or.

II

Ô pâle Ophélia! belle comme la neige!
Oui tu mourus, enfant, par un fleuve emporté!
   C'est que les vents tombant des grands monts de Norwège
T'avaient parlé tout bas de l'âpre liberté;

Ophelia

I

On the calm black waves where the bright stars sleep,
Like a great white lily Ophelia drifts,
Drifts so slowly, resting in her long veils...
—And from the far woods we hear hunting horns.

A thousand years and more, sad Ophelia has passed,
A pale wraith, on the river long and black.
A thousand years and more, her sweet madness
To the evening breeze has murmured its romance.

The wind kisses her breasts and spreads wide
Her clothes so limply borne by the waves;
On her shoulder the trembling willows weep,
To her wide pensive brow the reeds bend low.

All around her water lilies sigh;
Sometimes, in a dormant alder, she rouses
A nest, releasing the flick of a wing:
—From the golden stars falls a mysterious song.

II

O pale Ophelia, fair as snow!
You died still a child, the brook swept you away!
—Because the winds blowing from the mounts of Norway
Had whispered their song of harsh liberty;

C'est qu'un souffle, tordant ta grande chevelure,
A ton esprit rêveur portait d'étranges bruits;
Que ton cœur écoutait le chant de la Nature
Dans les plaintes de l'arbre et les soupirs des nuits;

C'est que la voix des mers folles, immense râle,
Brisait ton sein d'enfant, trop humain et trop doux;
C'est qu'un matin d'avril, un beau cavalier pâle,
Un pauvre fou, s'assit muet à tes genoux!

Ciel! Amour! Liberté! Quel rêve, ô pauvre Folle!
Tu te fondais à lui comme une neige au feu:
Tes grandes visions étranglaient ta parole
—Et l'Infini terrible effara ton œil bleu!

III

—Et le Poète dit qu'aux rayons des étoiles
Tu viens chercher, la nuit, les fleurs que tu cueillis;
Et qu'il a vu sur l'eau, couchée en ses longs voiles,
La blanche Ophélia flotter, comme un grand lys.

Because a breath, twisting your luxuriant hair,
To your dreaming mind carried mysterious sounds;
Because your heart listened to Nature's song
In the tree's laments and the nighttime sighs;

It's because the voice of mad seas, great rale,
Broke your childish breast, too soft and too frail;
Because one April morning, a pale fair prince,
A poor lunatic, laid his head on your lap!

Heaven! Love! Freedom! What a dream, you poor Fool!
In it you melted like snow in a flame:
Your grandiose visions strangled your words
—And your eye was alarmed by dread Infinity!

III

—And the Poet says that in the light of the stars
You come looking, at night, for the flowers you plucked;
And he's seen, resting in her long veils,
White Ophelia, a lily, adrift on the waves.

Bal des pendus

Au gibet noir, manchot aimable,
Dansent, dansent les paladins,
Les maigres paladins du diable,
Les squelettes de Saladins.

Messire Belzébuth tire par la cravate
Ses petits pantins noirs grimaçant sur le ciel,
Et, leur claquant au front un revers de savate,
Les fait danser, danser aux sons d'un vieux Noël!

Et les pantins choqués enlacent leurs bras grêles :
Comme des orgues noirs, les poitrines à jour
Que serraient autrefois les gentes damoiselles,
Se heurtent longuement dans un hideux amour.

Hurrah! les gais danseurs, qui n'avez plus de panse!
On peut cabrioler, les tréteaux sont si longs!
Hop! qu'on ne sache plus si c'est bataille ou danse!
Belzébuth enragé racle ses violons!

Ô durs talons, jamais on n'use sa sandale!
Presque tous ont quitté la chemise de peau;
Le reste est peu gênant et se voit sans scandale.
Sur les crânes, la neige applique un blanc chapeau:

Le corbeau fait panache à ces têtes fêlées,
Un morceau de chair tremble à leur maigre menton:
On dirait, tournoyant dans les sombres mêlées,
Des preux, raides, heurtant armures de carton.

The Hanged Man's Ball

On the cordial one-armed gibbet
Dance and dance the paladins,
The devil's scrawny champions,
The skeletons of Saladins.

Sire Beelzebub yanks about by the necktie
His black puppets, who grimace against the pale sky,
And, kicking their foreheads with his old shoe,
Makes them dance and dance to an ancient tune!

And the stunned puppets link their spindly arms
Like black hurdy-gurdies, their chests to the air
That once were held close by maidens fair
Collide and collide in a hideous kiss.

Hurrah, you gay dancers, your bellies now gone!
Cavort as you will, the trestles are long!
We no longer know if it's battle or dance!
Beelzebub scrapes his violins as they prance!

O heels hard as rock, in no need of clogs!
Since everyone here's shed his mantle of flesh,
The rest is no trouble and seen without shock.
The snow on their skulls is a cap white and fresh:

A crow somersaults on those fragmented heads,
A scrap of skin flutters from their narrow chins:
You'd think them knights errant, valiant but stiff,
Their cardboard arms clashing in some somber fray.

Hurrah! La bise siffle au grand bal des squelettes!
Le gibet noir mugit comme un orgue de fer!
Les loups vont répondant des forêts violettes:
À l'horizon, le ciel est d'un rouge d'enfer...

Holà, secouez-moi ces capitans funèbres
Qui défilent, sournois, de leurs gros doigts cassés
Un chapelet d'amour sur leurs pâles vertèbres:
Ce n'est pas un moustier ici, les trépassés!

Oh! voilà qu'au milieu de la danse macabre
Bondit dans le ciel rouge un grand squelette fou
Emporté par l'élan, comme un cheval se cabre:
Et, se sentant encor la corde raide au cou,

Crispe ses petits doigts sur son fémur qui craque
Avec des cris pareils à des ricanements,
Et, comme un baladin rentre dans la baraque,
Rebondit dans le bal au chant des ossements.

    Au gibet noir, manchot aimable,
    Dansent, dansent les paladins,
    Les maigres paladins du diable,
    Les squelettes de Saladins.

Hurrah, the wind blasts through the skeletons' ball!
The black gibbet shrieks like an organ of iron!
Wolves howl in answer to violet forests:
In the distance, the sky is a crimson from hell...

Ho, give those funereal captains a shake,
Who count, on the sly, with fat broken fingers
A rosary of love on their pale vertebrae:
That's enough, you cadavers, this isn't a wake!

And now from the midst of the macabre dance
A great crazy skeleton leaps to the sky
Impelled by the frenzy, as a horse might rear up:
Still feeling the tug of the noose round his neck,

Clenches his digits on femurs that crack
With clamors like snickers or indistinct moans,
And, like a stray minstrel rejoining the stage,
Jumps back in the ball to the song of the bones.

On the cordial one-armed gibbet
Dance and dance the paladins,
The devil's scrawny champions,
The skeletons of Saladins.

Morts de quatre-vingt-douze

...Français de soixante-dix, bonapartistes, républicains,
souvenez-vous de vos pères en 92, etc.
—Paul de Cassagnac, *Le Pays*

Morts de Quatre-vingt-douze et de Quatre-vingt-treize,
Qui, pâles du baiser fort de la liberté,
Calmes, sous vos sabots, brisiez le joug qui pèse
Sur l'âme et sur le front de toute humanité;

Hommes extasiés et grands dans la tourmente,
Vous dont les cœurs sautaient d'amour sous les haillons,
Ô Soldats que la Mort a semés, noble Amante,
Pour les régénérer, dans tous les vieux sillons;

Vous dont le sang lavait toute grandeur salie,
Morts de Valmy, Morts de Fleurus, Morts d'Italie,
Ô million de Christs aux yeux sombres et doux;

Nous vous laissions dormir avec la République,
Nous, courbés sous les rois comme sous une trique.
—Messieurs de Cassagnac nous reparlent de vous!

Fait à Mazas
3 Septembre 1870

Dead of '92

...Frenchmen of Seventy, Bonapartists, Republicans,
remember your forefathers of Ninety-two, etc.
—Paul de Cassagnac, *Le Pays*

Dead of Ninety-two and Ninety-three,
Who, pale with the strong kiss of liberty,
Crushed under calm clogs the yoke that weighs
On the soul and brow of all humanity;

Jubilant men, glorious in the storm,
You whose hearts burst with love under your rags,
O Soldiers whom Death, noble Lover, has sown
In all the old furrows, that you be reborn;

You whose blood washed away all soil from glory,
The Dead of Valmy, of Fleurus, of Italy,
O millions of Christs, your eyes gentle and dark;

We'd left you to sleep in Republican peace,
We, bent under kings as if under a mace.
—But the Cassagnacs now are calling you back!

Written in Mazas
September 3, 1870

Première Soirée

—Elle était fort déshabillée
Et de grands arbres indiscrets
Aux vitres jetaient leur feuillée
Malinement, tout près, tout près.

Assise sur ma grande chaise,
Mi-nue, elle joignait les mains.
Sur le plancher frissonnaient d'aise
Ses petits pieds si fins, si fins.

—Je regardai, couleur de cire,
Un petit rayon buissonnier
Papillonner dans son sourire
Et sur son sein,—mouche au rosier.

—Je baisai ses fines chevilles.
Elle eut un doux rire brutal
Qui s'égrenait en claires trilles,
Un joli rire de cristal.

Les petits pieds sous la chemise
Se sauvèrent: "Veux-tu finir!"
—La première audace permise,
Le rire feignait de punir!

—Pauvrets palpitants sous ma lèvre,
Je baisai doucement ses yeux:
—Elle jeta sa tête mièvre
En arrière: "Oh! c'est encor mieux!...

First Evening

—She was scantily dressed
And the big shameless trees
Scraped their leaves on the panes,
Cunningly, near and nearer.

Sat in my big chair,
Half nude, she clasped hands.
On the floor, trembling with pleasure,
Her tiny feet so fine, so fine.

—I watched as a fleeting
Shaft of waxen light
Flickered on her smile
And her breast—fly on a rose.

—I kissed her fine ankles.
She laughed soft and brutal
It chimed in clear trills,
A sweet laugh of crystal.

Small feet scampered back
Under her shift: "Will you quit!"
—That first liberty allowed,
Her laugh feigned punishment!

—Poor things quivering beneath my lips,
I kissed her eyelids with a whisper:
—She tossed back her mawkish head
Saying, "Oh, that's much better... !"

Monsieur, j'ai deux mots à te dire..."
—Je lui jetai le reste au sein
Dans un baiser, qui la fit rire
D'un bon rire qui voulait bien...

—Elle était fort déshabillée
Et de grands arbres indiscrets
Aux vitres jetaient leur feuillée
Malinement, tout près, tout près.

"Young man, I have just two words for you..."
—Then I went straight for her breast
With a kiss that made her laugh,
A good laugh promising better and best...

—She was scantily dressed
And the big shameless trees
Scraped their leaves on the panes,
Cunningly, near and nearer.

Roman

I

On n'est pas sérieux, quand on a dix-sept ans.
—Un beau soir, foin des bocks et de la limonade,
Des cafés tapageurs aux lustres éclatants!
—On va sous les tilleuls verts de la promenade.

Les tilleuls sentent bon dans les bons soirs de juin!
L'air est parfois si doux, qu'on ferme la paupière;
Le vent chargé de bruits,—la ville n'est pas loin,—
A des parfums de vigne et des parfums de bière...

II

—Voilà qu'on aperçoit un tout petit chiffon
D'azur sombre, encadré d'une petite branche,
Piqué d'une mauvaise étoile, qui se fond
Avec de doux frissons, petite et toute blanche...

Nuit de juin! Dix-sept ans! —On se laisse griser.
La sève est du champagne et vous monte à la tête...
On divague; on se sent aux lèvres un baiser
Qui palpite là, comme une petite bête...

III

Le cœur fou Robinsonne à travers les romans,
—Lorsque, dans la clarté d'un pâle réverbère,

Romance

I

No one's serious at seventeen.
—Nice evening out, to hell with beers and lemonade,
And rowdy cafés with glaring lights!
—Let's go to the green lindens on the promenade.

The lindens smell good on mild June nights!
The air so soft that you close your eyes;
Wind laden with sounds,—the town is near,—
Carries the scents of vineyard and beer...

II

—And there, a patch of darkest blue,
Framed by a little branch,
Pricked by a bad star, that diffuses
In soft shivers, small and white...

Night in June! Seventeen!—You're carried away.
The sap is champagne and it goes to your head...
You ramble; feel a kiss on your lips
That palpitates there like a minuscule beast...

III

Crazy heart Crusoes through romances galore,
—When, in the pale light of a tall streetlamp,

Passe une demoiselle aux petits airs charmants,
Sous l'ombre du faux col effrayant de son père...

Et, comme elle vous trouve immensément naïf,
Tout en faisant trotter ses petites bottines,
Elle se tourne, alerte et d'un mouvement vif...
—Sur vos lèvres alors meurent les cavatines...

IV

Vous êtes amoureux. Loué jusqu'au mois d'août.
Vous êtes amoureux.—Vos sonnets La font rire.
Tous vos amis s'en vont, vous êtes *mauvais goût.*
—Puis l'adorée, un soir, a daigné vous écrire!...

—Ce soir-là,...—vous rentrez aux cafés éclatants,
Vous demandez des bocks ou de la limonade...
—On n'est pas sérieux, quand on a dix-sept ans
Et qu'on a des tilleuls verts sur la promenade.

29 sept 70

A young miss passes, all charm and all airs,
In the unnerving shadow of Papa's stiff collar...

And, as she finds you immensely naïve,
While taking her booties out for a stroll,
She spins around, so quick and alive...
—The cavatinas on your lips die and fall...

IV

You're in love. Held up till August.
You're in love.—Your poems make Her laugh.
Your friends fall away, think you're a bore.
—Then one evening Beloved bothers to write...!

—That evening,...—you go back to glaring cafés,
You order beers or else lemonade...
—No one's serious at seventeen
When the lindens are green on the promenade.

Sept. 29, '70

Le Mal

Tandis que les crachats rouges de la mitraille
Sifflent tout le jour par l'infini du ciel bleu;
Qu'écarlates ou verts, près du Roi qui les raille,
Croulent les bataillons en masse dans le feu;

Tandis qu'une folie épouvantable, broie
Et fait de cent milliers d'hommes un tas fumant;
—Pauvres morts! dans l'été, dans l'herbe, dans ta joie,
Nature! ô toi qui fis ces hommes saintement!...—

—Il est un Dieu, qui rit aux nappes damassées
Des autels, à l'encens, aux grands calices d'or;
Qui dans le bercement des hosannah s'endort,

Et se réveille, quand des mères, ramassées
Dans l'angoisse, et pleurant sous leur vieux bonnet noir,
Lui donnent un gros sou lié dans leur mouchoir!

Evil

While vermillion sparks from machine guns spit
Dawn to dusk through the endless blue sky;
And red or green legions, jeered onward by Kings,
Crumble in masses under fire;

While a horrible folly annihilates men
Into steaming heaps by the thousands and more;
—The poor dead! in summer, in the grass, in your joy,
O holy Nature! you who created these beings!...

—There is a God, who laughs at frontals of damask
On altars, at incense, at chalices of gold;
Who cradled by hosannas drifts off to sleep,

Waking only when mothers, huddled in tears,
Grieving beneath their old black bonnets,
Hand him a coin that a kerchief enfolds!

Rêvé pour l'hiver

A *** Elle

L'hiver, nous irons dans un petit wagon rose
  Avec des coussins bleus.
Nous serons bien. Un nid de baisers fous repose
  Dans chaque coin moelleux.

Tu fermeras l'œil, pour ne point voir, par la glace,
  Grimacer les ombres des soirs,
Ces monstruosités hargneuses, populace
  De démons noirs et de loups noirs.

Puis tu te sentiras la joue égratignée...
Un petit baiser, comme une folle araignée,
  Te courra par le cou...

Et tu me diras: "Cherche!" en inclinant la tête,
—Et nous prendrons du temps à trouver cette bête
  —Qui voyage beaucoup...

En Wagon
le 7 octobre 70

Dream for Winter

for *** Her

We'll set off in winter in a pretty pink carriage
        With cushions blue.
And it will be good. Each soft corner a nest
        For kissing you.

You'll close your eyes, not to see through the glass
        The evening shadows grimace,
Those snarling monsters, black demons
        And black wolves, a populace.

Then on your cheek you'll feel a graze...
Like a mad little spider, a tiny kiss
        On your neck will rove...

"Find it!" you'll say, with a tilt of your head,
—And we'll take our time hunting that slippery beast
        —Who travels all over...

In a train compartment
October 7, '70

Le Dormeur du val

C'est un trou de verdure où chante une rivière,
Accrochant follement aux herbes des haillons
D'argent; où le soleil, de la montagne fière,
Luit: c'est un petit val qui mousse de rayons.

Un soldat jeune, bouche ouverte, tête nue,
Et la nuque baignant dans le frais cresson bleu,
Dort; il est étendu dans l'herbe, sous la nue,
Pâle dans son lit vert où la lumière pleut.

Les pieds dans les glaïeuls, il dort. Souriant comme
Sourirait un enfant malade, il fait un somme:
Nature, berce-le chaudement: il a froid.

Les parfums ne font pas frissonner sa narine;
Il dort dans le soleil, la main sur sa poitrine,
Tranquille. Il a deux trous rouges au côté droit.

Octobre 1870

Sleeper in the Valley

There's a little green hollow where a tuneful brook
Crazily sticks silver scraps on the weeds;
Where from the proud mountain the sun brightly shines:
The valley is modest, and frothy with rays.

A young soldier, mouth agape and head bare,
His neck bathing in fresh watercress blue,
Is sleeping; stretched out on the grass, beneath the skies,
Pale in his green bed with light raining down.

Feet in the irises, he rests. Smiling as
A sick child might smile, he dozes:
Nature, cradle him warmly: he's cold.

The scents do not cause his nostrils to stir;
He sleeps in the sun, a hand on his breast,
In peace. Right side pierced by two crimson holes.

October 1870

Au cabaret-vert

cinq heures du soir

Depuis huit jours, j'avais déchiré mes bottines
Aux cailloux des chemins. J'entrais à Charleroi.
—*Au Cabaret-Vert*: je demandai des tartines
De beurre et du jambon qui fût à moitié froid.

Bienheureux, j'allongeai les jambes sous la table
Verte: je contemplai les sujets très naïfs
De la tapisserie.—Et ce fut adorable,
Quand la fille aux tétons énormes, aux yeux vifs,

—Celle-là, ce n'est pas un baiser qui l'épeure! —
Rieuse, m'apporta des tartines de beurre,
Du jambon tiède, dans un plat colorié,

Du jambon rose et blanc parfumé d'une gousse
D'ail,—et m'emplit la chope immense, avec sa mousse
Que dorait un rayon de soleil arriéré.

Octobre 70

At the Green Tavern

5 in the afternoon

A week grinding down my boots
On the stones in my passway. Got into Charleroi.
—*At the Green Tavern*: I ordered bread,
Butter, and ham that was half chilled.

Legs stretched contentedly under the green
Table: I gazed at the artless scenes
On the wall.—And it was adorable,
When the waitress with huge tits and lively eyes

—Not one to be fazed by a kiss!—
Brought me bread and butter, all smiles,
And lukewarm ham on a colored dish,

The ham pink and white, flavored with garlic,
—And filled my towering mug, its foam
Gilded by the sun's lingering rays.

October '70

La Maline

Dans la salle à manger brune, que parfumait
Une odeur de vernis et de fruits, à mon aise
Je ramassais un plat de je ne sais quel met
Belge, et je m'épatais dans mon immense chaise.

En mangeant, j'écoutais l'horloge,—heureux et coi.
La cuisine s'ouvrit avec une bouffée,
—Et la servante vint, je ne sais pas pourquoi,
Fichu moitié défait, malinement coiffée

Et, tout en promenant son petit doigt tremblant
Sur sa joue, un velours de pêche rose et blanc,
En faisant, de sa lèvre enfantine, une moue,

Elle arrangeait les plats, près de moi, pour m'aiser;
—Puis, comme ça,—bien sûr, pour avoir un baiser,—
Tout bas: "Sens donc, j'ai pris *une* froid sur la joue…"

Charleroi
octobre 70

38

Cunning

In the brown dining room, smelling of
Polish and fruit, at my ease
I grabbed a plate of some Belgian
Dish, and spread out in my huge chair.

Eating, I listened to the clock,—quiet and calm.
The kitchen flew open in a puff of steam,
—And the serving girl came, don't ask me why,
Head scarf undone, cunningly coiffed

And running a trembling finger over
The pink-and-white fuzz of her cheek,
Her childish lips wearing a pout,

She cleared the dishes, for my ease;
—Then just like that,—for a kiss, no doubt,—
Murmured, "Feel my cheek, it *catched* a cold..."

Charleroi
October '70

39

Ma bohème

(Fantaisie)

Je m'en allais, les poings dans mes poches crevées;
Mon paletot aussi devenait idéal;
J'allais sous le ciel, Muse! et j'étais ton féal;
Oh! là! là! que d'amours splendides j'ai rêvées!

Mon unique culotte avait un large trou.
—Petit-Poucet rêveur, j'égrenais dans ma course
Des rimes. Mon auberge était à la Grande-Ourse.
—Mes étoiles au ciel avaient un doux frou-frou

Et je les écoutais, assis au bord des routes,
Ces bons soirs de septembre où je sentais des gouttes
De rosée à mon front, comme un vin de vigueur;

Où, rimant au milieu des ombres fantastiques,
Comme des lyres, je tirais les élastiques
De mes souliers blessés, un pied près de mon cœur!

My Bohemia

(A fantasy)

Off I went, fists in pockets and pockets in shreds;
My overcoat too had become an ideal;
I went 'neath the sky, Muse! to you I was loyal;
Oh, my, my! such incredible loves filled my head!

My one pair of trousers had sprung a big hole.
—Quixotic Tom Thumb, on my path I declaimed
New verses. I slept at the Big Dipper Inn.
—My stars in the sky made a delicate swish

And I listened to them, by the side of the road,
Those September nights, when I felt the dew
Pearled in drops on my brow, like restorative wine;

Where, rhyming amid the fantastic shadows,
I plucked, as if on a lyre, the distressed
Laces of my shoes, one foot close to my breast!

Oraison du soir

Je vis assis, tel qu'un ange aux mains d'un barbier,
Empoignant une chope à fortes cannelures,
L'hypogastre et le col cambrés, une Gambier
Aux dents, sous l'air gonflé d'impalpables voilures.

Tels que les excréments chauds d'un vieux colombier,
Mille Rêves en moi font de douces brûlures:
Puis par instants mon cœur triste est comme un aubier
Qu'ensanglante l'or jeune et sombre des coulures.

Puis, quand j'ai ravalé mes rêves avec soin,
Je me tourne, ayant bu trente ou quarante chopes,
Et me recueille, pour lâcher l'âcre besoin:

Doux comme le Seigneur du cèdre et des hysopes,
Je pisse vers les cieux bruns, très haut et très loin,
Avec l'assentiment des grands héliotropes.

Evening Prayer

I live seated, like an angel in a barber's chair,
Clutching a deeply fluted tankard,
Neck and hypogastrium arched, clay pipe clamped
Between my teeth, air thick with smoky veils.

Like warm droppings in an old dovecote,
A thousand Dreams leave gentle burns:
My sad heart is like a tender shoot
Stained by the leakage of dark young gold.

Then, carefully choking back my dreams,
I turn around, mugs quaffed by the dozens,
And take stock, to relieve the acrid need:

Gentle as the Lord of cedar and hyssop,
I piss to brown heavens, so high and so far,
Under the blessing of sunflower stalks.

Les Poètes de sept ans

à M. P. Demeny

Et la Mère, fermant le livre du devoir,
S'en allait satisfaite et très fière, sans voir,
Dans les yeux bleus et sous le front plein d'éminences,
L'âme de son enfant livrée aux répugnances.

Tout le jour il suait d'obéissance; très
Intelligent; pourtant des tics noirs, quelques traits
Semblaient prouver en lui d'âcres hypocrisies.
Dans l'ombre des couloirs aux tentures moisies,
En passant il tirait la langue, les deux poings
À l'aine, et dans ses yeux fermés voyait des points.
Une porte s'ouvrait sur le soir: à la lampe
On le voyait, là-haut, qui râlait sur la rampe,
Sous un golfe de jour pendant du toit. L'été
Surtout, vaincu, stupide, il était entêté
À se renfermer dans la fraîcheur des latrines:
Il pensait là, tranquille et livrant ses narines.

Quand, lavé des odeurs du jour, le jardinet
Derrière la maison, en hiver, s'illunait,
Gisant au pied d'un mur, enterré dans la marne
Et pour des visions écrasant son œil darne,
Il écoutait grouiller les galeux espaliers.
Pitié! Ces enfants seuls étaient ses familiers
Qui, chétifs, fronts nus, œil déteignant sur la joue,
Cachant de maigres doigts jaunes et noirs de boue
Sous des habits puant la foire et tout vieillots,
Conversaient avec la douceur des idiots!
Et si, l'ayant surpris à des pitiés immondes,
Sa mère s'effrayait; les tendresses, profondes,

Seven-Year-Old Poets

for P. Demeny

And his Mother, closing the exercise tome,
Went off satisfied and oh so proud,
Not seeing in the blue eyes beneath the prominent brow,
The soul of her child riddled with disgust.

All day he sweated obedience; such a smart boy;
And yet somber tics, the occasional trait
Hinted at bitter hypocrisies.
In dark halls lined with moldy draperies,
He pokes out his tongue in passing, fists dug
Into his groin, seeing stars in tight-shut eyes.
A door opened onto evening: by lamplight
They saw him, groaning at the upstairs rail,
In a gulf of light dropped from the ceiling. In summer
Especially, defeated and dull, he stubbornly
Locked himself in the cool of the latrines:
And there he pondered, alone at last, breathing deep.

In the little garden behind the house,
Washed by the day's odors, in winter, moonlit,
Lying at the foot of a wall, buried in marl,
Hoping for visions he pressed his dazed eye,
And in mangy espaliers listened to the swarm.
Pity! Those friendless kids were his familiars:
Puny and capless, eyes bleeding into their cheeks,
Hiding stubby fingers black and yellow with mud
In clothes outworn and reeking of dung,
They conversed with the tenderness of imbeciles!
And if, having caught him in these foul mercies,
His mother took fright; the child's affections,

De l'enfant se jetaient sur cet étonnement.
C'était bon. Elle avait le bleu regard,—qui ment!

À sept ans, il faisait des romans, sur la vie
Du grand désert, où luit la Liberté ravie,
Forêts, soleils, rives, savanes! —Il s'aidait
De journaux illustrés où, rouge, il regardait
Des Espagnoles rire et des Italiennes.
Quand venait, l'œil brun, folle, en robes d'indiennes,
—Huit ans—la fille des ouvriers d'à côté,
La petite brutale, et qu'elle avait sauté,
Dans un coin, sur son dos, en secouant ses tresses,
Et qu'il était sous elle, il lui mordait les fesses,
Car elle ne portait jamais de pantalons;
—Et, par elle meurtri des poings et des talons,
Remportait les saveurs de sa peau dans sa chambre.

Il craignait les blafards dimanches de décembre,
Où, pommadé, sur un guéridon d'acajou,
Il lisait une Bible à la tranche vert-chou;
Des rêves l'oppressaient chaque nuit dans l'alcôve.
Il n'aimait pas Dieu; mais les hommes, qu'au soir fauve,
Noirs, en blouse, il voyait rentrer dans le faubourg
Où les crieurs, en trois roulements de tambour,
Font autour des édits rire et gronder les foules.
—Il rêvait la prairie amoureuse, où des houles
Lumineuses, parfums sains, pubescences d'or,
Font leur remuement calme et prennent leur essor!

Et comme il savourait surtout les sombres choses,
Quand, dans la chambre nue aux persiennes closes,
Haute et bleue, âcrement prise d'humidité,
Il lisait son roman sans cesse médité,
Plein de lourds ciels ocreux et de forêts noyées,

Running deep, set upon that astonishment.
All good. She had those pale blue eyes,—that lie!

At seven, he made up stories, on the life
Of great deserts, where blissful Freedom shines,
Forests, suns, distant shores, savannas!—Took cues
From picture magazines where, cheeks burning red,
He saw Italian and Spanish girls, laughing.
Then came, brown-eyed, crazy, in a calico dress,
—Age eight—the workers' daughter next door,
A wild thing, who in a dark corner
Leapt onto his back, tossing her hair,
And when he was beneath her, he sank his teeth
Into her bottom, for no panties did she wear;
—And, bearing the marks of her fists and heels,
He smuggled the taste of her skin to his room.

He dreaded the pallid December Sundays,
When, hair gelled stiff, on a mahogany pew
He read a Bible with cabbage-green fore edge;
At night dreams oppressed him in his alcove.
He did not like God; but rather men, who on savage evenings,
Black, in smocks, returned to the outskirts
Where the criers, with three rolls of the drum,
Made the crowds grumble and laugh to proclamations.
—He dreamed of amorous fields, where luminous
Swells, wholesome aromas, golden pubescences
Move about calmly and take flight!

And as he especially savored dark things,
When, in the bare room with blinds firmly shut,
High-ceilinged and blue, and pungently damp,
He read in his much meditated romance,
Of ocherous skies and forests aflood,

De fleurs de chair aux bois sidérals déployées,
Vertige, écroulements, déroutes et pitié!
—Tandis que se faisait la rumeur du quartier,
En bas,—seul, et couché sur des pièces de toile
Écrue, et pressentant violemment la voile!

26 mai 1871

Flowers of flesh crawling through star-filled woods,
Raptures, collapses, mercies, and routs!
—While downstairs the neighborhood furthered its noise,
—He lay alone on canvas sheets,
And violently dreamed of setting sail!

May 26, 1871

Le Cœur supplicié

Mon triste cœur bave à la poupe…
Mon cœur est plein de caporal!
Ils y lancent des jets de soupe,
Mon triste cœur bave à la poupe…
Sous les quolibets de la troupe
Qui lance un rire général,
Mon triste cœur bave à la poupe,
Mon cœur est plein de caporal!

Ithyphalliques et pioupiesques
Leurs insultes l'ont dépravé;
À la vesprée, ils font des fresques
Ithyphalliques et pioupiesques;
Ô flots abracadabrantesques,
Prenez mon cœur, qu'il soit sauvé!
Ithyphalliques et pioupiesques
Leurs insultes l'ont dépravé.

Quand ils auront tari leurs chiques,
Comment agir, ô cœur volé?
Ce seront des refrains bachiques
Quand ils auront tari leurs chiques!
J'aurai des sursauts stomachiques
Si mon cœur triste est ravalé!
Quand ils auront tari leurs chiques
Comment agir, ô cœur volé?

Mai 1871

Tortured Heart

My sad heart slobbers at the poop . . .
My poor heart glutted with shag:
They pelt it with spurts of soup,
My sad heart slobbers at the poop . . .
Under the jeers of the troop
Who laugh and rag,
My sad heart slobbers at the poop,
My poor heart glutted with shag!

Ithyphallic and soldieresque
Their jeers have left it all depraved;
At nightfall they act out grotesques
Ithyphallic and soldieresque;
O waves abracadabrantesque,
Cleanse my heart, let it be saved!
Ithyphallic and soldieresque,
Their jeers have left it all depraved.

When all of them their wad have shot,
What then to do, my stolen heart?
There'll be bacchanalian glut
When all of them their wad have shot!
I'll have spasms in my gut
If I must swallow back my bile!
When all of them their wad have shot,
What then to do, my stolen heart?

May 1871

L'Orgie parisienne ou Paris se repeuple

Ô lâches, la voilà! Dégorgez dans les gares!
Le soleil essuya de ses poumons ardents
Les boulevards qu'un soir comblèrent les Barbares.
Voilà la Cité sainte, assise à l'occident!

Allez! on préviendra les reflux d'incendie,
Voilà les quais, voilà les boulevards, voilà
Les maisons sur l'azur léger qui s'irradie
Et qu'un soir la rougeur des bombes étoila!

Cachez les palais morts dans des niches de planches!
L'ancien jour effaré rafraîchit vos regards.
Voici le troupeau roux des tordeuses de hanches:
Soyez fous, vous serez drôles, étant hagards!

Tas de chiennes en rut mangeant des cataplasmes,
Le cri des maisons d'or vous réclame. Volez!
Mangez! Voici la nuit de joie aux profonds spasmes
Qui descend dans la rue. Ô buveurs désolés,

Buvez! Quand la lumière arrive intense et folle,
Fouillant à vos côtés les luxes ruisselants,
Vous n'allez pas baver, sans geste, sans parole,
Dans vos verres, les yeux perdus aux lointains blancs?

Avalez, pour la Reine aux fesses cascadantes!
Écoutez l'action des stupides hoquets
Déchirants! Écoutez sauter aux nuits ardentes
Les idiots râleux, vieillards, pantins, laquais!

Paris Repopulates (Parisian Orgy)

O cowards, there it is! Disgorge into the stations!
The sun has swept clean with its ardent lungs
The boulevards that one night the Barbarians thronged.
There is the Holy City, firmly fixed in the West!

Come on! They'll stamp out the fire next time,
There are the quays, there the boulevards, there
The houses against the lightening blue
Spangled one night by the rockets' red glare.

Hide the dead palaces behind warrens of planks!
The frightened old day will refresh your tired gaze.
And here comes the hennaed horde of hip-slingers:
Go for broke, you'll be comical, looking so dazed!

Bunch of bitches in rut gorging on cataplasms,
The song of the Gold House is calling for you.
Steal! Eat! Here's the joyous night filled with deep spasms
That descends to the streets. O desolate boozers,

Drink! When the light comes insane and intense,
Fumbling about you for riches galore,
Won't you drool, without moving, or saying a word,
In your glasses, eyes lost in some white distant shore?

Swallow down, for the Queen with her cascading bum!
Hark to the action of gut-rending flares!
Hear the idiots, oldsters, stooges, and lackeys
On ardent nights getting blown into the air!

Ô cœurs de saleté, bouches épouvantables,
Fonctionnez plus fort, bouches de puanteurs!
Un vin pour ces torpeurs ignobles, sur ces tables...
Vos ventres sont fondus de hontes, ô Vainqueurs!

Ouvrez votre narine aux superbes nausées!
Trempez de poisons forts les cordes de vos cous!
Sur vos nuques d'enfants baissant ses mains croisées
Le Poète vous dit: "Ô lâches, soyez fous!

Parce que vous fouillez le ventre de la Femme,
Vous craignez d'elle encore une convulsion
Qui crie, asphyxiant votre nichée infâme
Sur sa poitrine, en une horrible pression.

Syphilitiques, fous, rois, pantins, ventriloques,
Qu'est-ce que ça peut faire à la putain Paris,
Vos âmes et vos corps, vos poisons et vos loques?
Elle se secouera de vous, hargneux pourris!

Et quand vous serez bas, geignant sur vos entrailles,
Les flancs morts, réclamant votre argent, éperdus,
La rouge courtisane aux seins gros de batailles
Loin de votre stupeur tordra ses poings ardus!

Quand tes pieds ont dansé si fort dans les colères,
Paris! quand tu reçus tant de coups de couteau,
Quand tu gis, retenant dans tes prunelles claires
Un peu de la bonté du fauve renouveau,

Ô cité douloureuse, ô cité quasi morte,
La tête et les deux seins jetés vers l'Avenir
Ouvrant sur ta pâleur ses milliards de portes,
Cité que le Passé sombre pourrait bénir:

O hearts full of filth, O mouths appalling,
Pestiferous mouths, go at it some more!
Some wine for these vile torpors, on these tables ...
Your bellies are molten with shame, O Victors!

Open your nostrils to glorious nauseas!
Dip in strong poison the cords of your throats!
To your childish napes where he presses his hands
The Poet declares: "O cowards, go nuts!

Because you diddle at the belly of Woman,
You dread yet another convulsion in her
Who, crying out, smothers your brood on her bosom,
Your vile brood, with a horrendous pressure.

Lunatics, syphilitics, kings, puppets, surrogates,
What can they matter to Paris the Whore,
Your bodies and souls, your poisons, your rags?
She'll shed you like lice, you putrescent eyesores!

And when you're laid low, moaning over spilled guts,
Wrung out, howling loud for your money, and lost,
The red courtesan, her breasts swollen with battles,
Far from your stupors will shake arduous fists!

When your feet in a rage have so heavily danced,
Paris! after you've taken such jabs of the knife,
As you lie dying, holding in your clear pupils
Some good from the savage resurgence of life,

O dolorous city, O city half dead,
Head and two breasts thrust forth toward Destiny
Throwing wide to your pallor its millions of doors,
City that the dark Past could beatify:

Corps remagnétisé pour les énormes peines,
Tu rebois donc la vie effroyable! tu sens
Sourdre le flux des vers livides en tes veines,
Et sur ton clair amour rôder les doigts glaçants!

Et ce n'est pas mauvais. Les vers, les vers livides
Ne gêneront pas plus ton souffle de Progrès
Que les Stryx n'éteignaient l'œil des Cariatides
Où des pleurs d'or astral tombaient des bleus degrés."

Quoique ce soit affreux de te revoir couverte,
Ainsi; quoiqu'on n'ait fait jamais d'une cité
Ulcère plus puant à la Nature verte,
Le Poète te dit: "Splendide est ta Beauté!"

L'orage t'a sacrée suprême poésie;
L'immense remuement des forces te secourt;
Ton œuvre bout, la mort gronde, Cité choisie!
Amasse les strideurs au cœur du clairon sourd.

Le Poète prendra le sanglot des Infâmes,
La haine des Forçats, la clameur des Maudits;
Et ses rayons d'amour flagelleront les Femmes.
Ses strophes bondiront: Voilà! voilà! bandits!

—Société, tout est rétabli:—les orgies
Pleurent leur ancien râle aux anciens lupanars:
Et les gaz en délire, aux murailles rougies,
Flambent sinistrement vers les azurs blafards!

Mai 1871

Remagnetized body for gargantuan pains,
Once again you drink up horrid life! And you feel
Come surging the flow of pale worms in your veins,
And on your clear love prowl fingers of ice!

And it's not so bad. The worms, the pale worms
Will no more halt the Progress carried on your breath
Than the Striges could blind the Caryatids' eyes
Where tears of astral gold fell from blue ether."

Though it's awful to ponder you covered this way;
Though no one had ever dared make of a city
So fetid an ulcer on Nature's green earth,
The Poet cries unto you: "Splendid is thy Beauty!"

The storm consecrates your supreme poetry;
The vast movement of forces comes to your aid;
Your works seethe, your death rumbles, O chosen City!
Amass the sharp cries of your clarion call.

The Poet will take up the sobs of the Villains,
The hatred of Convicts, the cries of the Damned;
And his flashes of love will flagellate Women.
His verses will leap up: There! there go the thieves!

—Society, all is restored:—the orgies
In decrepit brothels rehash their death sighs:
And gas fires in folly, against reddened walls,
Flame ominously toward the anemic skies!

May 1871

Les Mains de Jeanne-Marie

Jeanne-Marie a des mains fortes,
Mains sombres que l'été tanna,
Mains pâles comme des mains mortes.
—Sont-ce des mains de Juana?

Ont-elles pris les crèmes brunes
Sur les mares des voluptés?
Ont-elles trempé dans des lunes
Aux étangs de sérénités?

Ont-elles bu des cieux barbares,
Calmes sur les genoux charmants?
Ont-elles roulé des cigares
Ou trafiqué des diamants?

Sur les pieds ardents des Madones
Ont-elles fané des fleurs d'or?
C'est le sang noir des belladones
Qui dans leur paume éclate et dort.

Mains chasseresses des diptères
Dont bombinent les bleuisons
Aurorales, vers les nectaires?
Mains décanteuses de poisons?

Oh! quel Rêve les a saisies
Dans les pandiculations?
Un rêve inouï des Asies,
Des Khenghavars ou des Sions?

Jeanne-Marie's Hands

Jeanne-Marie has sturdy hands,
Tanned and darkened by the sun,
Pale like fingers of the dead.
—Are these Juana's idle hands?

Have they slathered on brown creams
In unctuous pools of luxury?
Have they dipped in moonlight clear
In basins of serenity?

Have they drunk from savage skies,
Resting calm on gallant laps?
Have they ever rolled cigars
Or contrabanded diamonds?

On Madonnas' ardent feet
Have they wilted flowers of gold?
It's belladonnas' blackened blood
That in their palms blossoms and sleeps.

Hands that swat away the fly
Mizzing in auroral blue,
Toward the gaping nectaries?
Hands that decant poisons too?

Oh! What Dream has gotten hold
In their pandiculations?
A dream of Orients untold,
Of Kangavars or Zions?

—Ces mains n'ont pas vendu d'oranges,
Ni bruni sur les pieds des dieux:
Ces mains n'ont pas lavé les langes
Des lourds petits enfants sans yeux.

Ce ne sont pas mains de cousine
Ni d'ouvrières aux gros fronts
Que brûle, aux bois puant l'usine,
Un soleil ivre de goudrons.

Ce sont des ployeuses d'échines,
Des mains qui ne font jamais mal,
Plus fatales que des machines,
Plus fortes que tout un cheval!

Remuant comme des fournaises,
Et secouant tous ses frissons,
Leur chair chante des Marseillaises
Et jamais les Eleisons!

Ça serrerait vos cous, ô femmes
Mauvaises, ça broierait vos mains,
Femmes nobles, vos mains infâmes
Pleines de blancs et de carmins.

L'éclat de ces mains amoureuses
Tourne le crâne des brebis!
Dans leurs phalanges savoureuses
Le grand soleil met un rubis!

Une tache de populace
Les brunit comme un sein d'hier;
Le dos de ces Mains est la place
Qu'en baisa tout Révolté fier!

—These hands have sold no oranges
Nor tanned upon the feet of gods:
They have not washed the swaddling clothes
Of leaden children small and blind.

These are not a cousin's hands,
Or of workers with wide brows
Roasting in hot factories
Under the tar-besotted sun.

These are hands that fracture spines,
Hands that without malice act,
Deadlier than a machine,
Stronger than a stallion's kick!

Running hot like furnaces,
Spreading far and wide their shivers,
Their flesh rings out "La Marseillaise,"
But kyrie eleisons, never!

They'll squeeze your neck, O wicked wench,
They'll crush your hands, O nobles,
Your hands so full of villainy
And white and carmine red.

The dazzle in those loving hands
Wrenches round the skulls of sheep!
And in their wondrous phalanges
The great sun puts a ruby!

The people's mark has burnished them
As if upon a worn-out breast;
The backs of these Hands are the place
That any Rebel's proud to kiss.

Elles ont pâli, merveilleuses,
Au grand soleil d'amour chargé,
Sur le bronze des mitrailleuses
A travers Paris insurgé!

Ah! quelquefois, ô Mains sacrées,
A vos poings, Mains où tremblent nos
Lèvres jamais désenivrées,
Crie une chaîne aux clairs anneaux!

Et c'est un soubresaut étrange
Dans nos êtres, quand, quelquefois,
On veut vous déhâler, Mains d'ange,
En vous faisant saigner les doigts!

They have paled, so marvelous,
In the sun laden with love,
On the bronze of Gatling guns
Throughout Paris in revolt!

Ah! at times, O sacred Hands,
Hands on which our austere lips
Quiver lightly, links of chain
Wrap around your blazing fists!

And such a baffling jolt to feel
In our beings, when, indeed,
They'd whiten you, angelic Hands,
By making your fingers bleed!

Les Sœurs de charité

Le jeune homme dont l'œil est brillant, la peau brune,
Le beau corps de vingt ans qui devrait aller nu,
Et qu'eût, le front cerclé de cuivre, sous la lune
Adoré, dans la Perse un Génie inconnu,

Impétueux avec des douceurs virginales
Et noires, fier de ses premiers entêtements,
Pareil aux jeunes mers, pleurs de nuits estivales,
Qui se retournent sur des lits de diamants;

Le jeune homme, devant les laideurs de ce monde
Tressaille dans son cœur largement irrité,
Et plein de la blessure éternelle et profonde,
Se prend à désirer sa sœur de charité.

Mais, ô Femme, monceau d'entrailles, pitié douce,
Tu n'es jamais la Sœur de charité, jamais,
Ni regard noir, ni ventre où dort une ombre rousse,
Ni doigts légers, ni seins splendidement formés.

Aveugle irréveillée aux immenses prunelles,
Tout notre embrassement n'est qu'une question:
C'est toi qui pends à nous, porteuse de mamelles,
Nous te berçons, charmante et grave Passion.

Tes haines, tes torpeurs fixes, tes défaillances,
Et les brutalités souffertes autrefois,
Tu nous rends tout, ô Nuit pourtant sans malveillances,
Comme un excès de sang épanché tous les mois.

The Sisters of Mercy

The young man with bright eye and cinnamon skin,
Lithe body of twenty years made to go nude,
And who, forehead ringed with copper, under the moon,
By a nameless Genie in Persia was adored,

Impulsive, with a sweetness at once virginal
And dark, proud of his first obstinacies,
Like burgeoning seas, sobs of summer eves
Tossing and turning on diamond beds;

The young man, before the foulness of this world,
Feels shudders run through his irascible heart,
And filled with the deep and perpetual wound,
Conceives a desire for his sister of mercy.

But, O Woman, heap of entrails, gentle pity,
You are never the Sister of Mercy, no, never,
Not dark gaze, nor belly where red shadow sleeps,
Nor fingers so light, nor breasts nicely formed.

Unwoke and unseeing, with pupils enlarged,
All our embrace is merely a question:
It's you who hang from us, O bearer of udders,
It's we who rock you, grave and charming Passion.

Your hates, your set torpors, your deficiencies
And the brutalities that were suffered back then
You throw back at us, but without hostility,
O Night, like a mensual excess of blood.

—Quand la femme, portée un instant, l'épouvante,
Amour, appel de vie et chanson d'action,
Viennent la Muse verte et la Justice ardente
Le déchirer de leur auguste obsession.

Ah! sans cesse altéré des splendeurs et des calmes,
Délaissé des deux Sœurs implacables, geignant
Avec tendresse après la science aux bras almes,
Il porte à la nature en fleur son front saignant.

Mais la noire alchimie et les saintes études
Répugnent au blessé, sombre savant d'orgueil;
Il sent marcher sur lui d'atroces solitudes.
Alors, et toujours beau, sans dégoût du cercueil,

Qu'il croie aux vastes fins, Rêves ou Promenades
Immenses, à travers les nuits de Vérité,
Et t'appelle en son âme et ses membres malades,
Ô Mort mystérieuse, ô sœur de charité.

Juin 1871

—When woman, once wanted, leaves him horrified
Like love, song of life and signal for action,
Then come the Green Muse and impassioned Justice
To tear him apart with their noble obsession.

Ah! ceaselessly thirsting for splendors and calm,
Cast off by these two ruthless Sisters, he moans
Tenderly for science with beneficent arms,
And bends wounded brow to nature in bloom.

But black alchemy and studies religious
Disgust this hurt man, somber expert in pride;
He feels march upon him atrocious seclusions.
Then, good-looking still, unmoved by the casket,

He'll believe in grand exits, in Dreams or immense
Excursions, across the vast nightscapes of Truth,
And cry out to you with his soul and sick limbs,
O sister of mercy, O inscrutable Death.

June 1871

Voyelles

A noir, E blanc, I rouge, U vert, O bleu: voyelles,
Je dirai quelque jour vos naissances latentes:
A, noir corset velu des mouches éclatantes
Qui bombinent autour des puanteurs cruelles,

Golfes d'ombre; E, candeurs des vapeurs et des tentes,
Lances des glaciers fiers, rois blancs, frissons d'ombelles;
I, pourpres, sang craché, rire des lèvres belles
Dans la colère ou les ivresses pénitentes;

U, cycles, vibrements divins des mers virides,
Paix des pâtis semés d'animaux, paix des rides
Que l'alchimie imprime aux grands fronts studieux;

O, suprême Clairon plein des strideurs étranges,
Silences traversés des Mondes et des Anges;
—O l'Oméga, rayon violet de Ses Yeux!

Vowels

A black, E white, I red, U green, O blue:
Vowels, someday I'll relate your secret birth:
A, bristling black corset of shimmering flies
Mizzing about an unbearable stench,

Gulf of night; E, white of vapors and tents,
Proud glacier spears, ivory kings, Queen Anne's lace;
I, shades of crimson, spat blood, comely lips
Laughing in anger, or penitent drunks;

U, cycles, divine hum of viridian seas,
Peace of scrub-ground dotted with beasts, peace of lines
That alchemy etches in studious brows;

O, great Clarion so dissonant and shrill,
Silences crisscrossed by Angels and Worlds:
—O the Omega, violet beam of Your Eyes!

Les Chercheuses de poux

Quand le front de l'enfant, plein de rouges tourmentes,
Implore l'essaim blanc des rêves indistincts,
Il vient près de son lit deux grandes sœurs charmantes
Avec de frêles doigts aux ongles argentins.

Elles assoient l'enfant auprès d'une croisée
Grande ouverte où l'air bleu baigne un fouillis de fleurs,
Et dans ses lourds cheveux où tombe la rosée
Promènent leurs doigts fins, terribles et charmeurs.

Il écoute chanter leurs haleines craintives
Qui fleurent de longs miels végétaux et rosés,
Et qu'interrompt parfois un sifflement, salives
Reprises sur la lèvre ou désirs de baisers.

Il entend leurs cils noirs battant sous les silences
Parfumés; et leurs doigts électriques et doux
Font crépiter parmi ses grises indolences
Sous leurs ongles royaux la mort des petits poux.

Voilà que monte en lui le vin de la Paresse,
Soupirs d'harmonica qui pourrait délirer;
L'enfant se sent, selon la lenteur des caresses,
Sourdre et mourir sans cesse un désir de pleurer.

The Lice-Pickers

When the child's brow, teeming with torments red,
Longs for the swarm of vague pale dreams,
Two charming big sisters come to his bed
With slight tapered fingers and nails that gleam.

They settle the child near a large window frame
Wide open, where blue air bathes a jumble of flowers,
And through his thick hair on which dew descends
Their fine digits rove, bewitching and terrible.

He follows the song of their hesitant breaths
That bloom in long nectars vegetal and rosy
Interrupted sometimes by a whistle, saliva
Sucked back from a lip, or desire for a kiss.

In his gray languor, he hears their black lashes
Beat in perfumed silence; and their gentle fingers,
When between royal nails an electric crackle
Announces the death of each tiny louse.

And in him then flows the elixir of Sleep,
Harmonica sighs that meander along;
If caresses are late, the child always feels
Well up and die down a long yearning to weep.

Le Bateau ivre

Comme je descendais des Fleuves impassibles,
Je ne me sentis plus guidé par les haleurs:
Des Peaux-Rouges criards les avaient pris pour cibles,
Les ayant cloués nus aux poteaux de couleurs.

J'étais insoucieux de tous les équipages,
Porteur de blés flamands ou de cotons anglais.
Quand avec mes haleurs ont fini ces tapages,
Les Fleuves m'ont laissé descendre où je voulais.

Dans les clapotements furieux des marées,
Moi, l'autre hiver, plus sourd que les cerveaux d'enfants,
Je courus! Et les Péninsules démarrées
N'ont pas subi tohu-bohus plus triomphants.

La tempête a béni mes éveils maritimes.
Plus léger qu'un bouchon j'ai dansé sur les flots
Qu'on appelle rouleurs éternels de victimes,
Dix nuits, sans regretter l'œil niais des falots!

Plus douce qu'aux enfants la chair des pommes sûres,
L'eau verte pénétra ma coque de sapin
Et des taches de vins bleus et des vomissures
Me lava, dispersant gouvernail et grappin.

Et dès lors, je me suis baigné dans le Poème
De la Mer, infusé d'astres, et lactescent,
Dévorant les azurs verts; où, flottaison blême
Et ravie, un noyé pensif parfois descend;

The Drunken Boat

As I glided down impassive Rivers,
I no longer felt boatmen guiding my path:
Whooping Redskins had used them for targets,
And nailed their nude corpses to the colorful masts.

I couldn't care less about the crew or its cargo,
Flemish grain or English twill.
When my boatmen were gone and the ruckus all over,
The Rivers carried me at my will.

In the mad undulations of furious tides,
In the winter I ran, duller than a child's brain!
And in spring, the Peninsulas wrenching apart
Had never split to such triumphant strains.

My maritime wakings were blessed by the storm.
Lighter than cork I danced on the waves
That some call the eternal rollers of victims,
For ten nights, never missing the lamps' stupid rays!

Sweeter than to children the flesh of sour apples,
The green water entered my hull made of pine
And of stains of old vomit and indigo wine
Cleansed me, while scattering rudder and grapple.

And from then on, I immersed myself in the Poem
Of the Sea, infused by stars and lactescent,
Devouring the green azure; where a floater pale
And happy, a pensive carcass, might descend;

Où, teignant tout à coup les bleuités, délires
Et rhythmes lents sous les rutilements du jour,
Plus fortes que l'alcool, plus vastes que nos lyres,
Fermentent les rousseurs amères de l'amour!

Je sais les cieux crevant en éclairs, et les trombes
Et les ressacs et les courants: je sais le soir,
L'Aube exaltée ainsi qu'un peuple de colombes,
Et j'ai vu quelquefois ce que l'homme a cru voir!

J'ai vu le soleil bas, taché d'horreurs mystiques,
Illuminant de longs figements violets,
Pareils à des acteurs de drames très antiques
Les flots roulant au loin leurs frissons de volets!

J'ai rêvé la nuit verte aux neiges éblouies,
Baiser montant aux yeux des mers avec lenteurs,
La circulation des sèves inouïes,
Et l'éveil jaune et bleu des phosphores chanteurs!

J'ai suivi, des mois pleins, pareille aux vacheries
Hystériques, la houle à l'assaut des récifs,
Sans songer que les pieds lumineux des Maries
Pussent forcer le mufle aux Océans poussifs!

J'ai heurté, savez-vous, d'incroyables Florides
Mêlant aux fleurs des yeux de panthères à peaux
D'hommes! Des arcs-en-ciel tendus comme des brides
Sous l'horizon des mers, à de glauques troupeaux!

J'ai vu fermenter les marais énormes, nasses
Où pourrit dans les joncs tout un Léviathan!
Des écroulements d'eaux au milieu des bonaces,
Et les lointains vers les gouffres cataractant!

Where, suddenly tinting the blueness, the frenzies
And slow rhythms beneath the dazzle of day,
Stronger than liquor, vaster than lyres,
Love's bitter redness ferment and decay!

I know the skies bursting with flashes, and winds,
And the swells and currents: I know the dark eve,
Dawn in its glory and nations of doves,
And I've witnessed what men only thought they had seen!

I've seen the low sun, stained with mystical horrors,
Illuminate with frozen violet strains,
Like actors in dramas from antiquity,
The distant waves rolling their shuddering panes!

I dreamed of green nightscapes with dazzling snows,
A kiss slowly rising to the eyes of the sea,
The circulation of remarkable sap,
And quick phosphorescence in yellow and blue!

For months did I trail, like hysterical cattle,
The fierce swelling surges assaulting the reefs,
Not thinking that Virgins' luminous feet
Might drive on the muzzle of those sluggish Seas!

I crashed, don't you know, into fabulous Floridas
Where flowers combine with the eyes of black panthers
In human skin! Rainbows stretched taut like reins
'Neath the surface of oceans to greenish-blue herds!

I've seen great fermenting swamps, and fish traps
Amid bulrushes where a Leviathan rots!
I've seen torrents of water fall into flat calm,
And distant cascades rushing toward the abyss!

Glaciers, soleils d'argent, flots nacreux, cieux de braises!
Échouages hideux au fond des golfes bruns
Où les serpents géants dévorés des punaises
Choient, des arbres tordus, avec de noirs parfums!

J'aurais voulu montrer aux enfants ces dorades
Du flot bleu, ces poissons d'or, ces poissons chantants.
—Des écumes de fleurs ont bercé mes dérades
Et d'ineffables vents m'ont ailé par instants.

Parfois, martyr lassé des pôles et des zones,
La mer dont le sanglot faisait mon roulis doux
Montait vers moi ses fleurs d'ombre aux ventouses jaunes
Et je restais, ainsi qu'une femme à genoux…

Presque île, ballottant sur mes bords les querelles
Et les fientes d'oiseaux clabaudeurs aux yeux blonds.
Et je voguais, lorsqu'à travers mes liens frêles
Des noyés descendaient dormir, à reculons!

Or moi, bateau perdu sous les cheveux des anses,
Jeté par l'ouragan dans l'éther sans oiseau,
Moi dont les Monitors et les voiliers des Hanses
N'auraient pas repêché la carcasse ivre d'eau;

Libre, fumant, monté de brumes violettes,
Moi qui trouais le ciel rougeoyant comme un mur
Qui porte, confiture exquise aux bons poètes,
Des lichens de soleil et des morves d'azur,

Qui courais, taché de lunules électriques,
Planche folle, escorté des hippocampes noirs,
Quand les juillets faisaient crouler à coups de triques
Les cieux ultramarins aux ardents entonnoirs;

Glaciers, silver suns, pearly tides, ember skies!
Hideous wrecks in the depths of brown gulfs
Where monstrous serpents devoured by vermin
Fall from gnarled trees, giving off black perfumes!

I wish I could show these dorados to children,
These gold fish in blue tides, and these others that sing.
—Foaming florescence has lulled my unmooring
And ineffable winds sometimes given me wings.

At times, martyr weary of poles and of zones,
The vast sea whose sobbing caused my gentle roll
Lifted toward me its dark flowers with suckers pale
And I stayed, like a woman bent down on her knees...

Like an isle, tossing around on my decks the complaints
And droppings of mocking black birds with blond eyes.
And I navigated, when through my fragile rigging
Drowned bodies came creeping down backward to sleep!

Now I, a boat lost 'neath the swirled hair of coves,
By hurricanes tossed into featherless ether,
I, whom Hanseatic ships or clad Monitors
Wouldn't have fished from the depths of the sea;

Free, smoking, and rising in violet mists,
I, who pierced through the red sky like a wall
That offers—fine sweetmeats for proper young poets—
The mucus of azure and lichens of sun;

Who sailed on, a mad plank, dappled with crescents
Electric, escorted by seahorses black,
When July crushes down as if under a cudgel
Skies of ultramarine with blistering funnels;

Moi qui tremblais, sentant geindre à cinquante lieues
Le rut des Béhémots et les Maelstroms épais,
Fileur éternel des immobilités bleues,
Je regrette l'Europe aux anciens parapets!

J'ai vu des archipels sidéraux! et des îles
Dont les cieux délirants sont ouverts au vogueur:
—Est-ce en ces nuits sans fonds que tu dors et t'exiles,
Million d'oiseaux d'or, ô future Vigueur?

Mais, vrai, j'ai trop pleuré! Les Aubes sont navrantes.
Toute lune est atroce et tout soleil amer:
L'âcre amour m'a gonflé de torpeurs enivrantes.
Ô que ma quille éclate! Ô que j'aille à la mer!

Si je désire une eau d'Europe, c'est la flache
Noire et froide où vers le crépuscule embaumé
Un enfant accroupi plein de tristesse, lâche
Un bateau frêle comme un papillon de mai.

Je ne puis plus, baigné de vos langueurs, ô lames,
Enlever leur sillage aux porteurs de cotons,
Ni traverser l'orgueil des drapeaux et des flammes,
Ni nager sous les yeux horribles des pontons.

I, who trembled on hearing the moans from afar
Of the heavy Maelstroms and Behemoths in rut,
Spinner eternal of blue listlessness,
Of Europe I long for the old parapets!

I've seen archipelagos made up of stars!
And isles whose mad skies to the wanderer open:
—On those depthless nights do you sleep and depart,
Golden birds by the millions, O Vigor to come?

But enough of my tears! The Dawn is distressing.
Every moon is atrocious, and bleak every sun:
Bitter love has swelled me with dizzying torpors.
Let me go to the sea! Let my keel come undone!

If I miss any water in Europe, it's the puddle
Black and cold, at the hour when day slowly dies,
And a squatting child laden with sorrow lets loose
A boat light and frail like a May butterfly.

Waves, no longer can I, washed with your languor,
Follow the wake of the twill-bearing crafts,
Nor cross through the hubris of pennants and banners,
Nor drift past the haunted eyes of prison rafts.

"Qu'est-ce pour nous, mon cœur…"

Qu'est-ce pour nous, mon cœur, que les nappes de sang
Et de braise, et mille meurtres, et les longs cris
De rage, sanglots de tout enfer renversant
Tout ordre; et l'Aquilon encor sur les débris

Et toute vengeance? Rien!… —Mais si, toute encor,
Nous la voulons! Industriels, princes, sénats,
Périssez! puissance, justice, histoire, à bas!
Ça nous est dû. Le sang! le sang! la flamme d'or!

Tout à la guerre, à la vengeance, à la terreur,
Mon Esprit! Tournons dans la Morsure: Ah! passez,
Républiques de ce monde! Des empereurs,
Des régiments, des colons, des peuples, assez!

Qui remuerait les tourbillons de feu furieux,
Que nous et ceux que nous nous imaginons frères?
À nous! Romanesques amis: ça va nous plaire.
Jamais nous ne travaillerons, ô flots de feux!

Europe, Asie, Amérique, disparaissez.
Notre marche vengeresse a tout occupé,
Cités et campagnes! —Nous serons écrasés!
Les volcans sauteront! et l'océan frappé…

Oh! mes amis!—mon cœur, c'est sûr, ils sont des frères—,
Noirs inconnus, si nous allions! allons! allons!
Ô malheur! je me sens frémir, la vieille terre,
Sur moi de plus en plus à vous! la terre fond,

Ce n'est rien! j'y suis! j'y suis toujours.

"What's it to us, heart of mine..."

What's it to us, heart of mine, these pools of blood
And embers, and the multiple murders, and the long cries
Of rage, sobs of all hell toppling every order;
And the chill wind still howling over the rubble

And all the vengeance? Nothing!...—And yet, we do want it,
All of it! Princes, senators, industrialists,
Perish! power, justice, history, die!
Blood! blood! golden flames! It's our due.

Give over to war, to vengeance, to terror,
My Spirit! Tooth and nail in the Wound: Pass away,
Republics of this world! Of emperors,
Regiments, colonists, peoples, enough!

Who will stir the whirlwinds of this furious fire,
If not us and those we imagine brothers?
To us! Storybook friends: how happy we'll be.
Never will we work, O incendiary floods!

Europe, Asia, America, vanish.
Our vengeful march has occupied all,
Town and country!—We will be crushed!
Volcanoes will erupt! and the oceans rise...

Oh, my friends!—my heart, they are brothers for sure—
Black strangers, let us go on! go on! go on!
O misfortune! I feel myself shiver, the earth,
The old earth collapses, on me and on you!

No matter! I'm here! I'm still here.

La Rivière de Cassis

La Rivière de Cassis roule ignorée
   En des vaux étranges:
La voix de cent corbeaux l'accompagne, vraie
   Et bonne voix d'anges:
Avec les grands mouvements des sapinaies
   Quand plusieurs vents plongent.

Tout roule avec des mystères révoltants
   De campagnes d'anciens temps;
De donjons visités, de parcs importants:
   C'est en ces bords qu'on entend
Les passions mortes des chevaliers errants:
   Mais que salubre est le vent!

Que le piéton regarde à ces clairevoies:
   Il ira plus courageux.
Soldats des forêts que le Seigneur envoie,
   Chers corbeaux délicieux!
Faites fuir d'ici le paysan matois
   Qui trinqué d'un moignon vieux.

Mai 1872

The Cassis River

Unseen the Cassis River flows
　　　Through curious dales:
Along with the voice of a hundred crows
　　　And true sounds of angels:
With sweeping shifts in pinewood groves
　　　When many winds fall.

It flows in revolting mysteries
　　　From bold campaigns of olden times;
From dungeons viewed, great forestries:
　　　It's on these shores that we can hear
The passions past of errant knights:
　　　But oh, how healthful is the wind!

Let walkers through these openings peer:
　　　They'll move on more courageous.
Forest soldiers sent by the Lord,
　　　Dear crows so delicious!
Chase from here the peasant who toasts
　　　With aged claw malicious.

May 1872

Honte

Tant que la lame n'aura
Pas coupé cette cervelle,
Ce paquet blanc, vert et gras
À vapeur jamais nouvelle,

(Ah! Lui, devrait couper son
Nez, sa lèvre, ses oreilles,
Son ventre! et faire abandon
De ses jambes! ô merveille!)

Mais, non, vrai, je crois que tant
Que pour sa tête la lame
Que les cailloux pour son flanc
Que pour ses boyaux la flamme

N'auront pas agi, l'enfant
Gêneur, la si sotte bête,
Ne doit cesser un instant
De ruser et d'être traître

Comme un chat des Monts-Rocheux;
D'empuantir toutes sphères!
Qu'à sa mort pourtant, ô mon Dieu!
S'élève quelque prière!

Shame

As long as the blade
Hasn't sliced this brain,
That white, green, fatty mass,
Full of old hot air,

(Ah! *He* should sever
His nose, lips, ears,
And belly! and ditch
His legs! wonder of wonders!)

No, really, as long as
The blade hasn't done in his head
The stones his flank
Or the flame his guts,

Then that silly little beast,
That troublesome brat,
Will never quit
Using treachery and guile

Like a Rocky Mountain cat;
Or stinking up every sphere!
Yet, O my Lord! upon his death
Let someone say a prayer!

Mémoire

I

L'eau claire; comme le sel des larmes d'enfance,
L'assaut au soleil des blancheurs des corps de femmes;
la soie, en foule et de lys pur, des oriflammes
sous les murs dont quelque pucelle eut la défense;

l'ébat des anges;—Non...le courant d'or en marche,
meut ses bras, noirs, et lourds, et frais surtout, d'herbe. Elle
sombre, ayant le Ciel bleu pour ciel-de-lit, appelle
pour rideaux l'ombre de la colline et de l'arche.

II

Eh! l'humide carreau tend ses bouillons limpides!
L'eau meuble d'or pâle et sans fond les couches prêtes.
Les robes vertes et déteintes des fillettes
font les saules, d'où sautent les oiseaux sans brides.

Plus pure qu'un louis, jaune et chaude paupière
le souci d'eau—ta foi conjugale, ô l'Épouse! —
au midi prompt, de son terne miroir, jalouse
au ciel gris de chaleur la Sphère rose et chère.

III

Madame se tient trop debout dans la prairie
prochaine où neigent les fils du travail; l'ombrelle

Memory

I

Clear water; like salt from childish tears,
The sunlit assault of women's white forms;
silk, in droves and pure lily, banners on walls
that some vestal virgin was called to defend;

frolics angelic;—No...the gold current rolling,
moves her arms, black and heavy, and fresh with green grass.
She sinks darkly, blue Heaven for her canopy, summons
as drapes the deep shadows of hillside and arch.

II

The humid pane tenders its crystalline bubbling!
With pale gold the water arrays the beds deep.
The faded green dresses of girls still budding
form willows, from which unbridled swallows leap.

Purer than doubloons, eyelid warm and yellow,
the marsh marigolds—Bride, your conjugal faith!—
at noon sharp, from her cloudy mirror, begrudges
to the sultry gray sky the Sphere rosy and dear.

III

Madam stands too erect in the meadow
nearby where filaments of her labor snow; parasol

aux doigts; foulant l'ombelle; trop fière pour elle;
des enfants lisant dans la verdure fleurie

leur livre de maroquin rouge! Hélas, Lui, comme
mille anges blancs qui se séparent sur la route,
s'éloigne par delà la montagne! Elle, toute
froide, et noire, court! après le départ de l'homme!

IV

Regret des bras épais et jeunes d'herbe pure!
Or des lunes d'avril au cœur du saint lit! Joie
des chantiers riverains à l'abandon, en proie
aux soirs d'août qui faisaient germer ces pourritures!

Qu'elle pleure à présent sous les remparts! l'haleine
des peupliers d'en haut est pour la seule brise.
Puis, c'est la nappe, sans reflets, sans source, grise:
un vieux, dragueur, dans sa barque immobile, peine.

V

Jouet de cet œil d'eau morne, je n'y puis prendre,
ô canot immobile! oh! bras trop courts! ni l'une
ni l'autre fleur: ni la jaune qui m'importune,
là; ni la bleue, amie à l'eau couleur de cendre.

Ah! la poudre des saules qu'une aile secoue!
Les roses des roseaux dès longtemps dévorées!
Mon canot, toujours fixe; et sa chaîne tirée
Au fond de cet œil d'eau sans bords,—à quelle boue?

between her fingers rolled; careless stroll; too proud;
offspring reading on the flowering knoll

their books bound in red leather! Alas, He, like
a thousand white angels who part on the road,
is already setting off past the hills! She,
all frigid, and black, runs! after the man is gone!

IV

Longing for the thick young arms of pure grass! Gold of
April moons in the heart of the sacrosanct bed!
Joy of riverside worksites in dereliction, prey
to evenings in August that bred these decays!

Now she weeps under ramparts! The cool breath
of poplars above is the only breeze. Then,
it's the surface, with no source or reflections, gray:
an old dredger, in his still rowboat, toils away.

V

A pawn to that watery eye, I can't grasp,
O motionless boat! oh, short reach! either one
of these flowers: not the yellow that perturbs,
nor the blue, friend to water the color of ash.

Ah! white willow powder shaken off by a wing!
Rose of the reeds so long ago devoured!
My boat, ever still; its chain fast stuck
In the bed of this vast liquid eye,—to what muck?

A Season in Hell /
Une saison en enfer

♦

"Jadis, si je me souviens bien, ma vie était un festin où s'ouvraient tous les cœurs, où tous les vins coulaient. Un soir, j'ai assis la Beauté sur mes genoux.—Et je l'ai trouvée amère.—Et je l'ai injuriée.

Je me suis armé contre la justice.

Je me suis enfui. Ô sorcières, ô misère, ô haine, c'est à vous que mon trésor a été confié!

Je parvins à faire s'évanouir dans mon esprit toute l'espérance humaine. Sur toute joie pour l'étrangler j'ai fait le bond sourd de la bête féroce.

J'ai appelé les bourreaux pour, en périssant, mordre la crosse de leurs fusils. J'ai appelé les fléaux, pour m'étouffer avec le sable, le sang. Le malheur a été mon dieu. Je me suis allongé dans la boue. Je me suis séché à l'air du crime. Et j'ai joué de bons tours à la folie.

Et le printemps m'a apporté l'affreux rire de l'idiot.

Or, tout dernièrement m'étant trouvé sur le point de faire le dernier *couac*! j'ai songé à rechercher la clef du festin ancien, où je reprendrais peut-être appétit.

La charité est cette clef.—Cette inspiration prouve que j'ai rêvé!

"Tu resteras hyène, etc...," se récrie le démon qui me couronna de si aimables pavots. "Gagne la mort avec tous tes appétits, et ton égoïsme et tous les péchés capitaux."

Ah! j'en ai trop pris: —Mais, cher Satan, je vous en conjure, une prunelle moins irritée! et en attendant les quelques petites lâchetés en retard, vous qui aimez dans l'écrivain l'absence des facultés descriptives ou instructives, je vous détache ces quelques hideux feuillets de mon carnet de damné.

♦

"Back then, if I recall, my life was a feast in which every heart was open, every wine flowed. One evening, I sat Beauty on my knees.—And I found her bitter.—And I cursed her.

I took up arms against Justice.

I fled. O witches, O poverty, O hatred, to you I have entrusted my treasure!

I managed to expunge all human hope from my mind. I've pounced on every joy with the silent leap of the wild beast, and throttled it.

I've summoned executioners so that I could gnaw on the butt of their rifles as I died. I've called down plagues to choke me with blood and sand. Sorrow has been my god. I lay down in the mud, then dried off in the air of crime. And I played some fine tricks on madness.

And springtime brought me the appalling laugh of the idiot.

Now, having recently found myself on the verge of my last *croak!* it's occurred to me to seek the key to that former banquet, hoping I might regain some of my appetite.

Charity is that key.—This inspiration proves I must have been dreaming!

"You'll always be a hyena, etc . . . ," cries the demon who crowned me with such pleasant poppies. "Earn your death with all your appetites, your selfishness, and every cardinal sin."

Ah, I've had too much:—But, dear Satan, a less irritated eye, if you please! Meanwhile, to those who like their poets without descriptive or instructive faculties, and in anticipation of some last cowardly turpitudes, I've torn out for you these hideous pages from my notebook of the damned.

93

Mauvais Sang

J'ai de mes ancêtres gaulois l'œil bleu blanc, la cervelle étroite, et la maladresse dans la lutte. Je trouve mon habillement aussi barbare que le leur. Mais je ne beurre pas ma chevelure.

Les Gaulois étaient les écorcheurs de bêtes, les brûleurs d'herbes les plus ineptes de leur temps.

D'eux, j'ai: l'idolâtrie et l'amour du sacrilège;—oh! tous les vices, colère, luxure,—magnifique, la luxure;—surtout mensonge et paresse.

J'ai horreur de tous les métiers. Maîtres et ouvriers, tous paysans, ignobles. La main à plume vaut la main à charrue.—Quel siècle à mains! —Je n'aurai jamais ma main. Après, la domesticité mène trop loin. L'honnêteté de la mendicité me navre. Les criminels dégoûtent comme des châtrés: moi, je suis intact, et ça m'est égal.

Mais! qui a fait ma langue perfide tellement qu'elle ait guidé et sauvegardé jusqu'ici ma paresse? Sans me servir pour vivre même de mon corps, et plus oisif que le crapaud, j'ai vécu partout. Pas une famille d'Europe que je ne connaisse.—J'entends des familles comme la mienne, qui tiennent tout de la déclaration des Droits de l'Homme.—J'ai connu chaque fils de famille!

◆ ◆ ◆

Si j'avais des antécédents à un point quelconque de l'histoire de France!

Mais, non, rien.

Il m'est bien évident que j'ai toujours été de race inférieure. Je ne puis comprendre la révolte. Ma race ne se souleva jamais que pour piller: tels les loups à la bête qu'ils n'ont pas tuée.

Bad Blood

From my Gaulish ancestors I've inherited pale blue eyes, a narrow brain, and ineptitude in battle. I think my clothing is as barbarous as theirs. But I don't butter my hair.

The Gauls were the most incompetent slaughterers of beasts and burners of herbs in their day.

From them, I've got: idolatry and a love of sacrilege;—oh! every vice, anger, lust,—magnificent lust;—lying and laziness above all.

I loathe every trade. Masters and laborers, all peasants, ignoble. The writer's hand is worth the plowman's hand.— What a century of hands!—I'll never have a hand. Besides, domestic life leads you too far astray. The honesty of pan-handling grieves me. Criminals are as revolting as castrates: I'm intact, myself, and it's all the same to me.

But! who made my tongue deceitful enough to guide and guard my indolence for so long? I've lived all over, lazier than a toad, and put my body into it as little as possible. Not a single family in Europe I haven't met.—I mean families like mine, who owe it all to the Declaration of the Rights of Man.—I've known every mother's son!

◆ ◆ ◆

If only I had antecedents at some point in the history of France!

But no, not a one.

It's obvious I've always been of an inferior race. I can't understand revolt. My race never rose up except to pillage: like wolves onto prey they hadn't killed.

Je me rappelle l'histoire de la France fille aînée de l'Église. J'aurais fait, manant, le voyage de terre sainte, j'ai dans la tête des routes dans les plaines souabes, des vues de Byzance, des remparts de Solyme; le culte de Marie, l'attendrissement sur le crucifié s'éveillent en moi parmi les mille féeries profanes.—Je suis assis, lépreux, sur les pots cassés et les orties, au pied d'un mur rongé par le soleil.—Plus tard, reître, j'aurais bivaqué sous les nuits d'Allemagne.

Ah! encore: je danse le sabbat dans une rouge clairière, avec des vieilles et des enfants.

Je ne me souviens pas plus loin que cette terre-ci et le christianisme. Je n'en finirais pas de me revoir dans ce passé. Mais toujours seul; sans famille; même, quelle langue parlais-je? Je ne me vois jamais dans les conseils du Christ; ni dans les conseils des Seigneurs,—représentants du Christ.

Qu'étais-je au siècle dernier: je ne me retrouve qu'aujourd'hui. Plus de vagabonds, plus de guerres vagues. La race inférieure a tout couvert—le peuple, comme on dit, la raison; la nation et la science.

Oh! la science! On a tout repris. Pour le corps et pour l'âme,—le viatique,—on a la médecine et la philosophie,—les remèdes de bonnes femmes et les chansons populaires arrangées. Et les divertissements des princes et les jeux qu'ils interdisaient! Géographie, cosmographie, mécanique, chimie!...

La science, la nouvelle noblesse! Le progrès. Le monde marche! Pourquoi ne tournerait-il pas?

C'est la vision des nombres. Nous allons à l'*Esprit*. C'est très-certain, c'est oracle, ce que je dis. Je comprends, et ne sachant m'expliquer sans paroles païennes, je voudrais me taire.

◆　◆　◆

I remember the history of France, that eldest daughter of the Church. As a commoner, I would have made the trek to the Holy Land. I envision routes through the Swabian plains, views of Byzantium, the walls of Solyma; worship of the Virgin and tender pity for the Crucified One stir in my breast amid a slew of profane fantasies.—I'm sitting, a leper, on shattered pots and nettles, at the base of a wall eaten away by sunlight.—Later, as a mercenary thug, I'd have bivouacked under the German nights.

Ah! one more: I'm dancing on the Sabbath in a red clearing, with old women and children.

I can't remember anything beyond this land and Christianity. I'll never stop seeing myself in this past. But always alone; no family; and also, what language did I speak? I never see myself in the councils of Christ; or in the councils of Lords,—Christ's agents.

What was I in the last century: I only find myself in the here and now. No more vagabonds, no more vague wars. The inferior race has blotted out everything—the people, as they say, and reason; nation and science.

Oh! science! They've taken it all back. For body and soul,—the viaticum,—we have medicine and philosophy,—old wives' remedies and arranged popular songs. And the pastimes of princes and the entertainments they prohibited! Geography, cosmography, mechanics, chemistry! . . .

Science, the new nobility! Progress. The world marches on! Why can't it just turn?

It's a numerical vision. We're heading toward the *Spirit*. What I'm saying is very certain, oracular. I understand, and since I don't know how to express myself without pagan words, I'd just as soon shut up.

◆ ◆ ◆

Le sang païen revient! L'Esprit est proche, pourquoi Christ ne m'aide-t-il pas, en donnant à mon âme noblesse et liberté. Hélas! l'Évangile a passé! l'Évangile! l'Évangile.

J'attends Dieu avec gourmandise. Je suis de race inférieure de toute éternité.

Me voici sur la plage armoricaine. Que les villes s'allument dans le soir. Ma journée est faite; je quitte l'Europe. L'air marin brûlera mes poumons; les climats perdus me tanneront. Nager, broyer l'herbe, chasser, fumer surtout; boire des liqueurs fortes comme du métal bouillant,—comme faisaient ces chers ancêtres autour des feux.

Je reviendrai, avec des membres de fer, la peau sombre, l'œil furieux: sur mon masque, on me jugera d'une race forte. J'aurai de l'or: je serai oisif et brutal. Les femmes soignent ces féroces infirmes retour des pays chauds. Je serai mêlé aux affaires politiques. Sauvé.

Maintenant je suis maudit, j'ai horreur de la patrie. Le meilleur, c'est un sommeil bien ivre, sur la grève.

◆ ◆ ◆

On ne part pas.—Reprenons les chemins d'ici, chargé de mon vice, le vice qui a poussé ses racines de souffrance à mon côté, dès l'âge de raison—qui monte au ciel, me bat, me renverse, me traîne.

La dernière innocence et la dernière timidité. C'est dit. Ne pas porter au monde mes dégoûts et mes trahisons.

Allons! La marche, le fardeau, le désert, l'ennui et la colère.

À qui me louer? Quelle bête faut-il adorer? Quelle sainte image attaque-t-on? Quels cœurs briserai-je? Quel mensonge dois-je tenir? —Dans quel sang marcher?

Plutôt, se garder de la justice.—La vie dure, l'abrutissement simple,—soulever, le poing desséché, le couvercle du cercueil,

Pagan blood returns! The Spirit is near, why doesn't Christ help me, give my soul nobility and freedom. Alas! the Gospel has passed! the Gospel! the Gospel.

I await God gluttonously. I am of an inferior race for all eternity.

Here I am on Armorican shores. May the cities light up at dusk. My journey is over; I'm leaving Europe. The salt air will scorch my lungs; the lost climates will tan me. Swim, chew herbs, hunt, above all smoke; drink liquors strong as boiling metal,—as those dear ancestors of mine used to do around the fire.

I'll return with limbs of steel, dark skin, and furious eye: from my mask, they'll conclude I'm of a strong race. I'll have gold: I'll be lazy and brutal. Women care for those fierce invalids returning from hot climates. I'll dabble in politics. Saved.

Now I'm the damned, I despise the fatherland. The best thing is a good, drunken snooze on the strand.

◆ ◆ ◆

We're not leaving.—Let's set off again on these local roads, weighed down with my vice, the vice that has dug its painful roots into my side since the age of reason—that rises into the sky, pummels me, knocks me down, drags me along.

Utter innocence and utter timidity. I've said it. Don't bring my disgusts and my betrayals into the world.

On we go! March, burden, desert, boredom, and fury.

Who to rent myself out to? What beast should I adore? What sacred image is being attacked? What hearts shall I break? What lie must I maintain?—What blood shall I trample?

Rather, guard against justice.—Hard life, simple stupor,— prise open the coffin lid with desiccated fists, sit, suffocate. And so no old age, no dangers: terror is not French.

s'asseoir, s'étouffer. Ainsi point de vieillesse, ni de dangers: la terreur n'est pas française.

—Ah! je suis tellement délaissé que j'offre à n'importe quelle divine image des élans vers la perfection.

Ô mon abnégation, ô ma charité merveilleuse! ici-bas, pourtant!

De profundis Domine, suis-je bête!

◆ ◆ ◆

Encore tout enfant, j'admirais le forçat intraitable sur qui se referme toujours le bagne; je visitais les auberges et les garnis qu'il aurait sacrés par son séjour; je voyais *avec son idée* le ciel bleu et le travail fleuri de la campagne; je flairais sa fatalité dans les villes. Il avait plus de force qu'un saint, plus de bon sens qu'un voyageur—et lui, lui seul! pour témoin de sa gloire et de sa raison.

Sur les routes, par des nuits d'hiver, sans gîte, sans habits, sans pain, une voix étreignait mon cœur gelé: "Faiblesse ou force: te voilà, c'est la force. Tu ne sais ni où tu vas ni pourquoi tu vas, entre partout, réponds à tout. On ne te tuera pas plus que si tu étais cadavre." Au matin j'avais le regard si perdu et la contenance si morte, que ceux que j'ai rencontrés *ne m'ont peut-être pas vu.*

Dans les villes la boue m'apparaissait soudainement rouge et noire, comme une glace quand la lampe circule dans la chambre voisine, comme un trésor dans la forêt! Bonne chance, criais-je, et je voyais une mer de flammes et de fumées au ciel; et, à gauche, à droite, toutes les richesses flambant comme un milliard de tonnerres.

Mais l'orgie et la camaraderie des femmes m'étaient interdites. Pas même un compagnon. Je me voyais devant une foule exaspérée, en face du peloton d'exécution, pleurant du malheur qu'ils n'aient pu comprendre, et pardonnant!

Ah! I'm so abandoned that I offer my efforts at perfection to any graven image.

O my abnegation, O my marvelous charity! but, right down here!

De profundis Domine, silly me!

◆ ◆ ◆

When I was a small child, I admired the irredeemable criminal who always landed behind bars; I visited the inns and furnished rooms he sanctified with his stay; I saw *with his mind* the blue sky and floral handiwork of the countryside; I scented his fate in the cities. He had more strength than a saint, more savvy than a traveler—and he alone! was witness to his glory and his reason.

On the roads on winter nights, with no shelter, no clothes, no bread, a voice gripped my frozen heart: "Weakness or strength: here you are, it's strength. You don't know where you're going or why, enter everywhere, answer everything. They can't kill you any more than if you were a corpse." In the morning, I had such dazed eyes and dead countenance that I *might have passed unnoticed*.

In the cities, the mud suddenly appeared red and black, like a mirror when the lamp moves about in the next room, like a treasure in the woods! Good luck, I cried, and I saw a sea of flame and smoke billowing in the sky; and on all sides, riches ablaze like a billion lightning bolts.

But orgies and the friendship of women were denied me. Not even a companion. I saw myself before an enraged mob, facing the firing squad, weeping with a sorrow they couldn't comprehend, and forgiving!—Like Joan of Arc!—"Priests, professors, teachers, you are wrong to hand me over to justice. I've never belonged to this population; I've never been a Christian; I'm of the race who sang under torture; I don't

—Comme Jeanne d'Arc! —"Prêtres, professeurs, maîtres, vous vous trompez en me livrant à la justice. Je n'ai jamais été de ce peuple-ci; je n'ai jamais été chrétien; je suis de la race qui chantait dans le supplice; je ne comprends pas les lois; je n'ai pas le sens moral, je suis une brute: vous vous trompez..."

Oui, j'ai les yeux fermés à votre lumière. Je suis une bête, un nègre. Mais je puis être sauvé. Vous êtes de faux nègres, vous maniaques, féroces, avares. Marchand, tu es nègre; magistrat, tu es nègre; général, tu es nègre; empereur, vieille démangeaison, tu es nègre: tu as bu d'une liqueur non taxée, de la fabrique de Satan.—Ce peuple est inspiré par la fièvre et le cancer. Infirmes et vieillards sont tellement respectables qu'ils demandent à être bouillis.—Le plus malin est de quitter ce continent, où la folie rôde pour pourvoir d'otages ces misérables. J'entre au vrai royaume des enfants de Cham.

Connais-je encore la nature? me connais-je? —*Plus de mots*. J'ensevelis les morts dans mon ventre. Cris, tambour, danse, danse, danse, danse! Je ne vois même pas l'heure où, les blancs débarquant, je tomberai au néant.

Faim, soif, cris, danse, danse, danse, danse!

◆ ◆ ◆

Les blancs débarquent. Le canon! Il faut se soumettre au baptême, s'habiller, travailler.

J'ai reçu au cœur le coup de la grâce. Ah! je ne l'avais pas prévu!

Je n'ai point fait le mal. Les jours vont m'être légers, le repentir me sera épargné. Je n'aurai pas eu les tourments de l'âme presque morte au bien, où remonte la lumière sévère comme les cierges funéraires. Le sort du fils de famille, cercueil prématuré couvert de limpides larmes. Sans doute la débauche est bête, le vice est bête; il faut jeter la pourriture à l'écart. Mais l'horloge ne sera pas arrivée à ne plus sonner

understand your laws; I have no moral sense, I'm a brute: you're wrong..."

Yes, my eyes are shut to your light. I'm a beast, a nigger. But I can be saved. You, you ferocious, avaricious maniacs, you're false niggers. Merchant, you're a nigger; magistrate, you're a nigger; general, you're a nigger; emperor, you decrepit rash, you're a nigger, too: you've guzzled bootleg liquor from Satan's own still.—These people are inspired by fever and cancer. Invalids and oldsters are so respectable that they want boiling.—The smartest thing is to leave this continent, where madness goes prowling for hostages with which to furnish these wretches. I enter the true realm of the descendants of Ham.

Do I still know nature? do I know myself?—*No more words.* I bury the dead in my gut. Shouts, drumbeats, dance, dance, dance, dance! I can't even foresee the moment when, as the white men land, I'll tumble into the void.

Hunger, thirst, shouts, dance, dance, dance, dance!

◆　◆　◆

The white men have landed. Cannons! We must submit to baptism, wear clothes, go to work.

My heart has been smitten by grace. Didn't see that one coming!

I've done no harm. My days will be light, I shall be spared repentance. I'll avoid the torments of a soul nearly insensitive to good, one that gives off the astringent light of funeral candles. The fate of the dutiful son, an untimely casket bathed in limpid tears. No doubt debauchery is stupid, vice is stupid; we have to cast aside decay. But the clock can no longer strike the hour of pure pain alone! Will I be abducted like a child to play in Paradise, all sorrow forgotten!

Quick! are there other lives?—To sleep in wealth is

que l'heure de la pure douleur! Vais-je être enlevé comme un enfant, pour jouer au paradis dans l'oubli de tout le malheur!

Vite! est-il d'autres vies?—Le sommeil dans la richesse est impossible. La richesse a toujours été bien public. L'amour divin seul octroie les clefs de la science. Je vois que la nature n'est qu'un spectacle de bonté. Adieu chimères, idéals, erreurs.

Le chant raisonnable des anges s'élève du navire sauveur: c'est l'amour divin.—Deux amours! je puis mourir de l'amour terrestre, mourir de dévouement. J'ai laissé des âmes dont la peine s'accroîtra de mon départ! Vous me choisissez parmi les naufragés, ceux qui restent sont-ils pas mes amis?

Sauvez-les!

La raison est née. Le monde est bon. Je bénirai la vie. J'aimerai mes frères. Ce ne sont plus des promesses d'enfance. Ni l'espoir d'échapper à la vieillesse et à la mort. Dieu fait ma force, et je loue Dieu.

◆ ◆ ◆

L'ennui n'est plus mon amour. Les rages, les débauches, la folie, dont je sais tous les élans et les désastres,—tout mon fardeau est déposé. Apprécions sans vertige l'étendue de mon innocence.

Je ne serais plus capable de demander le réconfort d'une bastonnade. Je ne me crois pas embarqué pour une noce avec Jésus-Christ pour beau-père.

Je ne suis pas prisonnier de ma raison. J'ai dit: Dieu. Je veux la liberté dans le salut: comment la poursuivre? Les goûts frivoles m'ont quitté. Plus besoin de dévouement ni d'amour divin. Je ne regrette pas le siècle des cœurs sensibles. Chacun a sa raison, mépris et charité: je retiens ma place au sommet de cette angélique échelle de bon sens.

impossible. Wealth has always been a public good. Only divine love can bestow the keys to science. I see that Nature is but a spectacle of kindness. Farewell, wild fancies, ideals, errors.

The reasonable chant of angels rises from the salutary vessel: it's divine love.—Two loves! I can die of earthly love or of devotion. I've abandoned souls whose pain will swell with my departure! You've plucked me from among the shipwrecked, but aren't those left behind my friends?

Save them!

Reason is born. The world is good. I shall bless life. I shall love my brothers. These are no longer childish promises. Nor a bid to escape old age and death. God grants me strength, and I praise God.

◆ ◆ ◆

I'm no longer infatuated with boredom. Rages, debauchery, madness, of which I know every fit and disaster,—I've laid my whole burden down. Let us appreciate soberly the breadth of my innocence.

I can no longer ask for the comfort of a beating. I do not believe I'm off to get married and gain Jesus Christ as father-in-law.

I am not captive of my reason. I've said: God. I want freedom in salvation, but how do I pursue it? I've lost my taste for frivolity. No further need for devotion or divine love. I don't miss the century of sensitive hearts. To each his reason, contempt, and charity: I retain my spot at the top of this angelic ladder of good sense.

As for conventional happiness, domestic or otherwise... no, I can't. I'm too scattered and weak. Life flourishes in work, an old truism: my own life isn't weighty enough, it flits away and floats far above action, that dear point in the world.

Quant au bonheur établi, domestique ou non…non, je ne peux pas. Je suis trop dissipé, trop faible. La vie fleurit par le travail, vieille vérité: moi, ma vie n'est pas assez pesante, elle s'envole et flotte loin au-dessus de l'action, ce cher point du monde.

Comme je deviens vieille fille, à manquer du courage d'aimer la mort!

Si Dieu m'accordait le calme céleste, aérien, la prière,—comme les anciens saints.—Les saints! des forts! les anachorètes, des artistes comme il n'en faut plus!

Farce continuelle! Mon innocence me ferait pleurer. La vie est la farce à mener par tous.

◆ ◆ ◆

Assez! voici la punition.—*En marche!*

Ah! les poumons brûlent, les tempes grondent! la nuit roule dans mes yeux, par ce soleil! le cœur…les membres…

Où va-t-on? au combat? je suis faible! les autres avancent. Les outils, les armes…le temps!…

Feu! feu sur moi! Là! ou je me rends.—Lâches! —Je me tue! Je me jette aux pieds des chevaux!

Ah!…

—Je m'y habituerai.

Ce serait la vie française, le sentier de l'honneur!

What an old maid I'm becoming, lacking the courage to love death!

If God granted me celestial, aerial calm, prayer,—like the ancient saints.—The saints! the strong! the anchorites, artists of the sort we no longer need!

Constant farce! I weep at my innocence. Life is a farce led by everyone.

◆ ◆ ◆

Enough! here is punishment.—*Forward, march!*

Ah! my lungs are burning, temples thumping! Night fills my eyes, in broad daylight! heart...limbs...

Where are we going? to battle? I'm weak! let the others advance. Tools, weapons...time!...

Fire! fire on me! Over here! or I'll surrender.—Cowards!—I'll kill myself! throw myself under horses' hooves!

Ah!...

—I'll get used to it.

It would be the French thing to do, the path of honor!

Nuit de l'enfer

J'ai avalé une fameuse gorgée de poison.—Trois fois béni soit le conseil qui m'est arrivé! —Les entrailles me brûlent. La violence du venin tord mes membres, me rend difforme, me terrasse. Je meurs de soif, j'étouffe, je ne puis crier. C'est l'enfer, l'éternelle peine! Voyez comme le feu se relève! Je brûle comme il faut. Va, démon!

J'avais entrevu la conversion au bien et au bonheur, le salut. Puis-je décrire la vision, l'air de l'enfer ne souffre pas les hymnes! C'était des millions de créatures charmantes, un suave concert spirituel, la force et la paix, les nobles ambitions, que sais-je?

Les nobles ambitions!

Et c'est encore la vie! —Si la damnation est éternelle! Un homme qui veut se mutiler est bien damné, n'est-ce pas? Je me crois en enfer, donc j'y suis. C'est l'exécution du caté-chisme. Je suis esclave de mon baptême. Parents, vous avez fait mon malheur et vous avez fait le vôtre. Pauvre innocent! l'enfer ne peut attaquer les païens.—C'est la vie encore! Plus tard, les délices de la damnation seront plus profondes. Un crime, vite, que je tombe au néant, de par la loi humaine.

Tais-toi, mais tais-toi!...C'est la honte, le reproche, ici: Satan qui dit que le feu est ignoble, que ma colère est af-freusement sotte.—Assez!...Des erreurs qu'on me souffle, magies, parfums faux, musiques puériles.—Et dire que je tiens la vérité, que je vois la justice: j'ai un jugement sain et arrêté, je suis prêt pour la perfection...Orgueil.—La peau de ma tête se dessèche. Pitié! Seigneur, j'ai peur. J'ai soif, si soif! Ah! l'enfance, l'herbe, la pluie, le lac sur les pierres, *le clair de lune quand le clocher sonnait douze*...le diable est au clocher, à cette heure. Marie! Sainte-Vierge!...—Horreur de ma bêtise.

A Night of Hell

I drained a mighty cup of poison.—May the advice that came to me be three times blessed!—My guts are on fire. The violence of the venom twists my limbs in knots, leaves me misshapen, flat. I'm dying of thirst, I'm suffocating, I can't cry out. It's hell, eternal damnation! See how the fire is rising! I'm burning, as well I should. Off with you, demon!

I glimpsed the conversion to goodness and happiness, salvation. Let me describe the vision, the air of hell doesn't suffer hymns! There were millions of charming creatures, a mellow spiritual concert, peace and strength, noble ambitions, and who knows what else.

Noble ambitions!

And still it's life!—If damnation is eternal! A man who wishes to mutilate himself is truly damned, isn't he? I believe I'm in hell, therefore I am. The execution of catechism. I am a slave of my baptism. Parents, you have brought about my misfortune, and your own. The poor innocent! Hell cannot attack pagans.—It's life still! Later, the delights of damnation will run deeper. Quick, a crime, so I can tumble into nothingness, by human law.

Shut up, oh, shut up, already!...It's shame and reproach here: Satan says that fire is noble, that my anger is laughable.—Enough!...The errors being whispered to me, magic, false perfumes, childish music.—And to think that I hold the truth, that I see justice: I have a sane and settled sense of judgment, I am ready for perfection...Pride.—The skin on my scalp is drying out. Pity! Lord, I'm afraid. I'm thirsty, so thirsty! Ah! childhood, grass, rain, water on stones, *the moonlight when the clock struck twelve*...the devil is in the steeple, at that hour. Mary! Holy Virgin!...—Horror of my stupidity.

Là-bas, ne sont-ce pas des âmes honnêtes, qui me veulent du bien…Venez…J'ai un oreiller sur la bouche, elles ne m'entendent pas, ce sont des fantômes. Puis, jamais personne ne pense à autrui. Qu'on n'approche pas. Je sens le roussi, c'est certain.

Les hallucinations sont innombrables. C'est bien ce que j'ai toujours eu: plus de foi en l'histoire, l'oubli des principes. Je m'en tairai: poètes et visionnaires seraient jaloux. Je suis mille fois le plus riche, soyons avare comme la mer.

Ah çà! l'horloge de la vie s'est arrêtée tout à l'heure. Je ne suis plus au monde.—La théologie est sérieuse, l'enfer est certainement *en bas*—et le ciel en haut.—Extase, cauchemar, sommeil dans un nid de flammes.

Que de malices, dans l'attention dans la campagne… Satan, Ferdinand, court avec les graines sauvages…Jésus marche sur les ronces purpurines, sans les courber…Jésus marchait sur les eaux irritées. La lanterne nous le montra debout, blanc et des tresses brunes, au flanc d'une vague d'émeraude…

Je vais dévoiler tous les mystères: mystères religieux ou naturels, mort, naissance, avenir, passé, cosmogonie, néant. Je suis maître en fantasmagories.

Écoutez!…

J'ai tous les talents! —Il n'y a personne ici et il y a quelqu'un: je ne voudrais pas répandre mon trésor.—Veut-on des chants nègres, des danses de houris? Veut-on que je disparaisse, que je plonge à la recherche de l'*anneau*? Veut-on? Je ferai de l'or, des remèdes.

Fiez-vous donc à moi, la foi soulage, guide, guérit. Tous, venez,—même les petits enfants,—que je vous console, qu'on répande pour vous son cœur,—le cœur merveilleux! —Pauvres hommes, travailleurs! Je ne demande pas de prières; avec votre confiance seulement, je serai heureux.

—Et pensons à moi. Ceci me fait un peu regretter le monde.

Over there, aren't those honest souls who wish me well... Come...I have a pillow over my mouth, they can't hear me, they're ghosts. Besides, no one ever thinks about others. Don't come any nearer. I smell of char, that's for certain.

Countless hallucinations. It's indeed what I've always had: more faith in history, neglect of principles. I'll keep quiet about it: poets and visionaries will be jealous. I'm a thousand times richer, let's be miserly like the sea.

Ah, well! the clock of life just stopped. I'm no longer in the world.—Theology is serious business, hell is certainly *down there*—and heaven above.—Ecstasy, nightmare, slumber in a nest of flames.

So many tricks of attention in the country... Satan, Ferdinand, run with the bad seeds... Jesus walks on the purple brambles without bending them... Jesus walked on the agitated waters. The lantern showed him to us standing, white and with brown locks, on the flank of an emerald wave...

I shall unveil all the mysteries: mysteries religious or natural, death, birth, future, past, cosmogony, nothingness. I am a master at phantasmagoria.

Listen!...

I possess every talent!—There's no one here and there's someone: I wouldn't want to spread my treasure too thin.— Do you want Negro chants, houris' dances? Do you want me to disappear, dive deep in search of the *ring*? Do you? I'll make gold, and remedies.

So trust me, faith eases, guides, heals. Come one, come all,—even little children,—that I may console you, that a heart may be poured out to you,—marvelous heart!—Paupers, laborers! I'm not asking for prayers; just your trust will make me happy.

—And let's think of me. This makes me miss the world a little. I'm lucky I don't suffer more. My life was nothing but gentle follies, it's a shame.

J'ai de la chance de ne pas souffrir plus. Ma vie ne fut que folies douces, c'est regrettable.

Bah! faisons toutes les grimaces imaginables.

Décidément, nous sommes hors du monde. Plus aucun son. Mon tact a disparu. Ah! mon château, ma Saxe, mon bois de saules. Les soirs, les matins, les nuits, les jours... Suis-je las!

Je devrais avoir mon enfer pour la colère, mon enfer pour l'orgueil,—et l'enfer de la caresse; un concert d'enfers.

Je meurs de lassitude. C'est le tombeau, je m'en vais aux vers, horreur de l'horreur! Satan, farceur, tu veux me dissoudre, avec tes charmes. Je réclame. Je réclame! un coup de fourche, une goutte de feu.

Ah! remonter à la vie! Jeter les yeux sur nos difformités. Et ce poison, ce baiser mille fois maudit! Ma faiblesse, la cruauté du monde! Mon Dieu, pitié, cachez-moi, je me tiens trop mal!—Je suis caché et je ne le suis pas.

C'est le feu qui se relève avec son damné.

Bah! let's make every conceivable grimace.

We are decidedly out of the world. Not a sound. My tact has vanished. Ah! my castle, my Saxony, my willow forest. Evenings, mornings, nights, days... I'm so tired!

I should have a hell for my anger, a hell for my pride,—and the hell of caresses; a concert of hells.

I'm dying of weariness. It's the tomb, I'm going to the worms, horror of horrors! Satan, you old trickster, you want to melt me with your charms. I demand. I demand! a jab from the pitchfork, a drop of fire.

Ah! rise back up to life! Cast a glance at our deformities. And this poison, this kiss a thousand times cursed! My weakness, the cruelty of the world! My God, have pity, hide me, I'm holding up very poorly!—I am hidden and I am not.

It's the fire that rises with the damned.

Délires I

Écoutons, la confession d'un compagnon d'enfer:

"Ô divin Époux, mon Seigneur, ne refusez pas la confession de la plus triste de vos servantes. Je suis perdue. Je suis soûle. Je suis impure. Quelle vie!

"Pardon, divin Seigneur, pardon! Ah! pardon! Que de larmes! Et que de larmes encor plus tard, j'espère!

"Plus tard, je connaîtrai le divin Époux! Je suis née soumise à Lui.—L'autre peut me battre maintenant!

"À présent, je suis au fond du monde! Ô mes amies!... non, pas mes amies... Jamais délires ni tortures semblables... Est-ce bête!

"Ah! je souffre, je crie. Je souffre vraiment. Tout pourtant m'est permis, chargée du mépris des plus méprisables cœurs.

"Enfin, faisons cette confidence, quitte à la répéter vingt autres fois,—aussi morne, aussi insignifiante!

"Je suis esclave de l'Époux infernal, celui qui a perdu les vierges folles. C'est bien ce démon-là. Ce n'est pas un spectre, ce n'est pas un fantôme. Mais moi qui ai perdu la sagesse, qui suis damnée et morte au monde,—on ne me tuera pas! —Comment vous le décrire! Je ne sais même plus parler. Je suis en deuil, je pleure, j'ai peur. Un peu de fraîcheur, Seigneur, si vous voulez, si vous voulez bien!

"Je suis veuve...—J'étais veuve...—mais oui, j'ai été bien sérieuse jadis, et je ne suis pas née pour devenir squelette!...— Lui était presque un enfant... Ses délicatesses mystérieuses m'avaient séduite. J'ai oublié tout mon devoir humain pour le suivre. Quelle vie! La vraie vie est absente. Nous ne sommes pas au monde. Je vais où il va, il le faut. Et souvent il

Deliria I

THE FOOLISH VIRGIN
THE INFERNAL BRIDEGROOM

Let's hear the confession of a companion in hell:

"O divine Bridegroom, my Lord, do not refuse the confession of the most miserable of your servant maidens. I am lost. I am drunk. I am impure. What a life!

"Forgive me, divine Lord, forgive me! Ah, forgive me! So many tears! And so many more to come, I hope!

"Later, I shall know the divine Bridegroom! I was born to be His subject.—The other one can beat me now!

"For the moment I'm at the bottom of the world! O my friends!... no, not my friends... Never before such deliria or such tortures... It's so stupid!

"Ah! how I suffer and cry out. I'm truly suffering. Yet I'm allowed everything, burdened as I am with the contempt of the most contemptible hearts.

"Finally, let me tell you a secret, even if I have to repeat it twenty times over,—just as dreary, and as insignificant!

"I am the slave of the Infernal Bridegroom, the one who brought about the downfall of the foolish virgins. He is *that* demon. He's not a specter, not a ghost. But I, who have lost my wisdom, who am damned and dead to the world,—they will not kill me!—How can I describe him to you! I no longer even know how to speak. I am in mourning, I weep, I'm afraid. A little fresh air, Lord, if you would, if you would please!

"I'm a widow...—I was a widow...—oh yes, I was very serious once upon a time, and I wasn't meant to become a skeleton!... He was little more than a child... His mysterious thoughtfulness seduced me. I neglected all my human

s'emporte contre moi, *moi, la pauvre âme.* Le Démon! —C'est un Démon, vous savez, *ce n'est pas un homme.*

"Il dit: "Je n'aime pas les femmes. L'amour est à réinventer, on le sait. Elles ne peuvent plus que vouloir une position assurée. La position gagnée, cœur et beauté sont mis de côté: il ne reste que froid dédain, l'aliment du mariage, aujourd'hui. Ou bien je vois des femmes, avec les signes du bonheur, dont, moi, j'aurais pu faire de bonnes camarades, dévorées tout d'abord par des brutes sensibles comme des bûchers..."

"Je l'écoute faisant de l'infamie une gloire, de la cruauté un charme: "Je suis de race lointaine: mes pères étaient Scandinaves: ils se perçaient les côtes, buvaient leur sang.— Je me ferai des entailles par tout le corps, je me tatouerai, je veux devenir hideux comme un Mongol: tu verras, je hurlerai dans les rues. Je veux devenir bien fou de rage. Ne me montre jamais de bijoux, je ramperais et me tordrais sur le tapis. Ma richesse, je la voudrais tachée de sang partout. Jamais je ne travaillerai..." Plusieurs nuits, son démon me saisissant, nous roulions, je luttais avec lui! —Les nuits, souvent, ivre, il se poste dans des rues ou dans des maisons, pour m'épouvanter mortellement.—"On me coupera vraiment le cou; ce sera dégoûtant." Oh! ces jours où il veut marcher avec l'air du crime!

"Parfois il parle, en une façon de patois attendri, de la mort qui fait repentir, des malheureux qui existent certainement, des travaux pénibles, des départs qui déchirent les cœurs. Dans les bouges où nous enivrions, il pleurait en considérant ceux qui nous entouraient, bétail de la misère. Il relevait les ivrognes dans les rues noires. Il avait la pitié d'une mère méchante pour les petits enfants.—Il s'en allait avec des gentillesses de petite fille au catéchisme.—Il feignait d'être éclairé sur tout, commerce, art, médecine.—Je le suivais, il le faut!

"Je voyais tout le décor dont, en esprit, il s'entourait;

duties to follow him. What a life! Real life is absent. We are not in the world. I go where he goes, I have to. And often he flies off the handle at me, *me, the poor soul.* The Demon!— He's a Demon, you know, *he's not a man.*

"He said, 'I don't love women. We know love has to be reinvented. All they can do is wish for security. The minute they've got it, feelings and beauty go out the window: all that remains is cold disdain, the food of marriage these days. Or else I see women who show signs of happiness, whom I might have made into good comrades, devoured by brutes with all the sensitivity of funeral pyres...'

"I listen to him making a glory of infamy, a charm of cruelty: 'I am of a distant race: my forefathers were Scandinavians: they pierced their flanks, drank their blood.—I'll cover my body with gashes, I'll tattoo myself, I want to become hideous as a Mongol: you'll see, I'll howl in the streets. I want to go mad with rage. Never show me jewelry, I'll crawl and writhe on the carpet. I want my wealth spattered all over with blood. Never shall I work...' On several nights, when his demon grabbed me, we rolled around, I grappled with him!—Often at night, drunk, he hides in the street or in doorways, to scare me to death.—'They really will slit my throat; it'll be disgusting.' Oh! those days when he walks around trying to look like a criminal.

"Sometimes he speaks, in a kind of tender patois, of death that causes repentance, of the unfortunates who surely exist, of painful labors, heartrending departures. In the hovels where we get drunk, he wept at the thought of those around us, the cattle of poverty. He helped drunkards up from dark streets. He had a bad mother's pity for small children.—He would go to catechism as meekly as a little girl.—He claimed to know about all sorts of things, commerce, art, medicine.—I followed him; I had no choice!

"I saw the whole decor that he surrounded himself with

vêtements, draps, meubles: je lui prêtais des armes, une autre figure. Je voyais tout ce qui le touchait, comme il aurait voulu le créer pour lui. Quand il me semblait avoir l'esprit inerte, je le suivais, moi, dans des actions étranges et compliquées, loin, bonnes ou mauvaises: j'étais sûre de ne jamais entrer dans son monde. À côté de son cher corps endormi, que d'heures des nuits j'ai veillé, cherchant pourquoi il voulait tant s'évader de la réalité. Jamais l'homme n'eut pareil vœu. Je reconnaissais,—sans craindre pour lui,—qu'il pouvait être un sérieux danger dans la société.—Il a peut-être des secrets pour *changer la vie*? Non, il ne fait qu'en chercher, me répliquais-je. Enfin sa charité est ensorcelée, et j'en suis la prisonnière. Aucune autre âme n'aurait assez de force,—force de désespoir!—pour la supporter,—pour être protégée et aimée par lui. D'ailleurs, je ne me le figurais pas avec une autre âme: on voit son Ange, jamais l'Ange d'un autre,—je crois. J'étais dans son âme comme dans un palais qu'on a vidé pour ne pas voir une personne si peu noble que vous: voilà tout. Hélas! je dépendais bien de lui. Mais que voulait-il avec mon existence terne et lâche? Il ne me rendait pas meilleure, s'il ne me faisait pas mourir! Tristement dépitée, je lui dis quelquefois: "Je te comprends." Il haussait les épaules.

"Ainsi, mon chagrin se renouvelant sans cesse, et me trouvant plus égarée à mes yeux,—comme à tous les yeux qui auraient voulu me fixer, si je n'eusse été condamnée pour jamais à l'oubli de tous!—j'avais de plus en plus faim de sa bonté. Avec ses baisers et ses étreintes amies, c'était bien un ciel, un sombre ciel, où j'entrais, et où j'aurais voulu être laissée, pauvre, sourde, muette, aveugle. Déjà j'en prenais l'habitude. Je nous voyais comme deux bons enfants, libres de se promener dans le Paradis de tristesse. Nous nous accordions. Bien émus, nous travaillions ensemble. Mais, après une pénétrante caresse, il disait: "Comme ça te paraîtra drôle,

in his mind; clothes, sheets, furniture: I lent him weapons, another face. I saw everything that touched him, and how he wished he could create it for himself. When my mind seemed inert, I followed him, in strange and complicated deeds, far away, good or evil: I was sure I'd never enter his world. How many nighttime hours did I lie awake next to his dear sleeping body, trying to understand why he was so desperate to elude reality. Never had a man had such a wish. I recognized,—without fearing for him,—that he could pose a serious threat to society.—Did he perhaps hold the secrets to *change life*? No, he was only looking for them, I told myself. In short, his charity is bewitched, and I am its prisoner. No other soul would have the strength,—strength of despair!—to put up with him,—to be protected and loved by him. Besides, I never imagined him with another soul: one sees one's Angel, never another's Angel,—so I believe. I was in his soul as if in a palace that's been evacuated so you don't have to see someone as ignoble as yourself: that's all. Alas! I was very dependent on him. But what did he want with my dull, craven existence? He didn't make me any better, by not letting me die! Sometimes, in despair, I said to him, 'I understand you.' He merely shrugged.

"And so, my heartbreak constantly renewed, and finding myself increasingly lost in my own eyes,—as in all the eyes that would have stared at me, had I not been condemned to eternal neglect!—I had an ever greater hunger for his ministrations. With his kisses and tender embraces, it was indeed a heaven I entered, a somber heaven, where I would have liked to be left, poor, deaf, mute, and blind. I was already getting used to it. I saw us as two good children, free to walk around the Paradise of sadness. We meshed with each other. We worked together, deeply moved. But, after a penetrating caress, he said, 'How odd everything you've been through will seem, when I'm gone. When you no longer have my

quand je n'y serai plus, ce par quoi tu as passé. Quand tu n'auras plus mes bras sous ton cou, ni mon cœur pour t'y reposer, ni cette bouche sur tes yeux. Parce qu'il faudra que je m'en aille, très loin, un jour. Puis il faut que j'en aide d'autres: c'est mon devoir. Quoique ce ne soit guère ragoûtant..., chère âme..." Tout de suite je me pressentais, lui parti, en proie au vertige, précipitée dans l'ombre la plus affreuse: la mort. Je lui faisais promettre qu'il ne me lâcherait pas. Il l'a faite vingt fois, cette promesse d'amant. C'était aussi frivole que moi lui disant: "Je te comprends."

"Ah! je n'ai jamais été jalouse de lui. Il ne me quittera pas, je crois. Que devenir? Il n'a pas une connaissance; il ne travaillera jamais. Il veut vivre somnambule. Seules, sa bonté et sa charité lui donneraient-elles droit dans le monde réel? Par instants, j'oublie la pitié où je suis tombée: lui me rendra forte, nous voyagerons, nous chasserons dans les déserts, nous dormirons sur les pavés des villes inconnues, sans soins, sans peines. Ou je me réveillerai, et les lois et les mœurs auront changé,—grâce à son pouvoir magique,—le monde, en restant le même, me laissera à mes désirs, joies, nonchalances. Oh! la vie d'aventures qui existe dans les livres des enfants, pour me récompenser, j'ai tant souffert, me la donneras-tu? Il ne peut pas. J'ignore son idéal. Il m'a dit avoir des regrets, des espoirs: cela ne doit pas me regarder. Parle-t-il à Dieu? Peut-être devrais-je m'adresser à Dieu. Je suis au plus profond de l'abîme, et je ne sais plus prier.

"S'il m'expliquait ses tristesses, les comprendrais-je plus que ses railleries? Il m'attaque, il passe des heures à me faire honte de tout ce qui m'a pu toucher au monde, et s'indigne si je pleure.

"'Tu vois cet élégant jeune homme, entrant dans la belle et calme maison: il s'appelle Duval, Dufour, Armand, Maurice, que sais-je? Une femme s'est dévouée à aimer ce méchant idiot: elle est morte, c'est certes une sainte au ciel, à présent.

arms cradling your neck, or my heart to rest on, or this mouth on your eyes. Because I'll certainly have to go away, far away, someday. Then I'll have to help others: it's my duty. Although the prospect is not very appetizing . . . dear soul . . .' Suddenly I saw myself without him, overcome by vertigo, plunged into the most awful darkness: death. I made him promise never to leave me. He made them twenty times over, those lover's promises. They were just as shallow as me saying, 'I understand you.'

"Ah! I was never jealous of him. I don't think he'll ever leave me. To become what? He doesn't know anyone; he'll never hold a job. He wants to live as a sleepwalker. Would his goodness and charity alone qualify him for the real world? Sometimes I forget the pitiful state I've fallen into: he'll make me strong, we'll travel, we'll go hunting in the deserts, we'll sleep on the streets of unfamiliar cities, without cares or troubles. Yes, I'll awaken, and laws and customs will have changed,—thanks to his magical power,—the world, though remaining the same, will leave me to my desires, joys, and carefree ways. Oh! the adventurous life that exists in children's books: will you give this to me, as a reward for all my suffering? He cannot. I don't know his ideal. He says he has regrets, hopes: they must not concern me. Does he talk to God? Perhaps I should appeal to God. I'm in the depths of the abyss, and I no longer know how to pray.

"If he explained his sorrows to me, would I understand them better than his mockery? He attacks me, spends hours making me feel ashamed of everything in the world that might have touched me, and gets angry if I cry.

"'You see that elegant young man walking into the quiet, beautiful house: his name is Duval, Dufour, Armand, Maurice, whatever. Some woman dedicated herself to loving that paltry idiot: she's dead, she is surely a saint in heaven by now. You'll kill me off the way he killed that woman. That's the

Tu me feras mourir comme il a fait mourir cette femme. C'est notre sort, à nous, cœurs charitables...' Hélas! il avait des jours où tous les hommes agissant lui paraissaient les jouets de délires grotesques: il riait affreusement, longtemps.— Puis, il reprenait ses manières de jeune mère, de sœur aimée. S'il était moins sauvage, nous serions sauvés! Mais sa douceur aussi est mortelle. Je lui suis soumise.—Ah! je suis folle!

"Un jour peut-être il disparaîtra merveilleusement; mais il faut que je sache, s'il doit remonter à un ciel, que je voie un peu l'assomption de mon petit ami!"

Drôle de ménage!

fate of us charitable souls . . .' Alas! there were days when he considered any man who acted to be the plaything of grotesque delusions: he laughed, long and horribly.—Then he again assumed the manners of a young mother or beloved sister. If he were less savage, we'd be saved! But even his gentleness is deadly. I am his subject.—Ah, how foolish I am!

"Perhaps one day he'll miraculously disappear; but I'd have to know, if he were to ascend to some heaven; have to get a glimpse of my boyfriend's assumption!"

Peculiar couple!

Délires II

ALCHIMIE DU VERBE

À moi. L'histoire d'une de mes folies.

Depuis longtemps je me vantais de posséder tous les paysages possibles, et trouvais dérisoires les célébrités de la peinture et de la poésie moderne.

J'aimais les peintures idiotes, dessus des portes, décors, toiles de saltimbanques, enseignes, enluminures populaires; la littérature démodée, latin d'église, livres érotiques sans orthographe, romans de nos aïeules, contes de fées, petits livres de l'enfance, opéras vieux, refrains niais, rythmes naïfs.

Je rêvais croisades, voyages de découvertes dont on n'a pas de relations, républiques sans histoires, guerres de religion étouffées, révolutions de meurs, déplacements de races et de continents: je croyais à tous les enchantements.

J'inventai la couleur des voyelles! —*A* noir, *E* blanc, *I* rouge, *Ô* bleu, *U* vert.—Je réglai la forme et le mouvement de chaque consonne, et, avec des rythmes instinctifs, je me flattai d'inventer un verbe poétique accessible, un jour ou l'autre, à tous les sens. Je réservais la traduction.

Ce fut d'abord une étude. J'écrivais des silences, des nuits, je notais l'inexprimable, je fixais des vertiges.

◆　◆　◆

Loin des oiseaux, des troupeaux, des villageoises,
Que buvais-je, à genoux dans cette bruyère
Entourée de tendres bois de noisetiers,
Dans un brouillard d'après-midi tiède et vert?

Deliria II

ALCHEMY OF THE WORD

My turn. The tale of one of my follies.

For so long I boasted ownership of every possible landscape, sneered at the sacred cows of painting and modern poetry.

I loved inane paintings, lintel decorations, stage sets, acrobats' backdrops, shop signs, garish prints; outmoded literature, church Latin, pornographic booklets riddled with typos, the novels of our forebears, fairy tales, small children's books, old operas, corny refrains, naïve rhythms.

I dreamed of crusades, voyages of discovery that left no trace, republics with no history, suppressed religious wars, revolutions in mores, great drifts of races and continents; I believed unconditionally in magic.

I invented the color of vowels!—*A* black, *E* white, *I* red, *O* blue, *U* green—regulated the shape and movement of each consonant. With intuitive rhythms I prided myself on inventing the poetic Word that *all the senses* could access, someday. I reserved translation rights.

At first it was a study. I transcribed silences and nights, recorded the inexpressible. I captured whirlwinds.

◆ ◆ ◆

> Far from the birds, the herds, the village girls,
> What was I drinking, kneeling in that heather
> Circled by tender groves of hazel trees,
> In an afternoon mist warm and green?

Que pouvais-je boire dans cette jeune Oise,
—Ormeaux sans voix, gazon sans fleurs, ciel couvert!—
Boire à ces gourdes jaunes, loin de ma case
Chérie? Quelque liqueur d'or qui fait suer.

Je faisais une louche enseigne d'auberge.
—Un orage vint chasser le ciel. Au soir
L'eau des bois se perdait sur les sables vierges,
Le vent de Dieu jetait des glaçons aux mares;

Pleurant, je voyais de l'or—et ne pus boire.—

◆　◆　◆

À quatre heures du matin, l'été,
Le sommeil d'amour dure encore.
Sous les bocages s'évapore
L'odeur du soir fêté.

Là-bas, dans leur vaste chantier
Au soleil des Hespérides,
Déjà s'agitent—en bras de chemise—
Les Charpentiers.

Dans leurs Déserts de mousse, tranquilles,
Ils préparent les lambris précieux
Où la ville
Peindra de faux cieux.

Ô, pour ces Ouvriers charmants
Sujets d'un roi de Babylone,
Vénus! quitte un instant les Amants
Dont l'âme est en couronne.

What could I have drunk in that young River Oise,
—Voiceless elms, bloomless lawns, sky of lead!—
What drunk from those yellow flasks, far from my
Dear hut? Some golden liquor that makes you sweat.

I was a dubious signboard for an inn.
—A storm chased away the sky. That night
Forest waters sank into virgin sands,
God's winds glazed the ponds with hoar;

Weeping, I saw gold—and could drink no more.—

◆ ◆ ◆

At four o'clock on a summer's morn
Love's sleep lingers on.
Under the woods dissipate
The smells of honored night.

Yonder, in their vast workshop
In the sun of the Hesperides,
The Carpenters are bustling
In their shirtsleeves.

In their Deserts of foam, quiescent,
They prepare the precious panes
Where the city
Will paint bogus skies.

O, for these charming Workers
Subjects of a Babylonian king,
Venus! break away from your lovers
Whose souls form a ring.

Ô Reine des Bergers,
Porte aux travailleurs l'eau-de-vie,
Que leurs forces soient en paix
En attendant le bain dans la mer à midi.

◆ ◆ ◆

La vieillerie poétique avait une bonne part dans mon alchimie du verbe.

Je m'habituai à l'hallucination simple: je voyais très franchement une mosquée à la place d'une usine, une école de tambours faite par des anges, des calèches sur les routes du ciel, un salon au fond d'un lac; les monstres, les mystères; un titre de vaudeville dressait des épouvantes devant moi.

Puis j'expliquai mes sophismes magiques avec l'hallucination des mots!

Je finis par trouver sacré le désordre de mon esprit. J'étais oisif, en proie à une lourde fièvre: j'enviais la félicité des bêtes,—les chenilles, qui représentent l'innocence des limbes, les taupes, le sommeil de la virginité!

Mon caractère s'aigrissait. Je disais adieu au monde dans d'espèces de romances:

CHANSON DE LA PLUS HAUTE TOUR

Qu'il vienne, qu'il vienne,
Le temps dont on s'éprenne.

J'ai tant fait patience
Qu'à jamais j'oublie.
Craintes et souffrances
Aux cieux sont parties.
Et la soif malsaine
Obscurcit mes veines.

O Queen of the Shepherds,
Bring these men some brandy soon,
So that their strength might be at peace
Till they dive into the drink at noon.

◆ ◆ ◆

Poetic obsolescence played a huge part in my alchemy of the word.

I got used to simple hallucinations: I saw clear as day a mosque in place of a factory, drumming lessons led by angels, horse-drawn carriages on roads in the sky, a salon at the bottom of a lake; monsters, mysteries; a farcical title confronted me with horrors.

Then I explained my magical sophisms with verbal hallucinations!

I ended up deeming my mental disorder sacred. I was lazy, prey to a heavy fever: I envied beasts their happiness,—caterpillars, which represent the innocence of limbo; moles, the sleep of virginity!

My character turned sour. I bid the world farewell in various romances:

SONG OF THE HIGHEST TOWER

Let it come, let it come,
The time we dote upon.

I've been so patient
That I've forgot.
Fear and suffering
To heaven have gone.
And unholy thirst
Darkened my veins.

Qu'il vienne, qu'il vienne,
Le temps dont on s'éprenne.

Telle la prairie
À l'oubli livrée,
Grandie, et fleurie
D'encens et d'ivraies,
Au bourdon farouche
Des sales mouches.

Qu'il vienne, qu'il vienne,
Le temps dont on s'éprenne.

J'aimai le désert, les vergers brûlés, les boutiques fanées, les boissons tiédies. Je me traînais dans les ruelles puantes et, les yeux fermés, je m'offrais au soleil, dieu de feu.

"Général, s'il reste un vieux canon sur tes remparts en ruines, bombarde-nous avec des blocs de terre sèche. Aux glaces des magasins splendides! dans les salons! Fais manger sa poussière à la ville. Oxyde les gargouilles. Emplis les boudoirs de poudre de rubis brûlante … "

Oh! le moucheron enivré à la pissotière de l'auberge, amoureux de la bourrache, et que dissout un rayon!

FAIM

Si j'ai du goût, ce n'est guère
Que pour la terre et les pierres.
Je déjeune toujours d'air,
De roc, de charbons, de fer.

Mes faims, tournez. Paissez, faims,
     Le pré des sons.

Let it come, let it come,
The time we dote upon.

Like the prairie
To oblivion given,
Enlarged, in bloom
With scent and chaff,
To the buzzing fury
Of filthy flies.

Let it come, let it come,
The time we dote upon.

I loved the desert, burned-out orchards, faded shops, luke-
warm drinks. I dragged myself through fetid streets and, with
eyes closed, I offered myself to the sun, god of fire.

"General, if there remains one old cannon on your ruined
ramparts, bombard us with blocks of dried earth. In the
windows of splendid department stores! in salons! Make the
city eat its dust. Oxidize the gargoyles. Fill the boudoirs with
burning blood-red powder . . . "

Oh! the intoxicated gnat in the tavern urinal, besotted
with borage, dissolved by a sunbeam!

HUNGER

My taste is alone
For earth and for stone.
I always dine on air,
Rock, and iron, and coal.

Turn, my hungers. Hungers, graze
    In fields of seed.

Attirez le gai venin
    Des liserons.

Mangez les cailloux qu'on brise,
Les vieilles pierres d'églises;
Les galets des vieux déluges,
Pains semés dans les vallées grises.

           ◆ ◆ ◆

Le loup criait sous les feuilles
En crachant les belles plumes
De son repas de volailles:
Comme lui je me consume.

Les salades, les fruits
N'attendent que la cueillette;
Mais l'araignée de la haie
Ne mange que des violettes.

Que je dorme! que je bouille
Aux autels de Salomon.
Le bouillon court sur la rouille,
Et se mêle au Cédron.

Enfin, ô bonheur, ô raison, j'écartai du ciel l'azur, qui est
du noir, et je vécus, étincelle d'or de la lumière *nature*. De
joie, je prenais une expression bouffonne et égarée au pos-
sible:

Elle est retrouvée!
Quoi? l'éternité.
C'est la mer mêlée
    Au soleil.

Draw in the joyful poison
    Of bindweed.

Eat the stones we smash,
Old stones where we pray;
The pebbles of old floods,
Loaves scattered in valleys gray.

    ◆ ◆ ◆

Under leaves the wolf howled
Spitting out fine feathers
From his feast of fowls:
Like him I am devoured.

Salads and tree-ripened fruits
Wait only to be plucked;
But the spider in the hedge
Eats only violets.

May I sleep! may I boil
On the altars of Solomon.
The broth boils over the rust
And flows into the Kidron.

Finally, O bliss, O reason, from the sky I removed the
blue, which means black, and I lived, a spark of gold in
natural light. In a state of joy, I adopted as clownish and
disoriented a form of expression as possible:

Back it comes!
What? Eternity.
It's the blend of sea
    And sun.

Mon âme éternelle,
Observe ton vœu
Malgré la nuit seule
Et le jour en feu.

Donc tu te dégages
Des humains suffrages,
Des communs élans!
Tu voles selon…

—Jamais l'espérance.
    Pas d'*orietur*.
Science et patience,
Le supplice est sûr.

Plus de lendemain,
Braises de satin,
    Votre ardeur
    Est le devoir.

Elle est retrouvée!
—Quoi?—l'Éternité.
C'est la mer mêlée
    Au soleil.

◆　◆　◆

Je devins un opéra fabuleux: je vis que tous les êtres ont une fatalité de bonheur: l'action n'est pas la vie, mais une façon de gâcher quelque force, un énervement. La morale est la faiblesse de la cervelle.

À chaque être, plusieurs *autres* vies mes semblaient dues. Ce monsieur ne sait ce qu'il fait: il est un ange. Cette famille

My eternal soul,
Honor your vow
Despite lonely night
And fiery day.

So you break off again
From the sanctions of men,
From common consent!
You fly accordingly...

—No more hope.
    No *orietur*.
Patience and skill,
And torture sure.

No more tomorrows,
Satin embers,
    Duty is
    Your ardor.

Back it comes!
What? Eternity.
It's the blend of sea
    And sun.

◆ ◆ ◆

I became a fabulous opera: I saw that all creatures are fatally attracted to happiness: action isn't life, but a waste of energy, an irritation. Morality is a weakness of the brain.

It seemed to me that everyone was owed several *other* lives. That fellow has no idea what he's doing: he's an angel. That family is a litter of pups. With several men, I chatted

est une nichée de chiens. Devant plusieurs hommes, je causai tout haut avec un moment d'une de leurs autres vies.—Ainsi, j'ai aimé un porc.

Aucun des sophismes de la folie,—la folie qu'on enferme,—n'a été oublié par moi: je pourrais les redire tous, je tiens le système.

Ma santé fut menacée. La terreur venait. Je tombais dans des sommeils de plusieurs jours, et, levé, je continuais les rêves les plus tristes. J'étais mûr pour le trépas, et par une route de dangers ma faiblesse me menait aux confins du monde et de la Cimmérie, patrie de l'ombre et des tourbillons.

Je dus voyager, distraire les enchantements assemblés sur mon cerveau. Sur la mer, que j'aimais comme si elle eût dû me laver d'une souillure, je voyais se lever la croix consolatrice. J'avais été damné par l'arc-en-ciel. Le Bonheur était ma fatalité, mon remords, mon ver: ma vie serait toujours trop immense pour être dévouée à la force et à la beauté.

Le Bonheur! Sa dent, douce à la mort, m'avertissait au chant du coq,—*ad matutinum*, au *Christus venit*,—dans les plus sombres villes:

> Ô saisons, ô châteaux!
> Quelle âme est sans défauts?
>
> J'ai fait la magique étude
> Du bonheur, qu'aucun n'élude.
>
> Salut à lui, chaque fois
> Que chante le coq gaulois.
>
> Ah! je n'aurai plus d'envie:
> Il s'est chargé de ma vie.

aloud with a moment from one of their other lives.—And so, I loved a pig.

None of the sophisms of madness,—the sort of madness they lock up,—did I forget: I could repeat them all, I've got the system down.

My health was endangered. Terror came. I fell into slumbers that lasted days, and then, awake, I remained caught in the saddest dreams. I was ripe for demise, and my weakness led me along a dangerous road to the edge of the world and Cimmeria, land of darkness and vortices.

I had to travel, distract the enchantments gathered over my brain. On the ocean, which I loved as if it could cleanse me of a stain, I saw the consoling cross rise up. I had been damned by a rainbow. Happiness was my fate, my remorse, my worm: my life would always be too vast to devote itself to strength and beauty.

Happiness! Its tooth, sweet unto death, alerted me at cock's crow,—*ad matutinum*, at the *Christus venit*,—in the darkest of cities:

> O seasons, O châteaux!
> Who has a blameless soul?
>
> I have sought the magic shapes
> Of happiness, that none escapes.
>
> Greetings to it, every time
> That the Gallic cock chimes.
>
> Ah! of desire I'll have no more:
> My life he has taken over.

Ce charme a pris âme et corps
Et dispersé les efforts.

Ô saisons, ô châteaux!

L'heure de sa fuite, hélas!
Sera l'heure du trépas.

Ô saisons, ô châteaux!

◆ ◆ ◆

Cela s'est passé. Je sais aujourd'hui saluer la beauté.

Body and soul this charm has claimed
And made all efforts vain.

O seasons, O châteaux!

Alas! the moment when he leaves
Will be the hour of my decease.

O seasons, O châteaux!

◆ ◆ ◆

I'm past that now. These days I know how to welcome beauty.

L'Impossible

Ah! cette vie de mon enfance, la grande route par tous les temps, sobre surnaturellement, plus désintéressé que le meilleur des mendiants, fier de n'avoir ni pays, ni amis, quelle sottise c'était.—Et je m'en aperçois seulement!

—J'ai eu raison de mépriser ces bonshommes qui ne perdraient pas l'occasion d'une caresse, parasites de la propreté et de la santé de nos femmes, aujourd'hui qu'elles sont si peu d'accord avec nous.

J'ai eu raison dans tous mes dédains: puisque je m'évade!

Je m'évade!

Je m'explique.

Hier encore, je soupirais: "Ciel! sommes-nous assez de damnés ici-bas! Moi j'ai tant de temps déjà dans leur troupe! Je les connais tous. Nous nous reconnaissons toujours; nous nous dégoûtons. La charité nous est inconnue. Mais nous sommes polis; nos relations avec le monde sont très convenables." Est-ce étonnant? Le monde! les marchands, les naïfs! —Nous ne sommes pas déshonorés.—Mais les élus, comment nous recevraient-ils? Or il y a des gens hargneux et joyeux, de faux élus, puisqu'il nous faut de l'audace ou de l'humilité pour les aborder. Ce sont les seuls élus. Ce ne sont pas des bénisseurs!

M'étant retrouvé deux sous de raison—ça passe vite!—je vois que mes malaises viennent de ne m'être pas figuré assez tôt que nous sommes à l'Occident. Les marais occidentaux! Non que je croie la lumière altérée, la forme exténuée, le mouvement égaré...Bon! voici que mon esprit veut absolument se charger de tous les développements cruels qu'a subis l'esprit depuis la fin de l'Orient...Il en veut, mon esprit!

...Mes deux sous de raison sont finis! —L'esprit est au-

Impossibility

Ah! that childhood life of mine, the open road in all weather,
supernaturally sober, more impartial than the best of beggars,
proud of having neither country nor friends, what foolishness
it was.—And I'm noticing only now!

—I was right to despise those fellows who'd never pass
up a caress, parasites of the health and cleanliness of our
women, now that women are so out of sync with us.

I was right about all my disdains: since I'm escaping!

I'm escaping!

I'll explain.

Only yesterday, I could still sigh: "Heaven! how damned
we are here-below! I've already spent so much time in their
company! I know them all. We always recognize each other;
we disgust each other. We know no charity. But we're polite;
our relations with the world are very respectable." Surpris-
ing? The world! merchants, innocents!—We have not dis-
graced ourselves.—But how would we be received by the
chosen ones? Now, there are belligerent and joyful souls,
false chosen ones, since we'd need audacity or humility to
approach them. They are the sole chosen ones. They bestow
no benedictions!

Having regained two cents' worth of reason—it goes
fast!—I see that my malaise comes from not having figured
out soon enough that we are in the West. The Western
swamps! Not that I believe the light has changed, form been
exhausted, movement gone astray...Right! now my mind
is eager to take on all the cruel developments the mind has
suffered since the decline of the Orient...My mind can't get
enough!

...My two cents' worth of reason is over!—The mind is

torité, il veut que je sois en Occident. Il faudrait le faire taire pour conclure comme je voulais.

J'envoyais au diable les palmes des martyrs, les rayons de l'art, l'orgueil des inventeurs, l'ardeur des pillards; je retournais à l'Orient et à la sagesse première et éternelle.—Il paraît que c'est un rêve de paresse grossière!

Pourtant, je ne songeais guère au plaisir d'échapper aux souffrances modernes. Je n'avais pas en vue la sagesse bâtarde du Coran.—Mais n'y a-t-il pas un supplice réel en ce que, depuis cette déclaration de la science, le christianisme, l'homme *se joue*, se prouve les évidences, se gonfle du plaisir de répéter ces preuves, et ne vit que comme cela! Torture subtile, niaise; source de mes divagations spirituelles. La nature pourrait s'ennuyer, peut-être! M. Prudhomme est né avec le Christ.

N'est-ce pas parce que nous cultivons la brume! Nous mangeons la fièvre avec nos légumes aqueux. Et l'ivrognerie! et le tabac! et l'ignorance! et les dévouements! —Tout cela est-il assez loin de la pensée de la sagesse de l'Orient, la patrie primitive? Pourquoi un monde moderne, si de pareils poisons s'inventent!

Les gens d'Église diront: C'est compris. Mais vous voulez parler de l'Éden. Rien pour vous dans l'histoire des peuples orientaux.—C'est vrai; c'est à l'Éden que je songeais! Qu'est-ce que c'est pour mon rêve, cette pureté des races antiques!

Les philosophes: le monde n'a pas d'âge. L'humanité se déplace, simplement. Vous êtes en Occident, mais libre d'habiter dans votre Orient, quelque ancien qu'il vous le faille,—et d'y habiter bien. Ne soyez pas un vaincu. Philosophes, vous êtes de votre Occident.

Mon esprit, prends garde. Pas de partis de salut violents. Exerce-toi! —Ah! la science ne va pas assez vite pour nous!

—Mais je m'aperçois que mon esprit dort.

S'il était éveillé toujours à partir de ce moment, nous

authority, it wants me to be in the West. I'll have to keep it quiet if I'm to conclude as I wish.

I sent packing the palms of martyrs, the dazzle of art, the pride of inventors, the zeal of looters; I went back to the East and to primary, eternal wisdom.—Seems this is just a dream of gross laziness!

And yet, it wasn't about the pleasure of avoiding modern suffering. I wasn't thinking of the mongrel wisdom of the Koran.—But isn't this a real torture: that since the scientific declaration called Christianity, man *plays tricks on himself*, proves the obvious to himself, swells with the pleasure of repeating these proofs, and lives only that way! Subtle, inane torture; the source of my spiritual ramblings. Nature might get bored, perhaps! Sully Prudhomme was born alongside Christ.

Isn't it because we cultivate fog! We devour fever along with our watery vegetables. And drunkenness! and tobacco! and ignorance! and devotions!—Is all this distant enough from the thinking and wisdom of the East, the primary fatherland? Why a modern world at all, if it invents such poisons!

The clerics will say: We get it. You're talking about Eden. The history of Oriental peoples holds nothing for you.—It's true; it's Eden I was thinking of! What a dream it was, that purity of ancient races!

The philosophers: The world is ageless. Humanity simply moves around. You are in the West, but you're free to live in your East, however ancient you need it to be,—and you can live there comfortably. Don't be a loser. Philosophers, you really belong to your West.

Careful, mind of mine. No violent biases for health. Exert yourself!—Ah! science does not go fast enough for us!

—But now I see my mind is asleep.

If it stayed awake from this moment on, we would soon

serions bientôt à la vérité, qui peut-être nous entoure avec ses anges pleurant!...—S'il avait été éveillé jusqu'à ce moment-ci, c'est que je n'aurais pas cédé aux instincts délétères, à une époque immémoriale!...—S'il avait toujours été bien éveillé, je voguerais en pleine sagesse!...

Ô pureté! pureté!

C'est cette minute d'éveil qui m'a donné la vision de la pureté! —Par l'esprit on va à Dieu!

Déchirante infortune!

reach truth, which might be surrounding us even now with its weeping angels!...—If it had been awake until now, I wouldn't have succumbed to toxic instincts, back in time immemorial!...—If it had always been wide awake, I would navigate in total wisdom!...

O purity! purity!

It was that moment of lucidity that gave me the vision of purity!—With the mind one accedes to God!

Heartbreaking misfortune!

L'Éclair

Le travail humain! c'est l'explosion qui éclaire mon abîme de temps en temps.

"Rien n'est vanité; à la science, et en avant!" crie l'Ecclésiaste moderne, c'est-à-dire *Tout le monde*. Et pourtant les cadavres des méchants et des fainéants tombent sur le cœur des autres... Ah! vite, vite un peu; là-bas, par-delà la nuit, ces récompenses futures, éternelles... les échappons-nous?...

—Qu'y puis-je? Je connais le travail; et la science est trop lente. Que la prière galope et que la lumière gronde... je le vois bien. C'est trop simple, et il fait trop chaud; on se passera de moi. J'ai mon devoir, j'en serai fier à la façon de plusieurs, en le mettant de côté.

Ma vie est usée. Allons! feignons, fainéantons, ô pitié! Et nous existerons en nous amusant, en rêvant amours monstres et univers fantastiques, en nous plaignant et en querellant les apparences du monde, saltimbanque, mendiant, artiste, bandit,—prêtre! Sur mon lit d'hôpital, l'odeur de l'encens m'est revenue si puissante; gardien des aromates sacrés, confesseur, martyr...

Je reconnais là ma sale éducation d'enfance. Puis quoi!... Aller mes vingt ans, si les autres vont vingt ans...

Non! non! à présent je me révolte contre la mort! Le travail paraît trop léger à mon orgueil: ma trahison au monde serait un supplice trop court. Au dernier moment, j'attaquerais à droite, à gauche...

Alors,—oh!—chère pauvre âme, l'éternité serait-elle pas perdue pour nous!

Lightning

Human labor! It's the explosion that lights my abyss now and again.

"Nothing is vanity; on to science, and forward ho!" cries the modern Ecclesiastes, in other words, *Everybody*. And yet the corpses of the wicked and the idle fall onto the hearts of others...Ah! please, a bit of speed; over there, past the darkness, those future, eternal rewards...can we escape them?...

—What can I do? I know all about work; and science is too slow. May prayer gallop and light rumble on...I see it perfectly well. It's too simple, and the temperature is too hot; they can do without me. I have my duty; like some others, I'll be proud to lay it aside.

My life is used up. Come on! let's loll, let's lollygag, O pity! And we'll exist while having fun, dreaming of monstrous loves and fantastic universes, while complaining and feuding with the appearances of the world, street performer, beggar, artist, thief,—priest! In my hospital bed, the odor of incense came back to me so strong; guardian of sacred aromatics, confessor, martyr...

That's where I recognize my shitty childhood education. And anyway!...Let's make it to twenty, if others are making it to twenty...

No! no! for now I'm rebelling against death! Work seems too frivolous for my pride: my betrayal of the world would be too short a torment. At the last moment, I'd lash out left and right...

And so,—oh!—poor dear soul, won't eternity be lost to us!

Matin

N'eus-je pas *une fois* une jeunesse aimable, héroïque, fabu-leuse, à écrire sur des feuilles d'or,—trop de chance! Par quel crime, par quelle erreur, ai-je mérité ma faiblesse actuelle? Vous qui prétendez que des bêtes poussent des sanglots de chagrin, que des malades désespèrent, que des morts rêvent mal, tâchez de raconter ma chute et mon sommeil. Moi, je ne puis pas plus m'expliquer que le mendiant avec ses con-tinuels *Pater* et *Ave Maria*. *Je ne sais plus parler!*

Pourtant, aujourd'hui, je crois avoir fini la relation de mon enfer. C'était bien l'enfer; l'ancien, celui dont le fils de l'homme ouvrit les portes.

Du même désert, à la même nuit, toujours mes yeux las se réveillent à l'étoile d'argent, toujours, sans que s'émeuvent les Rois de la vie, les trois mages, le cœur, l'âme, l'esprit. Quand irons-nous, par-delà les grèves et les monts, saluer la naissance du travail nouveau, la sagesse nouvelle, la fuite des tyrans et des démons, la fin de la superstition, adorer—les premiers!—Noël sur la terre!

Le chant des cieux, la marche des peuples! Esclaves ne maudissons pas la vie.

Morning

Didn't I *once upon a time* have a pleasant, heroic, fabulous youth, to inscribe on leaves of gold,—too much luck! What crime, what error made me deserve my current weakness? You who claim that animals sob in pain, that the sick despair, that the dead have bad dreams, try to recount my fall and my slumber. As for me, I can't explain myself any better than the beggar with his continual Paters and Ave Marias. *I've forgotten how to talk!*

And yet, today, I believe I've finished the story of my hell. It was indeed Hell; the old kind, the one whose doors the Son of Man threw open.

From the same desert, from the same night, my weary eyes still awaken to the silver star, always, without it affecting the Kings of life, the three magi: heart, soul, and mind. When will we go, past beaches and mountains, to greet the birth of the new labor, the new wisdom, the flight of tyrants and demons, the end of superstition, and be the first to adore Christmas on earth!

The heavens' song, the people's march! Slaves, let us not curse life.

Adieu

L'automne déjà! —Mais pourquoi regretter un éternel soleil, si nous sommes engagés à la découverte de la clarté divine,— loin des gens qui meurent sur les saisons.

L'automne. Notre barque élevée dans les brumes immobiles tourne vers le port de la misère, la cité énorme au ciel taché de feu et de boue. Ah! les haillons pourris, le pain trempé de pluie, l'ivresse, les mille amours qui m'ont crucifié! Elle ne finira donc point cette goule reine de millions d'âmes et de corps morts *et qui seront jugés*! Je me revois la peau rongée par la boue et la peste, des vers plein les cheveux et les aisselles et encore de plus gros vers dans le cœur, étendu parmi les inconnus sans âge, sans sentiment... J'aurais pu y mourir... L'affreuse évocation! J'exècre la misère.

Et je redoute l'hiver parce que c'est la saison du comfort!

—Quelquefois je vois au ciel des plages sans fin couvertes de blanches nations en joie. Un grand vaisseau d'or, au-dessus de moi, agite ses pavillons multicolores sous les brises du matin. J'ai créé toutes les fêtes, tous les triomphes, tous les drames. J'ai essayé d'inventer de nouvelles fleurs, de nouveaux astres, de nouvelles chairs, de nouvelles langues. J'ai cru acquérir des pouvoirs surnaturels. Eh bien! je dois enterrer mon imagination et mes souvenirs! Une belle gloire d'artiste et de conteur emportée!

Moi! moi qui me suis dit mage ou ange, dispensé de toute morale, je suis rendu au sol, avec un devoir à chercher, et la réalité rugueuse à étreindre! Paysan!

Suis-je trompé, la charité serait-elle sœur de la mort, pour moi?

Enfin, je demanderai pardon pour m'être nourri de mensonge. Et allons.

Mais pas une main amie! et où puiser le secours?

Farewell

Autumn already!—But why long for an eternal sun, if we're out to discover divine clarity,—far from those who die by the seasons.

Autumn. Our boat risen in the still mists turns toward the port of indigence, the enormous city in the sky spattered with fire and mud. Ah! the decaying rags, rain-drenched bread, drunkenness, the thousand loves that crucified me! So she'll never stop, that ghoul, queen of millions of dead souls and bodies *that will be judged*! I can still see myself, skin ravaged by mud and pestilence, hair and armpits crawling with maggots and the biggest maggot of all in my heart, lying among strangers with no age or feelings...I could have died there...Horrible recollection! I abhor poverty.

And I dread winter because it's the season of comforts!

—Sometimes I see in the sky endless beaches covered with joyous white nations. A great golden vessel, above me, waves its multicolored banners in the morning breezes. I've created every feast, every triumph, every drama. I tried to invent new flowers, new stars, new fleshes, new languages. I believed I'd acquired supernatural powers. Well! I have to bury my imagination and my memories! What fine glory I've won, as an artist and storyteller! I! I, who called myself magus or angel, exempt from any morality, I've crashed back down to earth, with a duty to find, and a coarse reality to embrace! Peasant!

Was I wrong, would charity be the sister of death, for me?

Anyway, I'll ask forgiveness for having nourished myself on lies. And on we go.

But not a single friendly hand! where can I turn for help?

Oui, l'heure nouvelle est au moins très sévère.

Car je puis dire que la victoire m'est acquise: les grince-ments de dents, les sifflements de feu, les soupirs empestés se modèrent. Tous les souvenirs immondes s'effacent. Mes derniers regrets détalent,—des jalousies pour les mendiants, les brigands, les amis de la mort, les arriérés de toutes sortes.— Damnés, si je me vengeais!

Il faut être absolument moderne.

Point de cantiques: tenir le pas gagné. Dure nuit! le sang séché fume sur ma face, et je n'ai rien derrière moi, que cet horrible arbrisseau!...Le combat spirituel est aussi brutal que la bataille d'hommes; mais la vision de la justice est le plaisir de Dieu seul.

Cependant c'est la veille. Recevons tous les influx de vigueur et de tendresse réelle. Et à l'aurore, armés d'une ardente patience, nous entrerons aux splendides villes.

Que parlais-je de main amie! un bel avantage, c'est que je puis rire des vieilles amours mensongères, et frapper de honte ces couples menteurs,—j'ai vu l'enfer des femmes là-bas;—et il me sera loisible de *posséder la vérité dans une âme et un corps.*

Avril–août, 1873

⬥ ⬥ ⬥

Yes, these new times are harsh, to say the least.

For I can assert that victory is mine: the gnashing of teeth, whistling gunfire, and reeking sighs are abating. All the squalid memories are fading. My last regrets are scurrying off,—envy over beggars, bandits, friends of death, backward sorts of every stripe.—All damned, if I took my revenge!

We have to be absolutely modern.

No hymns: hold the ground that's been won. Hard night! dried blood steams on my face, and I have nothing behind me but that horrid shrub!...Spiritual combat is just as brutal as the battles of men; but the vision of justice is a pleasure for God alone.

Nevertheless, it's the night before. Let us receive every influx of vigor and true tenderness. And at dawn, armed with fervent patience, we'll enter the splendid cities.

What was I saying about a friendly hand! a fine advantage, it's just that I can laugh about deceitful old loves, and heap scorn upon those lying couples,—I've seen the hell of women there;—and I will be free to *possess the truth in one soul and one body.*

April–August, 1873

Illuminations

Après le déluge

Aussitôt que l'idée du Déluge se fut rassise,

Un lièvre s'arrêta dans les sainfoins et les clochettes mouvantes et dit sa prière à l'arc-en-ciel à travers la toile de l'araignée.

Oh! les pierres précieuses qui se cachaient,—les fleurs qui regardaient déjà.

Dans la grande rue sale les étals se dressèrent, et l'on tira les barques vers la mer étagée là-haut comme sur les gravures.

Le sang coula, chez Barbe-Bleue,—aux abattoirs,—dans les cirques, où le sceau de Dieu blêmit les fenêtres. Le sang et le lait coulèrent.

Les castors bâtirent. Les "mazagrans" fumèrent dans les estaminets.

Dans la grande maison de vitres encore ruisselante les enfants en deuil regardèrent les merveilleuses images.

Une porte claqua, et sur la place du hameau, l'enfant tourna ses bras, compris des girouettes et des coqs des clochers de partout, sous l'éclatante giboulée.

Madame *** établit un piano dans les Alpes. La messe et les premières communions se célébrèrent aux cent mille autels de la cathédrale.

Les caravanes partirent. Et le Splendide Hôtel fut bâti dans le chaos de glaces et de nuit du pôle.

Depuis lors, la Lune entendit les chacals piaulant par les déserts de thym,—et les églogues en sabots grognant dans le verger. Puis, dans la futaie violette, bourgeonnante, Eucharis me dit que c'était le printemps.

—Sourds, étang,—Écume, roule sur le pont, et par-dessus les bois;—draps noirs et orgues,—éclairs et tonnerre,—montez et roulez;—Eaux et tristesses, montez et relevez les Déluges.

After the Flood

Once the idea of the Flood had subsided,

A hare froze in the clover and wavering bellflowers, and prayed to the rainbow through a spider's web.

Oh, the precious stones that hid!—flowers already peeking through.

Market stalls sprouted in the grubby main street, and rowboats were dragged to sea, layered at the top as in bookplates.

Blood flowed in Bluebeard's castle—in slaughterhouses—in circuses, where God's seal blanched the windowpanes. Blood and milk flowed.

Beavers built. Spiked coffees steamed in taverns.

In the great, streaming house of windows, children in mourning dress gazed at marvelous pictures.

A door slammed, and the child windmilled his arms through the town square, understood by the weathervanes and steeple cocks from all over, in the brilliant downpour.

Madam * * * installed a piano in the Alps. Masses and first communions were celebrated at the hundred thousand altars of the cathedral.

The caravans pulled out. And the Splendide Hotel was built in a tumult of glaciers and polar night.

Since then, the Moon has heard jackals mewling in thyme-covered deserts—and bucolics in clogs grumbling in the orchard. Then, in a forest of budding violets, Eucharis told me it was spring.

—Pond, well up,—Foam, roll over the bridge and through the woods;—black flags and pipe organs—thunder and lightning—rise and roll;—Water and sorrows, rise up and raise the Floods.

Car depuis qu'ils se sont dissipés,—oh les pierres précieuses s'enfouissant, et les fleurs ouvertes!—c'est un ennui! et la Reine, la Sorcière qui allume sa braise dans le pot de terre, ne voudra jamais nous raconter ce qu'elle sait, et que nous ignorons.

For since they've receded—oh, the precious stones have fled, and the flowers in bloom—it's so boring! and the Queen, the Sorceress who stokes her embers in an earthen pot, will never deign to tell us what she knows, and we do not.

Enfance

I

Cette idole, yeux noirs et crin jaune, sans parents ni cour, plus noble que la fable, mexicaine et flamande; son domaine, azur et verdure insolents, court sur des plages nommées, par des vagues sans vaisseaux, de noms férocement grecs, slaves, celtiques.

À la lisière de la forêt—les fleurs de rêve tintent, éclatent, éclairent,—la fille à lèvre d'orange, les genoux croisés dans le clair déluge qui sourd des prés, nudité qu'ombrent, traversent et habillent les arcs-en-ciel, la flore, la mer.

Dames qui tournoient sur les terrasses voisines de la mer; enfantes et géantes, superbes noires dans la mousse vert-de-gris, bijoux debout sur le sol gras des bosquets et des jardinets dégelés—jeunes mères et grandes sœurs aux regards pleins de pèlerinages, sultanes, princesses de démarche et de costume tyranniques, petites étrangères et personnes doucement malheureuses.

Quel ennui, l'heure du "cher corps" et "cher cœur".

II

C'est elle, la petite morte, derrière les rosiers.—La jeune maman trépassée descend le perron.—La calèche du cousin crie sur le sable.—Le petit frère—(il est aux Indes!) là, devant le couchant, sur le pré d'œillets.—Les vieux qu'on a enterrés tout droits dans le rempart aux giroflées.

L'essaim des feuilles d'or entoure la maison du général. Ils sont dans le midi.—On suit la route rouge pour arriver à

Childhood

I

That idol, black eyes and blond mane, no parents or hearth, nobler than the Mexican or Flemish fable; his domain, insolent azure and greenery, runs over beaches named by waves with no ships, names that are ferociously Greek, or Slavic, or Celtic.

At the edge of the forest—dream flowers ring out, burst, brighten—the girl with orange lip, knees crossed in the clear flood welling up from the fields, nudity shadowed, traversed, clothed by rainbows, flora, the sea.

Ladies twirling on balconies near the sea; children and giantesses, superb black women in the verdigris foam, jewelry erect on the greasy soil of thawed groves and gardens—young mothers and big sisters with eyes full of pilgrimages, sultanas, princesses tyrannical in gait and dress, diminutive foreigners, and gently unhappy creatures.

The hour of "dear body" and "dear heart"—what a drag.

II

There's the little dead girl, behind the rosebushes.—The deceased young mom descends the mansion steps.—The cousin's carriage squeals on the sand.—The little brother—(he's in India!) there, before the sunset, on the field of carnations.—The oldsters they've buried upright in the rampart covered in wallflowers.

The swarm of golden leaves surrounds the general's house. They are in the South.—You follow the red path to reach the

l'auberge vide. Le château est à vendre; les persiennes sont détachées.—Le curé aura emporté la clef de l'église.—Autour du parc, les loges des gardes sont inhabitées. Les palissades sont si hautes qu'on ne voit que les cimes bruissantes. D'ailleurs il n'y a rien à voir là-dedans.

Les prés remontent aux hameaux sans coqs, sans enclumes. L'écluse est levée. Ô les calvaires et les moulins du désert, les îles et les meules.

Des fleurs magiques bourdonnaient. Les talus le berçaient. Des bêtes d'une élégance fabuleuse circulaient. Les nuées s'amassaient sur la haute mer faite d'une éternité de chaudes larmes.

III

Au bois il y a un oiseau, son chant vous arrête et vous fait rougir.

Il y a une horloge qui ne sonne pas.

Il y a une fondrière avec un nid de bêtes blanches.

Il y a une cathédrale qui descend et un lac qui monte.

Il y a une petite voiture abandonnée dans le taillis, ou qui descend le sentier en courant, enrubannée.

Il y a une troupe de petits comédiens en costumes, aperçus sur la route à travers la lisière du bois.

empty inn. The castle is for sale; the blinds have fallen off.—The priest absconded with the key to the church.— Around the park, the guards' lodges stand empty. The fences are so tall that you can't see past the rustling peaks. Anyway, there's nothing to see in there.

The meadows stretch back to hamlets with no cocks, no anvils. The sluice is up. O the wayside crosses and desert mills, the islands and millstones.

Magic flowers were abuzz. The embankment cradled him. Fabulously elegant beasts milled about. Thick clouds formed over high seas made of an eternity of hot tears.

III

In the woods there is a bird; its song makes you stop and blush.

There is a clock that doesn't chime.

There is a rut with a nest of small white creatures.

There is a cathedral that goes down and a lake that goes up.

There is a little cart abandoned in the copse, or that rushes headlong down the path, beribboned.

There is a troupe of diminutive actors in costume, spotted on the road past the edge of the woods.

Il y a enfin, quand l'on a faim et soif, quelqu'un qui vous chasse.

IV

Je suis le saint, en prière sur la terrasse,—comme les bêtes pacifiques paissent jusqu'à la mer de Palestine.

Je suis le savant au fauteuil sombre. Les branches et la pluie se jettent à la croisée de la bibliothèque.

Je suis le piéton de la grand'route par les bois nains; la rumeur des écluses couvre mes pas. Je vois longtemps la mélancolique lessive d'or du couchant.

Je serais bien l'enfant abandonné sur la jetée partie à la haute mer, le petit valet, suivant l'allée dont le front touche le ciel.

Les sentiers sont âpres. Les monticules se couvrent de genêts. L'air est immobile. Que les oiseaux et les sources sont loin! Ce ne peut être que la fin du monde, en avançant.

V

Qu'on me loue enfin ce tombeau, blanchi à la chaux avec les lignes du ciment en relief—très loin sous terre.

Je m'accoude à la table, la lampe éclaire très vivement ces journaux que je suis idiot de relire, ces livres sans intérêt.

There is, finally, when you're hungry and thirsty, someone to chase you away.

IV

I am the saint, praying on the terrace,—like peaceful beasts grazing up to the Sea of Palestine.

I am the scholar in the dark armchair. Branches and rain hurl themselves at the library windowpanes.

I am the wanderer of open roads by the dwarf woods; the noise of sluice gates buries my footsteps. I gaze endlessly at the wistful golden wash of sunset.

I would gladly be the child abandoned on the jetty cast out to the high seas, the little valet in the walkway whose forehead touches the sky.

The paths are bitter. The hillocks are shrouded in broom. The air is still. How distant the birds and springs! It can only be the end of the world, marching on.

V

May they finally rent me this tomb, whitewashed and with cement lines in relief—way deep underground.

I rest my elbows on the table, the lamp throws a bright light on these newspapers that I'm dumb enough to reread, these unimpressive books.

À une distance énorme au-dessus de mon salon souterrain, les maisons s'implantent, les brumes s'assemblent. La boue est rouge ou noire. Ville monstrueuse, nuit sans fin!

Moins haut, sont des égouts. Aux côtés, rien que l'épaisseur du globe. Peut-être les gouffres d'azur, des puits de feu. C'est peut-être sur ces plans que se rencontrent lunes et comètes, mers et fables.

Aux heures d'amertume je m'imagine des boules de saphir, de métal. Je suis maître du silence. Pourquoi une apparence de soupirail blêmirait-elle au coin de la voûte?

Far above my subterranean salon, houses settle in, mists assemble. The mud is red or black. Monstrous city, endless night!

Not so high up, are the sewers. Nothing on either side but the thickness of the globe. Perhaps blue abysses, fiery pits. It might be on this level that moons meet comets, seas meet fables.

In my bitterest hours I picture balls of sapphire, or of metal. I am the lord of silence. Why would a seeming aperture pale at the crest of the vault?

Conte

Un Prince était vexé de ne s'être employé jamais qu'à la perfection des générosités vulgaires. Il prévoyait d'étonnantes révolutions de l'amour, et soupçonnait ses femmes de pouvoir mieux que cette complaisance agrémentée de ciel et de luxe. Il voulait voir la vérité, l'heure du désir et de la satisfaction essentiels. Que ce fût ou non une aberration de piété, il voulut. Il possédait au moins un assez large pouvoir humain.

Toutes les femmes qui l'avaient connu furent assassinées. Quel saccage du jardin de la beauté! Sous le sabre, elles le bénirent. Il n'en commanda point de nouvelles.—Les femmes réapparurent.

Il tua tous ceux qui le suivaient, après la chasse ou les libations.—Tous le suivaient.

Il s'amusa à égorger les bêtes de luxe. Il fit flamber les palais. Il se ruait sur les gens et les taillait en pièces.—La foule, les toits d'or, les belles bêtes existaient encore.

Peut-on s'extasier dans la destruction, se rajeunir par la cruauté! Le peuple ne murmura pas. Personne n'offrit le concours de ses vues.

Un soir il galopait fièrement. Un Génie apparut, d'une beauté ineffable, inavouable même. De sa physionomie et de son maintien ressortait la promesse d'un amour multiple et complexe! d'un bonheur indicible, insupportable même! Le Prince et le Génie s'anéantirent probablement dans la santé essentielle. Comment n'auraient-ils pas pu en mourir? Ensemble donc ils moururent.

Mais ce Prince décéda, dans son palais, à un âge ordinaire. Le prince était le Génie. Le Génie était le Prince.

La musique savante manque à notre désir.

Tale

A Prince was annoyed at never having applied himself to anything but perfecting vulgar generosities. He envisioned astounding revolutions of love, and suspected his wives could do better than those indulgences of theirs, adorned with heavens and luxury. He wanted to see the truth, the moment of essential desire and satisfaction. Whether this was an aberration of piety or not, he wanted it. He was endowed with considerable human power, to say the least.

All the women who had known him were killed. Such devastation in the garden of beauty! Under the blade, they blessed him. He ordered no replacements.—Women reappeared.

He did away with everyone who followed him, after the hunt or the libations.—Everyone followed him.

He got a thrill from slaughtering luxurious animals. He sent palaces up in flames. He pounced on people and sliced them to pieces.—Crowds, gilded rooftops, lovely animals still existed.

How one can go into raptures over destruction, grow younger in cruelty! Not a murmur was spoken. No one offered a concordant viewpoint.

One evening he was galloping proudly. A Genie appeared, of ineffable, even unspeakable beauty. His features and bearing exuded the promise of a multifarious and complex love! an inexpressible, even unendurable happiness! The Prince and the Genie annihilated each other, no doubt in fundamental well-being. What could they do but die from it? And so together they died.

But the Prince passed away, in his palace, at an ordinary age. The prince was the Genie. The Genie was the Prince.

Our desire lacks learned music.

Parade

Des drôles très solides. Plusieurs ont exploité vos mondes. Sans besoins, et peu pressés de mettre en œuvre leurs brillantes facultés et leur expérience de vos consciences. Quels hommes mûrs! Des yeux hébétés à la façon de la nuit d'été, rouges et noirs, tricolores, d'acier piqué d'étoiles d'or; des faciès déformés, plombés, blêmis, incendiés; des enrouements folâtres! La démarche cruelle des oripeaux! —Il y a quelques jeunes,—comment regarderaient-ils Chérubin?—pourvus de voix effrayantes et de quelques ressources dangereuses. On les envoie prendre du dos en ville, affublés d'un *luxe* dégoûtant.

Ô le plus violent Paradis de la grimace enragée! Pas de comparaison avec vos Fakirs et les autres bouffonneries scéniques. Dans des costumes improvisés avec le goût du mauvais rêve ils jouent des complaintes, des tragédies de malandrins et de demi-dieux spirituels comme l'histoire ou les religions ne l'ont jamais été. Chinois, Hottentots, bohémiens, niais, hyènes, Molochs, vieilles démences, démons sinistres, ils mêlent les tours populaires, maternels, avec les poses et les tendresses bestiales. Ils interpréteraient des pièces nouvelles et des chansons "bonnes filles". Maîtres jongleurs, ils transforment le lieu et les personnes, et usent de la comédie magnétique. Les yeux flambent, le sang chante, les os s'élargissent, les larmes et des filets rouges ruissellent. Leur raillerie ou leur terreur dure une minute, ou des mois entiers.

J'ai seul la clef de cette parade sauvage.

Sideshow

Solidly built scoundrels. Some of them have exploited your worlds. Wanting for nothing, in no rush to engage their brilliant faculties and experience of your consciousness. Such mature fellows! Eyes dazed like a summer's night, red and black, tricolored, eyes of steel spangled with gold stars; faces deformed, leaden, washed out, burned out; hoarse exuberance! The cruel practice of trumpery!—A few youths,—what could they make of Cherubino?—endowed with terrifying voices and some dangerous assets. We send them to get their kicks in town, decked out with *appalling* gaudiness.

O most violent Paradise of enraged grimaces! No comparison with your Fakirs and other scenic buffooneries. In improvised costumes with nightmarish taste, they perform their laments, their tragedies of brigands and demigods, witty, as history or religions have never been. Chinese, Hottentots, Bohemians, simpletons, hyenas, Molochs, old dementias, sinister demons, they mix popular, maternal numbers with poses and bestial tenderness. They'd gladly perform new plays and "family-friendly" ditties. Master jugglers, they transform places and people, use magnetic comedy. Eyes flame, blood sings, bones expand, tears and crimson trickles flow down. Their mockery or their terror lasts a minute, or entire months.

Only I hold the key to this savage parade.

Being Beauteous

Devant une neige un Être de Beauté de haute taille. Des sifflements de mort et des cercles de musique sourde font monter, s'élargir et trembler comme un spectre ce corps adoré; des blessures écarlates et noires éclatent dans les chairs superbes. Les couleurs propres de la vie se foncent, dansent, et se dégagent autour de la Vision, sur le chantier. Et les frissons s'élèvent et grondent, et la saveur forcenée de ces effets se chargeant avec les sifflements mortels et les rauques musiques que le monde, loin derrière nous, lance sur notre mère de beauté,—elle recule, elle se dresse. Oh! nos os sont revêtus d'un nouveau corps amoureux.

◆

Ô la face cendrée, l'écusson de crin, les bras de cristal! Le canon sur lequel je dois m'abattre à travers la mêlée des arbres et de l'air léger!

Being Beauteous

Before a snowfall, a tall Beauteous Being. Whistles of the dead and muffled music circles make this adored body rise up, expand, tremble like a ghost; scarlet-and-black wounds blossom from this superb flesh. The proper colors of life rush forward, dance, disperse around the Vision, on the scaffolding. And shivers rise and grumble, and the frenzied tang of these effects takes on the mortal wheezing and hoarse music that the world, far behind us, hurls at our mother of beauty,— she recoils, rears up. Oh! our bones are clothed in a loving new body.

◆

O the ashen face, fur badge, crystal arms! The cannon onto which I must flop down through the tangle of trees and light air!

Vies

I

Ô les énormes avenues du pays saint, les terrasses du temple! Qu'a-t-on fait du brahmane qui m'expliqua les Proverbes? D'alors, de là-bas, je vois encore même les vieilles! Je me souviens des heures d'argent et de soleil vers les fleuves, la main de la campagne sur mon épaule, et de nos caresses debout dans les plaines poivrées.—Un envol de pigeons écarlates tonne autour de ma pensée —Exilé ici, j'ai eu une scène où jouer les chefs-d'œuvre dramatiques de toutes les littératures. Je vous indiquerais les richesses inouïes. J'observe l'histoire des trésors que vous trouvâtes. Je vois la suite! Ma sagesse est aussi dédaignée que le chaos. Qu'est mon néant, auprès de la stupeur qui vous attend?

II

Je suis un inventeur bien autrement méritant que tous ceux qui m'ont précédé; un musicien même, qui ai trouvé quelque chose comme la clef de l'amour. À présent, gentilhomme d'une campagne aigre au ciel sobre, j'essaye de m'émouvoir au souvenir de l'enfance mendiante, de l'apprentissage ou de l'arrivée en sabots, des polémiques, des cinq ou six veuvages, et quelques noces où ma forte tête m'empêcha de monter au diapason des camarades. Je ne regrette pas ma vieille part de gaîté divine: l'air sobre de cette aigre campagne alimente fort activement mon atroce scepticisme. Mais comme ce scepticisme ne peut désormais être mis en œuvre, et que d'ailleurs je suis dévoué à un trouble nouveau,—j'attends de devenir un très méchant fou.

Lives

I

O the broad avenues of this holy land, the squares before the temple! What have they done with the Brahmin who taught me the Proverbs? From then, from there, I still see even the old women! I remember hours of silver and sunshine near the rivers, a country hand on my shoulder, and our caresses while standing in the peppery plains.—A flight of scarlet pigeons thunders in my brain—Here in exile, I've had a stage to perform the dramatic masterpieces of every literature. I could describe for you untold riches. I observe the history of the treasures you found. I see what's coming! My wisdom is as scorned as chaos. What is my nothingness, next to the stupor awaiting you?

II

I am an inventor vastly more deserving than any before me; a musician, too, who has found something like the key of love. These days, a country gentleman in a bitter land with sober skies, I try to be moved by the memory of an impoverished childhood, of apprenticeship or arrival in wooden shoes, of polemics, of five or six widowhoods, and of a few marriages in which my hotheadedness kept me from getting in step with my comrades. I don't miss my former share of divine happiness: the sober air of this acrid countryside actively feeds my awful skepticism. But since this skepticism can no longer be practiced, and since at any rate I'm devoted to a new turmoil,—I expect to turn into a very mean lunatic.

III

Dans un grenier où je fus enfermé à douze ans j'ai connu le monde, j'ai illustré la comédie humaine. Dans un cellier j'ai appris l'histoire. À quelque fête de nuit dans une cité du Nord, j'ai rencontré toutes les femmes des anciens peintres. Dans un vieux passage à Paris on m'a enseigné les sciences classiques. Dans une magnifique demeure cernée par l'Orient entier j'ai accompli mon immense œuvre et passé mon illustre retraite. J'ai brassé mon sang. Mon devoir m'est remis. Il ne faut même plus songer à cela. Je suis réellement d'outre-tombe, et pas de commissions.

III

In an attic where I was cloistered at age twelve I came to know the world, I illustrated the human comedy. In a cellar I learned history. At some nocturnal revelry in a northern city, I met all the ancient painters' women. In an old passageway in Paris they taught me classical sciences. In a sumptuous dwelling surrounded by all the Orient, I completed my vast labors and lived out my illustrious retirement. I've stirred my blood. I'm relieved of my duties. No point even thinking about it anymore. I really am from beyond the grave, and take no assignments.

Départ

Assez vu. La vision s'est rencontrée à tous les airs.

Assez eu. Rumeurs des villes, le soir, et au soleil, et toujours.

Assez connu. Les arrêts de la vie.—Ô Rumeurs et Visions!
Départ dans l'affection et le bruit neufs!

Departure

Seen enough. Vision met with every climate.

Owned enough. Sounds of the city, in the evening, in the sun, and always.

Known enough. The pauses of life.—O Sounds and Visions!

Departure amid new noises and feelings!

Matinée d'ivresse

Ô *mon* Bien! Ô *mon* Beau! Fanfare atroce où je ne trébuche point! Chevalet féerique! Hourra pour l'œuvre inouïe et pour le corps merveilleux, pour la première fois! Cela commença sous les rires des enfants, cela finira par eux. Ce poison va rester dans toutes nos veines même quand, la fanfare tournant, nous serons rendu à l'ancienne inharmonie. Ô maintenant, nous si digne de ces tortures! rassemblons fervemment cette promesse surhumaine faite à notre corps et à notre âme créés: cette promesse, cette démence! L'élégance, la science, la violence! On nous a promis d'enterrer dans l'ombre l'arbre du bien et du mal, de déporter les honnêtetés tyranniques, afin que nous amenions notre très pur amour. Cela commença par quelques dégoûts et cela finit,—ne pouvant nous saisir sur-le-champ de cette éternité,—cela finit par une débandade de parfums.

Rire des enfants, discrétion des esclaves, austérité des vierges, horreur des figures et des objets d'ici, sacrés soyez-vous par le souvenir de cette veille. Cela commençait par toute la rustrerie, voici que cela finit par des anges de flamme et de glace.

Petite veille d'ivresse, sainte! quand ce ne serait que pour le masque dont tu nous as gratifié. Nous t'affirmons, méthode! Nous n'oublions pas que tu as glorifié hier chacun de nos âges. Nous avons foi au poison. Nous savons donner notre vie tout entière tous les jours.

Voici le temps des *Assassins*.

Morning Intoxication

O *my* Good! O *my* Beauty! Horrid fanfare in which I never stumble! Magical canvas! Hooray for the singular work and the marvelous body, for the first time! It began amid children's laughter and it will end the same way. The poison will stay in our veins long after the fanfare turns and we revert to our former disharmony. And we—so deserving of these tortures!— let us fervently gather the superhuman promise made to our created body and soul: this promise, this dementia! This elegance, this science, this violence! They promised they'd bury the tree of good and evil in the shadows, expel tyrannical decencies, so that we could enact our most pure love. It began with nausea and it ends—since we can't seize that eternity all at once—it ends in a riot of perfumes.

Laughter of children, discretion of slaves, austerity of virgins, horror of local faces and objects, made sacred by the memory of that sleepless night. It began in brutality, it ends with angels of fire and ice.

Little intoxicated vigil, holy! holy if only for the mask you bestowed on us. We affirm you, method! We won't forget that yesterday you glorified each of our ages. We have faith in the poison. We are ready to devote our entire life, every single day.

Comes the hour of the *Assassins*.

Phrases

Quand le monde sera réduit en un seul bois noir pour nos quatre yeux étonnés,—en une plage pour deux enfants fidèles,—en une maison musicale pour notre claire sympathie,—je vous trouverai.

Qu'il n'y ait ici-bas qu'un vieillard seul, calme et beau, entouré d'un "luxe inouï,"—et je suis à vos genoux.

Que j'aie réalisé tous vos souvenirs,—que je sois celle qui sait vous garrotter,—je vous étoufferai.

◆ ◆ ◆

Quand nous somme très forts,—qui recule? très gais, qui tombe de ridicule? Quand nous sommes très méchants, que ferait-on de nous?

Parez-vous, dansez, riez,—je ne pourrai jamais envoyer l'Amour par la fenêtre.

◆ ◆ ◆

—Ma camarade, mendiante, enfant monstre! comme ça t'est égal, ces malheureuses et ces manœuvres, et mes embarras. Attache-toi à nous avec ta voix impossible, ta voix! unique flatteur de ce vil désespoir.

Une matinée couverte, en Juillet. Un goût de cendres vole dans l'air;—une odeur de bois suant dans l'âtre,—les fleurs rouies,—le saccage des promenades,—la bruine des canaux par les champs—pourquoi pas déjà les joujoux et l'encens?

Phrases

When the world is reduced to a single black wood for our four astonished eyes,—to a beach for two faithful children,—to a musical house for our clear sympathy,—I will find you.

Let there be but a solitary old man here-below, calm and handsome, surrounded by "untold luxury,"—and I am at your feet.

May I realize all your memories,—may I be she who can tie you down,—I will smother you.

♦ ♦ ♦

When we are very strong,—who recoils? Very buoyant, who drops from ridicule? When we're very wicked, what will become of us?

Dress up, cavort, laugh,—I'll never manage to toss Love out the window.

♦ ♦ ♦

—Comrade mine, beggar girl, monster child! how little you care about these unfortunates and these undertakings, and my troubles. Latch on to us with your impossible voice, your voice! sole flatterer of this vile despair.

An overcast morning in July. A taste of ash floats in the air;—an odor of wood sweating in the hearth,—flowers withered,—pillage of walks,—the drizzle of canals along the fields—why not toys and incense, while we're at it?

◆

J'ai tendu des cordes de clocher à clocher; des guirlandes de fenêtre à fenêtre; des chaînes d'or d'étoile à étoile, et je danse.

◆

Le haut étang fume continuellement. Quelle sorcière va se dresser sur le couchant blanc? Quelles violettes frondaisons vont descendre?

◆

Pendant que les fonds publics s'écoulent en fêtes de fraternité, il sonne une cloche de feu rose dans les nuages.

◆

Avivant un agréable goût d'encre de Chine, une poudre noire pleut doucement sur ma veillée,—je baisse les feux du lustre, je me jette sur le lit, et tourné du côté de l'ombre je vous vois, mes filles! mes reines!

◆

◆

I've stretched ropes from steeple to steeple; garlands from window to window; gold chains from star to star, and I dance.

◆

Continual smoke from the upper pond. What sorceress will rise in the white sunset? What violet foliage will rain down?

◆

While public funds are poured into celebrations of fraternity, a bell of pink fire tolls in the clouds.

◆

Stirring up a pleasant taste of India ink, black powder rains softly on my evening,—I lower the lamplight, throw myself on the bed, and, turned toward the shadows, I see you, my beauties! my queens!

◆

Les Ponts

Des ciels gris de cristal. Un bizarre dessin de ponts, ceux-ci droits, ceux-là bombés, d'autres descendant ou obliquant en angles sur les premiers, et ces figures se renouvelant dans les autres circuits éclairés du canal, mais tous tellement longs et légers que les rives, chargées de dômes s'abaissent et s'amoindrissent. Quelques-uns de ces ponts sont encore chargés de masures. D'autres soutiennent des mâts, des signaux, de frêles parapets. Des accords mineurs se croisent, et filent, des cordes montent des berges. On distingue une veste rouge, peut-être d'autres costumes et des instruments de musique. Sont-ce des airs populaires, des bouts de concerts seigneuriaux, des restants d'hymnes publics? L'eau est grise et bleue, large comme un bras de mer.—Un rayon blanc, tombant du haut du ciel, anéantit cette comédie.

Bridges

Crystal-gray skies. A weird drawing of bridges, some straight, others curved, still others angling over them slantwise—these figures repeated in other bright circuits of the canal, but all so long and light that the banks, weighted with domes, sink and diminish. Some of these bridges are still laden with hovels. Others support masts, signals, fragile parapets. Minor chords intersect and vanish; cords snake up from shore. We can spot a red jacket, maybe other costumes as well, and musical instruments. Are these popular tunes, snatches of lordly concerts, remnants of public hymns? The water is gray and blue, as wide as a branch of the sea.—A white ray, falling from the sky, obliterates this farce.

Ville

Je suis un éphémère et point trop mécontent citoyen d'une métropole crue moderne parce que tout goût connu a été éludé dans les ameublements et l'extérieur des maisons aussi bien que dans le plan de la ville. Ici vous ne signaleriez les traces d'aucun monument de superstition. La morale et la langue sont réduites à leur plus simple expression, enfin! Ces millions de gens qui n'ont pas besoin de se connaître amènent si pareillement l'éducation, le métier et la vieillesse, que ce cours de vie doit être plusieurs fois moins long que ce qu'une statistique folle trouve pour les peuples du continent. Aussi comme, de ma fenêtre, je vois des spectres nouveaux roulant à travers l'épaisse et éternelle fumée de charbon,—notre ombre des bois, notre nuit d'été!—des Érinnyes nouvelles, devant mon cottage qui est ma patrie et tout mon cœur puisque tout ici ressemble à ceci,—la Mort sans pleurs, notre active fille et servante, et un Amour désespéré, et un joli Crime piaulant dans la boue de la rue.

City

I am the transitory and not too disgruntled citizen of a metropolis considered modern because any appreciable taste has been evaded, in the furnishings and fronts of houses as in the city plan. You'll find no trace here of any monument to superstition. Morals and language have been reduced to their simplest expression, at last! These millions of people, who don't need to know one another, conduct their education, trade, and old age so uniformly that their life-spans must be many times shorter than the insane statistics for continental populations. And so as I watch from my window new specters, new Furies, gliding through the dense, eternal soot—our sylvan shade, our summer night!—past my cottage which is my country and all my heart, since everything here looks the same: Death without tears, our active maidservant; and a desperate Cupid; and a handsome Crime whimpering in the street filth.

Vagabonds

Pitoyable frère! Que d'atroces veillées je lui dus! "Je ne me saisissais pas fervemment de cette entreprise. Je m'étais joué de son infirmité. Par ma faute nous retournerions en exil, en esclavage." Il me supposait un guignon et une innocence très bizarres, et il ajoutait des raisons inquiétantes.

Je répondais en ricanant à ce satanique docteur, et finissais par gagner la fenêtre. Je créais, par delà la campagne traversée par des bandes de musique rare, les fantômes du futur luxe nocturne.

Après cette distraction vaguement hygiénique, je m'étendais sur une paillasse. Et, presque chaque nuit, aussitôt endormi, le pauvre frère se levait, la bouche pourrie, les yeux arrachés,—tel qu'il se rêvait!—et me tirait dans la salle en hurlant son songe de chagrin idiot.

J'avais en effet, en toute sincérité d'esprit, pris l'engagement de le rendre à son état primitif de fils du soleil,—et nous errions, nourris du vin des cavernes et du biscuit de la route, moi pressé de trouver le lieu et la formule.

Vagabonds

My pitiful brother! How many awful nights he caused me! "I did not embrace this undertaking fervently enough! I made light of his infirmity. It would be my fault if we went back into exile, into slavery." He fancied I was endowed with very weird innocence and rotten luck, then piled on some worrisome rationales.

I answered this satanic doctor with snickers, and ended up moving to the window. Beyond the countryside crisscrossed by bands of rare music, I conjured the ghosts of my future nocturnal luxury.

After that vaguely hygienic distraction, I stretched out on a mattress. And almost every night, no sooner had I fallen asleep than the poor brother got up, bug-eyed and with stinking breath,—his dream of himself!—and dragged me into the other room screeching his idiotic fantasy of heartache.

Actually, in all sincerity, I had sought to return him to his primal state as Child of the Sun,—and we wandered, living on Adam's ale and road biscuits, I restless to find the place and the formula.

Mystique

Sur la pente du talus les anges tournent leurs robes de laine dans les herbages d'acier et d'émeraude.

Des prés de flammes bondissent jusqu'au sommet du mamelon. À gauche le terreau de l'arête est piétiné par tous les homicides et toutes les batailles, et tous les bruits désastreux filent leur courbe. Derrière l'arête de droite la ligne des orients, des progrès.

Et tandis que la bande en haut du tableau est formée de la rumeur tournante et bondissante des conques des mers et des nuits humaines,

La douceur fleurie des étoiles et du ciel et du reste descend en face du talus, comme un panier,—contre notre face, et fait l'abîme fleurant et bleu là-dessous.

Mystic

On the embankment slope, angels twirl their woolen robes in pastures of emerald and steel.

Fields of flame leap to the crest of the knoll. To the left, the fertile ground of the ridge is trampled by hordes of murder and war, and all the sounds of disaster curve off in their wake. Behind the right-hand ridge is the eastern line, the line of progress.

And while the swirling, leaping roar of conch shells and human nights forms the upper part of the scene,

The gentle flowering of the stars and sky and everything else descends toward the embankment, like a basket, against our face, and fashions the blue floral abyss down below.

Aube

J'ai embrassé l'aube d'été.

Rien ne bougeait encore au front des palais. L'eau était morte. Les camps d'ombres ne quittaient pas la route du bois. J'ai marché, réveillant les haleines vives et tièdes, et les pierreries regardèrent, et les ailes se levèrent sans bruit.

La première entreprise fut, dans le sentier déjà empli de frais et blêmes éclats, une fleur qui me dit son nom.

Je ris au wasserfall blond qui s'échevela à travers les sapins: à la cime argentée je reconnus la déesse.

Alors je levai un à un les voiles. Dans l'allée, en agitant les bras. Par la plaine, où je l'ai dénoncée au coq. À la grand'ville elle fuyait parmi les clochers et les dômes, et courant comme un mendiant sur les quais de marbre, je la chassais.

En haut de la route, près d'un bois de lauriers, je l'ai entourée avec ses voiles amassés, et j'ai senti un peu son immense corps. L'aube et l'enfant tombèrent au bas du bois.

Au réveil il était midi.

Dawn

I kissed the summer dawn.

Nothing stirring on the palace front. The water was dead.
Camps of shadows clung to the path in the woods. I walked,
rousing lively, warm breaths, and gemstones watched, and
wings took flight without a sound.

The first venture, on a trail strewn with fresh, pale bursts,
was a flower telling me its name.

I laughed at the blond wasserfall whose hair came undone
amid the pines: at the silvery crest I knew the goddess.

Then one by one I lifted the veils. In the alley, my arms
flailing. On the plain, where I denounced her to the cockerel.
In the big city, she fled among the spires and domes and I
chased after, running like a beggar down the marble quays.

At the top of the road, near a laurel grove, I encircled her
with her gathered veils, and briefly I felt her massive body.
Dawn and the child tumbled into a hollow.

When I awoke it was noon.

Nocturne vulgaire

Un souffle ouvre des brèches opéradiques dans les cloisons,—brouille le pivotement des toits rongés,—disperse les limites des foyers,—éclipse les croisées.—Le long de la vigne, m'étant appuyé du pied à une gargouille,—je suis descendu dans ce carrosse dont l'époque est assez indiquée par les glaces convexes, les panneaux bombés et les sophas contournés. Corbillard de mon sommeil, isolé, maison de berger de ma niaiserie, le véhicule vire sur le gazon de la grande route effacée; et dans un défaut en haut de la glace de droite tournoient les blêmes figures lunaires, feuilles, seins;—Un vert et un bleu très foncés envahissent l'image. Dételage aux environs d'une tache de gravier.

—Ici, va-t-on siffler pour l'orage, et les Sodomes,—et les Solymes,—et les bêtes féroces et les armées,

—(Postillon et bêtes de songe reprendront-ils sous les plus suffocantes futaies, pour m'enfoncer jusqu'aux yeux dans la source de soie).

—Et nous envoyer, fouettés à travers les eaux clapotantes et les boissons répandues, rouler sur l'aboi des dogues...

—Un souffle disperse les limites du foyer.

Ordinary Nocturne

A gust of wind rips operatically through the walls,—twists and scatters the worm-eaten rooftops,—blows open the rooms,—blots out the casements.—One foot resting on a gargoyle, I rolled through the vineyard in this coach whose vintage is told by its convex mirrors, bulging panes, and contoured sofas. Private hearse for my sleep, shepherd's hut for my foolishness, the coach veers onto the grass leaving the highway behind; and spinning around in a flaw at the top of the right-hand mirror are pale lunar figures, leaves, breasts;—Dark green and blue invade the picture. Unhitched near a patch of gravel.

—Here, they'll whistle for the tempest, and the Sodoms,—and the Solymas,—and wild beasts, and armies.

—(Coachman and dreamlike animals will set off again in stifling forests, sinking me to my eyeballs in silken springs.)

—And send us whipping across lapping waters and spilled drinks, to roll on the barking of bulldogs...

—A gust of wind blows open the rooms.

Angoisse

Se peut-il qu'Elle me fasse pardonner les ambitions continu-
ellement écrasées,—qu'une fin aisée répare les âges d'indigence,
—qu'un jour de succès nous endorme sur la honte de notre
inhabileté fatale ?

(Ô palmes! diamant! —Amour, force!—plus haut que
toutes joies et gloires!—de toutes façons, partout,—Démon,
dieu,—Jeunesse de cet être-ci; moi!)

Que des accidents de féerie scientifique et des mouvements
de fraternité sociale soient chéris comme restitution progres-
sive de la franchise première? . . .

Mais la Vampire qui nous rend gentils commande que
nous nous amusions avec ce qu'elle nous laisse, ou qu'autrement
nous soyons plus drôles.

Rouler aux blessures, par l'air lassant et la mer; aux sup-
plices, par le silence des eaux et de l'air meurtriers; aux
tortures qui rient, dans leur silence atrocement houleux.

Anguish

Could She have me pardoned for my ever quashed ambitions, —could a comfortable end remedy ages of poverty,—could one day of success dull us to the shame of our fatal ineptitude?

(O palms! diamond!—Love, strength!—higher than every joy and glory!—in every way, everywhere,—Demon, deity,— The youth of this person; me!)

Could accidents of scientific enchantment and movements of social fraternity be cherished as a gradual restitution of original honesty? . . .

But the Vampire who makes us docile commands us to amuse ourselves with what she leaves us, or anyway to be more entertaining.

Give over to traumas, through the tedious air and the sea; to torments, through the silence of murderous water and air; to tortures, jeering in their horrible, turbulent silence.

Métropolitain

Du détroit d'indigo aux mers d'Ossian, sur le sable rose et orange qu'a lavé le ciel vineux viennent de monter et de se croiser des boulevards de cristal habités incontinent par de jeunes familles pauvres qui s'alimentent chez les fruitiers. Rien de riche.—La ville!

Du désert de bitume fuient droit en déroute avec les nappes de brumes échelonnées en bandes affreuses au ciel qui se recourbe, se recule et descend, formé de la plus sinistre fumée noire que puisse faire l'Océan en deuil, les casques, les roues, les barques, les croupes.—La bataille!

Lève la tête: ce pont de bois, arqué; les derniers potagers de Samarie; ces masques enluminés sous la lanterne fouettée par la nuit froide; l'ondine niaise à la robe bruyante, au bas de la rivière: les crânes lumineux dans les plans de pois—et les autres fantasmagories—la campagne.

Des routes bordées de grilles et de murs, contenant à peine leurs bosquets, et les atroces fleurs qu'on appellerait cœurs et sœurs, Damas damnant de longueur,—possessions de féeriques aristocraties ultra-Rhénanes, Japonaises, Guaranies, propres encore à recevoir la musique des anciens—et il y a des auberges qui pour toujours n'ouvrent déjà plus—il y a des princesses, et si tu n'es pas trop accablé, l'étude des astres—le ciel.

Le matin où avec Elle, vous vous débattîtes parmi les éclats de neige, les lèvres vertes, les glaces, les drapeaux noirs et les rayons bleus, et les parfums pourpres du soleil des pôles,—ta force.

Metropolitan

From indigo straits to the seas of Ossian, on the pink-and-orange sands washed by vinous skies, crystal boulevards spring up and intersect, soon inhabited by poor young families subsisting on fruit. Nothing rich.—City!

From the asphalt desert, fleeing forward in defeat, through layers of fog stretched in horrible bands across a sky that curves, recoils, descends, formed by the foulest black smoke that the bereaved Ocean can generate: helmets, cartwheels, rowboats, hindquarters.—Battle!

Raise your head: this arched wooden bridge; the last vegetable gardens in Samaria; these flame-lit masks under the lantern whipped by the cold night; the silly mermaid with the loud dress, at the bottom of the river; luminous skulls in flats of peas—and other phantasmagoria—country.

Roads lined with fences and walls, barely containing their groves, and the horrid blooms you might call plumes or wombs, Damas damning in doom,—possessions of magical Rhenish, Japanese, or Guarani aristocracies, still fit to receive the music of the ancients—and already there are inns that shall remain closed forevermore—there are princesses, and if you aren't too stricken, the study of astral bodies—the heavens.

The morning when you and She wrestled in the blinding snow, lips green, ice, black flags and blue sunbeams, and purple scents of the polar sun,—your strength.

Jeunesse

I

DIMANCHE

Les calculs de côté, l'inévitable descente du ciel, et la visite des souvenirs et la séance des rythmes occupent la demeure, la tête et le monde de l'esprit.

—Un cheval détale sur le turf suburbain, et le long des cultures et des boisements, percé par la peste carbonique. Une misérable femme de drame, quelque part dans le monde, soupire après des abandons improbables. Les desperadoes languissent après l'orage, l'ivresse et les blessures. De petits enfants étouffent des malédictions le long des rivières.—

Reprenons l'étude au bruit de l'œuvre dévorante qui se rassemble et remonte dans les masses.

II

SONNET

Homme de constitution ordinaire, la chair n'était-elle pas un fruit pendu dans le verger,—ô journées enfantes ! le corps un trésor à prodiguer;—ô aimer, le péril ou la force de Psyché? La terre avait des versants fertiles en princes et en artistes, et la descendance et la race nous poussaient aux crimes et aux deuils: le monde, votre fortune et votre péril. Mais à présent, ce labeur comblé,—toi, tes calculs, toi, tes impatiences,—ne sont plus que votre danse et votre voix, non fixées et point forcées, quoique d'un double événement d'invention et de succès une saison,—en l'humanité fraternelle

Youth

I

SUNDAY

Calculations set aside, the inevitable descent from heaven, and visitations of memory and the session of rhythms fill your dwelling, your head, and the realm of the mind.

—A horse bolts on the suburban turf and along woods and farmlands, pierced by carbonic plague. Somewhere in the world, a miserable drama queen sighs over unlikely abandonments. Desperadoes laze about after storms, drunks, and injuries. Small children stifle curses up and down the rivers.—

Back to our studies, to the sound of all-consuming labors that come together and rise into the masses.

II

SONNET

Man of plain constitution, was flesh not a fruit hanging low in the orchard;—O childish days! the body a treasure to grant lavishly;—O love, Psyche's peril or vigor? The earth had slopes rich in princes and artists; relations and race pushed you into bereavements and crimes: the world your estate and your peril. But now, this labor fulfilled,—you, with your calculations, your rashness—the only remains are your dance and your voice, never fixed and not ever forced, though yet from a dual event of invention and success a season,—in fraternal, discreet humanity, blank universe;—

et discrète par l'univers sans images;—la force et le droit réfléchissent la danse et la voix à présent seulement appréciées.

III

Les voix instructives exilées... L'ingénuité physique amèrement rassise... —Adagio—Ah! l'égoïsme infini de l'adolescence, l'optimisme studieux: que le monde était plein de fleurs cet été! Les airs et les formes mourant... —Un chœur, pour calmer l'impuissance et l'absence! Un chœur de verres, de mélodies nocturnes... En effet les nerfs vont vite chasser.

IV

Tu es encore à la tentation d'Antoine. L'ébat du zèle écourté, les tics d'orgueil puéril, l'affaissement et l'effroi.

Mais tu te mettras à ce travail: toutes les possibilités harmoniques et architecturales s'émouvront autour de ton siège. Des êtres parfaits, imprévus, s'offriront à tes expériences. Dans tes environs affluera rêveusement la curiosité d'anciennes foules et de luxes oisifs. Ta mémoire et tes sens ne seront que la nourriture de ton impulsion créatrice. Quant au monde, quand tu sortiras, que sera-t-il devenu? En tout cas, rien des apparences actuelles.

strength and law ponder the dance and the voice, esteemed only now.

III

AT TWENTY

Instructive voices exiled...Physical ingenuity bitterly wanes...—Adagio—Ah! the boundless egotism of adolescence, its studious optimism: how the world was full of flowers that summer! Airs and dying forms...—A chorus, to assuage impotence and absence! A chorus of glasses, of nocturnes... Sure enough, our nerves will soon be listing badly.

IV

You're still at the temptations of Anthony. The frolic of zeal curtailed, tics of childish pride, collapse and dread.

But you'll get down to work: every harmonic and architectural possibility will agitate around your seat. Perfect creatures will offer themselves unbidden for your experiments. The curiosity of ancient crowds and idle luxuries will flock dreamily to your surroundings. Your memory and senses will only nourish your creative impulse. As for the world, when you emerge, what will it have become? Nothing like its current appearance, in any case.

Bottom

La réalité étant trop épineuse pour mon grand caractère,—je me trouvai néanmoins chez ma dame, en gros oiseau gris bleu s'essorant vers les moulures du plafond et traînant l'aile dans les ombres de la soirée.

Je fus, au pied du baldaquin supportant ses bijoux adorés et ses chefs-d'œuvre physiques, un gros ours aux gencives violettes et au poil chenu de chagrin, les yeux aux cristaux et aux argents des consoles.

Tout se fait ombre et aquarium ardent.

Au matin,—aube de juin batailleuse,—je courus aux champs, âne, claironnant et brandissant mon grief, jusqu'à ce que les Sabines de la banlieue vinrent se jeter à mon poitrail.

Bottom

Reality being too thorny for my grand personality,—I none-theless found myself at milady's, a huge blue-gray bird shaking dry his plumage toward the moldings on the ceiling and dragging his wings through the evening's shadows.

At the foot of the four-poster bed supporting her adored jewelry and her physical masterworks, I was a great bear with purple gums and fur hoary with sorrow, eyes on the crystal and silver of the console tables.

It all turns to shadow and brilliant aquarium.

In the morning,—an embattled June dawn,—I took to the fields, an ass, trumpeting and brandishing my grievance, until suburban Sabines came to throw themselves at my neck.

H

Toutes les monstruosités violent les gestes atroces d'Hortense. Sa solitude est la mécanique érotique, sa lassitude, la dynamique amoureuse. Sous la surveillance d'une enfance elle a été, à des époques nombreuses, l'ardente hygiène des races. Sa porte est ouverte à la misère. Là, la moralité des êtres actuels se décorpore en sa passion ou en son action —Ô terrible frisson des amours novices, sur le sol sanglant et par l'hydrogène clarteux! trouvez Hortense.

H

All monstrosities her odious motions violate. Hortense: her solitude is erotic mechanics, her lassitude amorous dynamics. Under the watchful eyes of childhood, she has been, so many times, an ardent racial hygiene. Her door stands open to misery. There, the morality of today's creatures is disembodied by her passion or action—Terrible thrill of novice loves on bloody floors, in hydrogen glare! find Hortense.

Dévotion

À ma sœur Louise Vanaen de Voringhem: —Sa cornette bleue tournée à la mer du Nord.—Pour les naufragés.

À ma sœur Léonie Aubois d'Ashby. Baou—l'herbe d'été bourdonnante et puante.—Pour la fièvre des mères et des enfants.

À Lulu,—démon—qui a conservé un goût pour les oratoires du temps des Amies et de son éducation incomplète. Pour les hommes! À madame ***.

À l'adolescent que je fus. À ce saint vieillard, ermitage ou mission.

À l'esprit des pauvres. Et à un très haut clergé.

Aussi bien à tout culte en telle place de culte mémoriale et parmi tels événements qu'il faille se rendre, suivant les aspirations du moment ou bien notre propre vice sérieux,

Ce soir à Circeto des hautes glaces, grasse comme le poisson, et enluminée comme les dix mois de la nuit rouge,—(son cœur ambre et spunk),—pour ma seule prière muette comme ces régions de nuit et précédant des bravoures plus violentes que ce chaos polaire.

À tout prix et avec tous les airs, même dans des voyages métaphysiques.—Mais plus *alors*.

Devotion

To my sister Louise Vanaen of Voringhem:—Her blue cornette turned toward the North Sea.—For the shipwrecked.

To my sister Léonie Aubois of Ashby. Baou—summer grasses buzzing and fetid.—For the fevers of mothers and children.

To Lulu,—demon—who preserved a liking for shrines from the time of Girlfriends and her incomplete education. For men! To Madam ***.

To the adolescent I once was. To the holy graybeard, hermitage or mission.

To the spirit of the poor. And to a clergy most high.

As well as to every faith, in such a memorial place of worship and among such events that we must depart, following momentary aspirations or else our own serious vice,

This evening to Circeto and her glacial heights, fat as a fish, and lit like the ten months of red night,—(her heart of ambergris and spunk),—for my sole prayer silent like those nocturnal regions, before exploits more violent than this polar chaos.

At any price, in every place, even on metaphysical journeys.—But then *no more*.

Génie

Il est l'affection et le présent puisqu'il a fait la maison ouverte à l'hiver écumeux et à la rumeur de l'été, lui qui a purifié les boissons et les aliments, lui qui est le charme des lieux fuyant et le délice surhumain des stations. Il est l'affection et l'avenir, la force et l'amour que nous, debout dans les rages et les ennuis, nous voyons passer dans le ciel de tempête et les drapeaux d'extase.

Il est l'amour, mesure parfaite et réinventée, raison merveilleuse et imprévue, et l'éternité: machine aimée des qualités fatales. Nous avons tous eu l'épouvante de sa concession et de la nôtre: ô jouissance de notre santé, élan de nos facultés, affection égoïste et passion pour lui, lui qui nous aime pour sa vie infinie...

Et nous nous le rappelons et il voyage... Et si l'Adoration s'en va, sonne, sa promesse, sonne: "Arrière ces superstitions, ces anciens corps, ces ménages et ces âges. C'est cette époque-ci qui a sombré!"

Il ne s'en ira pas, il ne redescendra pas d'un ciel, il n'accomplira pas la rédemption des colères de femmes et des gaîtés des hommes et de tout ce pêché: car c'est fait, lui étant, et étant aimé.

Ô ses souffles, ses têtes, ses courses; la terrible célérité de la perfection des formes et de l'action.

Ô fécondité de l'esprit et immensité de l'univers!

Son corps! Le dégagement rêvé, le brisement de la grâce croisée de violence nouvelle!

Sa vue, sa vue! tous les agenouillages anciens et les peines *relevées* à sa suite.

Son jour! l'abolition de toutes souffrances sonores et mouvantes dans la musique plus intense.

Genius

He is affection and the present since he threw open the house to frothy winter and the sounds of summer—he who purified food and drink—he who is the charm of fleeting places and the superhuman delight of stations.—He is affection and the future, the strength and love that we, standing in rage and boredom, see pass in the stormy sky and ecstatic banners.

He is love, perfect and reinvented measure, marvelous and unexpected reason, and eternity: beloved instrument of fatal qualities. We have all felt the horror of his concession and ours: O delight of our well-being, surge of our faculties, selfish affection and passion for him,—he who loves us his whole endless life long...

And we call him back and he travels... And if Adoration leaves us, his Promise rings out: "Get thee behind me, superstitions, ancient bodies, households, and ages. It is this era that has capsized!"

He will not leave us, will not come down from some heaven, will not redeem women's anger and men's gaiety and all that sin: for it is done, he is, he is loved.

O his breaths, his heads, his journeys; the terrible swiftness of perfected forms and action.

O fecundity of the mind and immensity of the universe!

His body! The ideal disengagement, the shattering of grace shot through with new violence!

His sight, the sight of him! all the old genuflections and sorrows *risen* in his wake.

His light! the abolition of every resonant and unstable suffering in more intense music.

Son pas! les migrations plus énormes que les anciennes invasions.

Ô Lui et nous! l'orgueil plus bienveillant que les charités perdues.

Ô monde! et le chant clair des malheurs nouveaux!

Il nous a connus tous et nous a tous aimés. Sachons, cette nuit d'hiver, de cap en cap, du pôle tumultueux au château, de la foule à la plage, de regards en regards, forces et sentiments las, le héler et le voir, et le renvoyer, et sous les marées et au haut des déserts de neige, suivre ses vues,—ses *souffles*— son corps,—son jour.

His step! migrations vaster than ancient invasions.

O Him and us! pride more benevolent than lost charities.

O world!—and the clear song of new misfortunes!

He has known us all and loved us all, and let us know, on this winter's night, from cape to cape, from tumultuous pole to castle, from crowd to seashore, from glances to glances, energies and emotions weary, how to hail him and see him, and echo him, and beneath the tides and the crest of snowy deserts, follow his sight,—his *breaths*—his body,—his light.

Selected Letters

1870–1875

To Théodore de Banville

Charleville (Ardennes), May 24, 1870

Honored Sir,

We are in the months of love; I'm nearly seventeen. The age of hopes and dreams, as they say,—and so I've decided, as a child touched by the finger of the Muse,—pardon the banality,—to tell you my most cherished beliefs, hopes, sensations, all those poet things—I call that springtime.

So if I send you a few of my verses,—which I do via the kindness of publisher Alph. Lemerre,—it's because I love all poets, all the good Parnassians,—since a poet is a Parnassian,—smitten with ideal beauty; it's what I love in you, quite naïvely, a descendant of Ronsard, a brother of our masters of 1830, a true Romantic, a true poet. That's why.— Stupid, isn't it, but anyway? . . .

In two years, or perhaps one year, I'll be in Paris.

—Anch'io, gentlemen of the press, I shall be a Parnassian!—No idea what I've got here . . . but it wants to come up . . . —I pledge, honored sir, to adore the two goddesses, Muse and Freedom.

Don't make too sour a face when reading these poems: . . . You'd leave me wild with joy and hope, if you would agree, honored Sir, to *make* a little room among the Parnassians for the piece "Credo in unam" . . . I would come in the last volume of *Parnasse*: it would be the poets' Creed! . . . O mad Ambition!

ARTHUR RIMBAUD

[. . .] Do you think these verses could find a place in the *Parnasse contemporain*?

—Aren't they the poets' act of faith?

—I'm not well known; but so what? all poets are brothers.
These verses believe; they love; they hope: that's all.

—Honored Sir, my turn: Lift me up a little: I am young:
give me your hand...

To Georges Izambard

Charleville, August 25, 70

Sir,

You're so lucky not to live in Charleville anymore!—My hometown is the most supremely idiotic of all the provincial towns. I no longer harbor any illusions about this, you see. Because it's next to Mézières,—a town you can barely find,— and because it has two or three hundred soldier boys wandering its streets, this sanctimonious population gesticulates, sharp-tongued banalities at the ready, much more than the besieged of Metz and Strasbourg! It's terrifying to see those retired greengrocers squeezed back in their uniforms! How wonderfully chic they look, all those notaries, glaziers, tax collectors, carpenters, and other paunches, blunderbuss clutched to their breast, practicing their patridiotism at the gates of Mézières; my nation is rising up!...Personally, I'd rather it stay seated: don't get your boots in a stir! that's my motto.

I'm a fish out of water, sick, furious, dumb, down and out; I was hoping to lie in the sun, take endless walks, rest, travel, have adventures, to gypsify, in short; I especially hoped for newspapers and books...Nothing! Nothing! The mail isn't delivering a thing to the bookstores; Paris is having a good guffaw at our expense: not a single new book! it's deathly! For newspapers, I'm reduced to the honorable *Courrier des Ardennes*,—A. Pouillard, owner, manager, publisher, and editor in chief all in one! The paper epitomizes the aspirations, wishes, and opinions of the populace: judge for yourself! a fine thing!...Exiled in my own homeland!!!

[...] I'm sending you some poems; read them one morning,

in the sun, as I wrote them: you're no longer teaching these days, I hope!

[...] So long, send me a 25-page letter—general delivery—and fast!

A. RIMBAUD

PS—Soon, some revelations on the life I'm going to lead after...this vacation...

To Georges Izambard

Paris, September 5, 1870

Dear Sir,

· What you advised me not to do, I did: I went to Paris, leaving the maternal household! I performed this feat on August 29.

I was arrested as I got off the train for being broke and owing thirteen francs in railway fare, taken into custody, and today I'm awaiting sentencing in Mazas! oh!—*I place my hopes in you* as I do in my mother; you have always been like a brother to me: I urge you to give me the help you once offered. I've written to my mother, the imperial prosecutor, and the police commissioner in Charleville; if you don't receive word from me by Wednesday, before the train from Douai to Paris, *take that train, come here to claim me by letter, or by going to see the prosecutor*, plead my case, *vouch for me, pay my debt! Do whatever you can*, and also, when you get this letter, *I order you*, yes, *to write to my poor mother* (5 Quai de la Madeleine, Charlev[ille]) *to console her. Write to me* too; do all the above! I love you like a brother, I will love you like a father.

With fondest greetings
Your poor
ARTHUR RIMBAUD
in Mazas

(and if you manage to get me free, you'll take me to Douai with you.)

To Georges Izambard

Charleville, November 2, 1870

Sir,

—This to you alone.—

I got back to Charleville the day after leaving you. My mother took me in, and here I am...idle as can be. My mother doesn't plan to send me to boarding school until January '71.

Well, I've kept my promise!

I'm dying, decomposing in dullness, badness, grayness. What can I say, I horribly insist on adoring total freedom, and...so many things that are "such a pity," right? I was supposed to leave again today; I could have: I had all new clothes, I could have sold my watch, and long live freedom!— And then I stayed! I stayed!—and I'll want to leave again many times more.—Off we go, hat, coat, fists in pockets, and out.—But I'll stay, I'll stay. I never promised to! But I'll do it to earn your affection: you told me so. I'll earn it.

I can't express how grateful I am to you any better today than the other day. I'll prove it. It would mean doing something for you, something I would die in order to do,—I give you my word.—I still have so much to say...

That "heartless"

A. RIMBAUD

War:—no siege yet in Mézières. For when? No one's talking about it. I gave Mr. Deverrière your message, and, if there's more to be done, I'll do it.—Potshots here, potshots there.— The general mind-set is a hideous rash of idiocy. You hear some good ones, let me tell you. Numbs the brain.

To Paul Demeny

Charleville, April 17, 1871

Your letter arrived yesterday, the 16th. Many thanks.—As for what I requested, how silly I was! With no clue of what one needs to know, determined not to do what needs doing, I'm doomed, since forever and for always. Long live today, long live tomorrow!

Since the 12th, I've been sorting mail at the *Progrès des Ardennes*: it's true that publication has been suspended. But I was able to appease the Mouth of Darkness for a while.

Yes, you sure are a lucky one. Mark my words,—and also there are miserable wretches who will never find the Sister of Mercy, wife or ideal.

For the rest, for now, I'd advise you to immerse yourself in these verses from Ecclesiastes, chs. 11–12, as wise as they are romantic: "He who has seven waves of folly in his soul, who, having hung his clothes in the sun, moans when come the rains," but enough with the wisdom of 1830: let's talk about Paris.

I saw some recent publications at Lemerre's [...] At the Artistique bookshop,— I went to get Vermersch's address,— they asked after you. As far as I knew, you were in Abbeville at the time.

Every publisher has its *Siege* book, its *Siege Journal,*—Sarcey's *Siege* is in its 14th prtg.;—and I saw such a dreary torrent of photographs and drawings about the Siege,—you'd never believe how many. [...]—As for the theaters, abomination of desolation.—The latest things of note were *Le Mot d'ordre* and admirable fancies by Vallès and Vermersch in the *Cri du Peuple*.

Such was the state of literature,—February 25 to March 10.—Besides, I might not be telling you anything you don't know.

In which case, let us turn our brows to the lances of the rain, our souls to ancient wisdom.

And may Belgian literature whisk us off under its arm.

So long,

A. RIMBAUD

To Georges Izambard

Charleville, May [13,] 1871

Dear Sir!

So you're a teacher again. One owes a debt to Society, you said; you are part of the teaching profession: you're rolling in a good rut.—I, too, am following a principle: I'm cynically letting myself be supported; I dredge up old morons from school, feed them all sorts of stupid, dirty, or evil words or deeds that I make up on the spot, and they pay me in beers and bottles. *Stat mater dolorosa, dum pendet filius.*—I owe a debt to Society, that's a fact,—and I'm right.—You're right, too, for now. Basically, in principle you recognize only subjective poetry; your obstinacy in returning to the academic trough,—sorry!—proves it! But you'll still end up self-satisfied, not having accomplished anything, never having tried to accomplish anything. Not to mention that your subjective poetry will always be horribly insipid. Someday, I hope,— many others hope the same,—I'll see some objective poetry in your principles, I'll see it more sincerely than you'd make it!—I'll be a worker: that's the thought that holds me back, when wild rages urge me toward the fighting in Paris—where so many workers are still dying even as I write! Work now— never, never; I'm on strike.

For now, I'm filthifying myself as best I can. Why? I want to be a poet, and I'm working on becoming a *seer*: you won't understand any of it, and I can hardly explain. It's about reaching the unknown by the disordering of *all the senses.* It involves considerable suffering, but you have to be strong, be born a poet, and I have recognized myself as a poet. It's not my fault. It's false to say: I think: one should say: I am thought.—Pardon the word games.—

I is an Other. Too bad for the wood that turns into a violin, and to hell with oblivious fools who split hairs over things they know nothing about!

To me, you are not a *Teacher*. I'll send you this: is it a satire, as you'd say? Is it poetry? It's just fancy, as always.— But, I beg you, don't underline it, either in pencil or with too much thought:

TORTURED HEART
My sad heart slobbers at the poop [...]

It doesn't mean just nothing.—ANSWER ME: c/o Mr. Deverrière, for A.R.

Warm regards,
AR. RIMBAUD

To Paul Demeny

Charleville, May 15, 1871

[...]—Here's some prose about the future of poetry—

All ancient poetry leads to Greek poetry, Life in harmony.—From Greece to the Romantic movement,—Middle Ages,—there are men of letters, versifiers. From Ennius to Turoldus, from Turoldus to Casimir Delavigne, it's all rhymed prose, a game, flaccidity and glory of countless idiotic generations: Racine the pure, the strong, the great.—If they'd puffed on his rhymes, messed with his caesuras, the Divine Dope would be as forgotten today as your basic contributor to *Origins*.—After Racine, the game gets stale. It's lasted for two thousand years!

No joke or paradox. Reason inspires more certainties in me about this topic than the young Romantics have ravings. Moreover, it's up to the *newcomers*! to despise their ancestors: we're at home here and we have plenty of time.

No one has ever judged Romanticism appropriately. Who would have judged it? the critics!! The Romantics, who so rightly prove that the song is seldom the work, in other words a thought not only sung *but understood* by the singer?

For I is an Other. If copper wakes up as a clarion, it's hardly its fault. That seems clear to me: I'm there to see my thought burst forth: I watch it, listen to it: I attack with my bow: the symphony stirs in the depths, or leaps onto the stage.

If the old fools had found more in the Self than false meaning, we wouldn't have to clear away these millions of skeletons, who since time immemorial have stacked up the products of their nearsighted intelligence, and boasted of being their authors!

229

As I was saying, in Greece, verses and lyres *gave rhythm to Action*. After that, music and rhymes are just games, pastimes. The study of this past charms the curious: some delight in reviving such antiquities:—they can have them. Universal intelligence has always generated ideas, naturally; people gathered up some of those fruits of the mind: they acted on them, wrote books from them: that's how it went, man didn't strain too hard, as he was neither awake yet nor fully in the great dream. Writers, functionaries. Author, creator, poet—this man has never existed!

The primary study of someone who wants to be a poet is his own consciousness, in its entirety; he searches his soul, inspects it, tries it out, learns it. Once he knows it, he has to cultivate it; this seems easy: every brain undergoes a natural development; so many *egotists* proclaim themselves authors; there are many others who attribute their intellectual progress to *themselves*!—But the point is to make your soul monstrous: like Hugo's Comprachicos! Imagine someone planting and cultivating warts on his face.

What I'm *saying* is that one must be a *seer*, make oneself a *seer*.

The Poet makes himself a *seer* by a long, massive, and reasoned *disordering* of *all the senses*. Every form of love, suffering, madness; he searches himself, drinks every poison in him to the dregs, retaining only the quintessences. Unspeakable torture that will require all his faith, all his superhuman strength, in which he becomes the greatest invalid, the greatest criminal, the most accursed of all,—and the supreme Scientist!—For he has attained the *unknown*! Since, more than anyone, he has cultivated his already fertile soul! He attains the unknown, and even when he ultimately loses his mind and stops understanding his visions, he will have seen them! So what if he dies while striving toward new and unnameable things: other horrible toilers will appear in his stead; they'll begin on the horizons where the first one keeled over! [...]

So the poet is truly the thief of fire.

He is responsible for humanity, even for *animals*; he has to make people feel, touch, heed his inventions; if what he brings back *from over there* has shape, he gives shape: if it's shapeless, he gives shapelessness. Find a language;

—What's more, all words being ideas, the time of a universal language will come! You have to be an academician,—deader than a fossil,—to perfect a dictionary, in whatever language. The weak would set *to thinking* on the first letter of the alphabet, which could quickly veer into madness!—

This language will be by the soul for the soul, encompassing everything, scents, sounds, colors, thought linking to thought and tugging on it. The poet, in his time, would define how much of the unknown awakens in the universal soul: he would give more—than the formula of his thinking, than the record *of his march toward Progress*! As enormity becomes norm and is absorbed by all, he would truly be *a multiplier of progress!*

This future will be materialist, you see;—Always filled with *Number* and *Harmony*, these poems will be made to last.—Basically, this would still be a bit of Greek poetry. Eternal art would have its uses; just as poets are citizens. Poetry will no longer give rhythm to action; it will lead it.

These poets will be! When the endless serfdom of woman is toppled, when she can live for herself and by herself, and man,—who until now has been reprehensible,—discharges her, she too will be a poet! Woman will find the unknown! Will the worlds of her ideas differ from ours?—She will find strange, unfathomable, repulsive, delightful things; we will apprehend them, and comprehend them.

Meanwhile, let us demand that *poets* give us *new* ideas and forms. The clever ones will soon think they've satisfied this demand.—Far from it!

The first Romantics were *seers* without quite realizing it: the cultivation of their souls began as accidents: locomotives, abandoned but burning hot, that the rails guide for a while.—Lamartine is sometimes a seer, but strangled by old forms.—Hugo, *too pigheaded*, definitely has some VISION in his latest volumes: *Les Misérables* is a real *poem*. I've got the *Châtiments* at hand; "Stella" gives some idea of Hugo's *vision*. Too much Belmontet and Lamennais, Jehovahs and columns, crumbling old enormities.

Musset is abhorrent fourteen times over for us, painful generations subject to visions,—which his angelic laziness has insulted! O! the insipid stories and proverbs! O those *Nuits*! O *Rolla*, O *Namouna*, O *La Coupe*! It's all so French, in other words contemptible to the highest degree; French, not Parisian! Yet another body of work from the same hateful ingenuity that sparked Rabelais, Voltaire, Jean [de] La Fontaine, as commented by Mr. Taine! So springlike, Musset's mind! So charming, his love! And there you have it, from painting to enamel, some solid poetry! Long will *French* poetry be savored, but only in France. Every shop assistant is able to spew out a Rollesque declamation; every seminarian carries its five hundred rhymes in a secret notebook. At age fifteen, these passionate declamations get young people horny; at sixteen, they're already content to recite them with *heart*; at eighteen, or even seventeen, any schoolboy with half a brain makes his own Rolla, writes a Rolla! A few might still be dying from it. Musset didn't know what to do with it: his visions were behind gauze curtains: he shut his eyes. French, wishy-washy, dragged from the tavern to the school lectern, the good-looking corpse is dead, and let's not even bother reviving it for our abuse!

The second wave of Romantics are very *visionary*: Th. Gautier, Lec. de Lisle, Th. de Banville. But since inspecting the invisible and hearing the unheard is not the same as recapturing the spirit of dead things, Baudelaire is the first seer, king of poets, *a real God*. Even so, he lived in too artistic a milieu; and his much vaunted form is petty: inventing the unknown demands new forms.

Schooled in old forms, among the innocents, A. Renaud,—did his Rolla,—L. Grandet—did his Rolla;—The Gauls and the Mussets, G. Lafenestre, Coran, Cl. Popelin, Soulary, L. Salles; The schoolboys, Marc, Aicard, Theuriet; the dead and the idiots, Autran, Barbier, L. Pichat, Lemoyne, the Deschamps, the Desessarts; The journalists, L. Cladel, Robert Luzarches, X. de Ricard; the fantasists, C. Mendès; the bohemians; the women; the talents, Léon Dierx, Sully Prudhomme, Coppée,—the new, so-called Parnassian school boasts two seers, Albert Mérat and Paul Verlaine, a true poet. That's it.—And so I'm working on becoming a *seer*. […]

It would be despicable of you not to answer; quick, 'cause a week from now I might be in Paris.

So long. A. RIMBAUD

To Paul Demeny

Charleville, June 10, 1871

[…] Here,—don't get mad,—an intentionally humorous sketch: an antithesis to perennially sweet ditties where Cupids frolic and blazing hearts take flight, with green flowers, wet birds, promontories on Lefkada, etc.—These triplets, too, by the by, will go

Where perennial ditties,
Where sweet verses.

Here:—don't get mad—

HEART OF A CLOWN
My sad heart slobbers at the poop […]

So that's what I'm up to.

I have three requests for you: burn, *I mean it*, and I believe you'll respect my wishes as if I were dead, burn *all the poems I was dumb enough* to give you when I was in Douai: be good enough to send me, if you can and if you would, a copy of your *Glaneuses*, which I'd like to reread and which I'm unable to buy, my mother not having graced me with a single bronze farthing in six months,—pity!—and finally, kindly answer, however you please, both this letter and the one before.

I wish you a good day, which is damn nice of me.

Write to: Mr. Deverrière, 95, sous les Allées, for

A. RIMBAUD

To Théodore de Banville

Charleville, Ardennes, August 15, 1871
[…]
Honored Sir and dear Master,
Do you recall receiving from the provinces, in June 1870, a hundred or hundred-fifty mythological hexameters entitled "Credo in unam"? You were kind enough to reply!

Here's the same idiot now sending you the above verses, signed Alcide Bava.—Sorry.

I'm eighteen years old.—I will love Banville's poetry forever.

Last year I was only seventeen!

Have I progressed?

ALCIDE BAVA
A. R.

My address:
M. Charles Bretagne,
Avenue de Mézières, in Charleville,
for
A. RIMBAUD

To Paul Demeny

Charleville (Ardennes), August [28,] 1871

Sir,

You're making me renew my request: so be it. Here's the whole sad story. I'm trying to find calm words: but my skill is not very developed. Anyway, here goes:

Situation of the accused: it's been more than a year since I turned my back on ordinary life, you know for what. Cooped up in that unspeakable Ardennes region, not a soul for company, trapped in a vile job, inept, obstinate, cryptic, answering people's questions and their mean, vulgar insults with stony silence, proving myself worthy in my extralegal position, I ended up provoking horrible resolutions from a mother as rigid as seventy-three lead-helmeted administrations.

She tried to make me take a job,—a permanent one, in Charleville (Ardennes)! Get hired by such-and-such a date, she said, or out the door.—I rejected that life; without giving my reasons: it would have been pathetic. Up to now, I've been able to skirt such ultimatums. She, has come to this: constantly wishing for me to run away, to escape! Broke and inexperienced, I'd wind up in a correctional facility. And then, last you'd hear of me!

That's the disgusting snot-rag they've stuffed in my mouth. Simple as can be.

I'm not asking for anything, I just need information. I want to work as a free man; but in Paris, which I love. Listen: I'm a walker, nothing more; I arrive in the big city with no material resources: but it was you who told me: Whoever wants to be a laborer at fifteen sous a day, show up here, do this, live like that. So I show up, I do this, I live like that. I asked you to suggest occupations that aren't too demanding, since thinking requires large chunks of time. As it gets the poet off the hook, such bread-and-butter nonsense becomes lovable. I'm in Paris: I need a positive *economy*! Don't you find that sincere? Personally, I think it's so strange that I should have to convince you how serious I am!

That was my idea: the only one that seemed sensible: I'm sending it back in different words. I'm of good faith, I do what I can, I'm putting this as straightforwardly as any wretch! Why scold the child who's not good in zoology and wishes for a five-winged bird? They could make him believe in birds with six tails, or three beaks! They could lend him the *Family Buffon*: that'd disabuse him.

So, not knowing what you might tell me, I'll cut this short and trust in your experience, your benevolence that I blessed fervently, when I got your letter, and I'm enlisting you to follow my ideas,—if you'd be so kind...

Would you mind terribly if I sent you some samples of my work?

A. RIMBAUD

To Paul Verlaine [fragments]

[Charleville, September 1871]
[...] I've hatched a plan to make a great poem, and I can't work in Charleville. I'm unable to come to Paris, as I have no resources. My mother is a widow and extremely devout. She only gives me ten centimes every Sunday for my seat in church.

[...] Little filth [...]

[...] less bother than a Zanetto.

To Paul Verlaine [fragments]

[Charleville, April 1872]
[...] The idea of work is as distant from me as my fingernail
is from my eye. Shit for me! Shit for me! Shit for me! Shit
for me? Shit for me! Shit for me! Shit for me! Shit for me!
....

Only when you see me positively eating shit will you quit
thinking I'm expensive to feed!...

To Ernest Delahaye

Parishit, Junphe 72

My friend,

Surprising indeed is existence in the Arduene cosmorama. The provinces, where they subsist on starches and mud, where they drink regional wines and local brew, are not what I miss. You're quite right to constantly dump on them. But this place here: distillation, composition, all forms of narrowness; and oppressive summer: the heat isn't very constant, but since good weather is apparently in everyone's interest, and everyone is a swine, I hate summer, which kills me when it even begins to show its face. I'm so thirsty I'm worried I've got gangrene: the rivers and caves of the Ardennes and Belgium, that's what I miss.

Still, there is one watering hole here that I'm fond of. Long live the Academy of Absomphe, despite the ill-tempered waiters! Intoxication by virtue of that sage leaf of the glaciers, absomphe [absinthe], is the most delicate and tremulous of attires! But, afterward, you lie down in shit!

Always the same moan and groan! What's for certain is: screw Perrin! And screw the Univers bar, whether facing the square or not. That said, nothing against the Univers.—I fervently hope the Ardenne is occupied and squeezed inordinately hard. But all that is still piddling.

What's serious is that you're feeling so down. Maybe you should spend your time walking and reading. In any case, best not to cloister yourself in offices and family homes. Stupors have to be induced far from such places. I'm hardly one to peddle balms, but I don't think habits offer much consolation, in our pitiful moments.

These days, I do my toilations at night. Midnight to five in the morning. Last month, my room on rue Monsieur-le-Prince looked onto the garden of the Lycée Saint-Louis. There were huge trees beneath my narrow window. At three in the morning, the candle grows dim; all the birds in the trees start shrieking at once: it's over. No more work. All I could do was gaze at the trees and sky, transfixed by that inexpressible first hour of morning. I saw the school dormitories, absolutely silent. And already the staccato, ringing, delightful sound of the tipcarts on the boulevards.—I smoked my hammerhead pipe and spat on the roof tiles, as my room was a garret. At five o'clock, I'd go down to buy some bread; that time of day. Workers scurrying all around. For me, it was time to get shit-faced at the wine shop. I'd go home to eat and crawl into bed at 7 a.m., when the sun's heat forced the woodlice out from under the tiles. The first morning of summer and December evenings, that's what I've always loved here.

But for now, I have a pretty room, over a bottomless courtyard but only three meters square.—Rue Victor-Cousin abuts Place de la Sorbonne, with the Bas-Rhin Café on the corner, and runs into rue Soufflot at the other end.—Here, I drink water all night long, I don't see morning, I don't sleep, I'm suffocating. And there you have it.

Your demand shall certainly be granted! Don't forget to shit on *La Renaissance*, artistic and literary periodical, should you come across it. Up to now I've avoided émigrés from Carolopolishit like the plague. Fuck the seasons. And colrage.

Courage.

A.R.

Rue Victor-Cousin, Hôtel de Cluny

To Ernest Delahaye

Laïtou, (Roches) (canton of Attigny)
May 73

Dear friend, you can glimpse my current existence in the watercolor below.

O Nature! O my mother!

What a fucking drag! and what horrible innocints these

peasants are. In the evening, you have to walk for miles just to get a lousy drink. *La Mother* has landed me in a sorry shithole.

I don't know how I'll get out: but I'll get out. I miss that awful Charlestown, the Univers, the Liberry, etc.... Still, I'm working pretty regularly; I'm writing little tales in prose, overall title: *Pagan Book*, or *Negro Book*. It's stupid and innocent. O innocence! Innocence; innocence, innoc...pestilence!

Verlaine has surely given you the unfortunate task of bargaining with sire Devin, printer of the *Nôress*. I think this Devin could do Verlaine's book fairly cheaply and almost correctly. (If he doesn't use the shitty typeface from the *Nôress*. I wouldn't put it past him to stick in a picture or an ad!)

I have nothing more to tell you, the contemplostation of Nature is absorbuggering me whole. I am yours, O Nature, O my mother!

Warmest regards, in hopes of a re-viewing that I'll activate as best I can.

R.

PS. Verlaine must have suggested a meet-up on Sunday the 18th, in Boulion [*sic*]. I can't go, myself. If you go, he'll probably burden you with a few prose fraguemints of mine or his, to give back to me.

Mother Rimb. will be back in Charlestown sometime in June, for sure, and I'll attempt to stay in that lovely burg for a while.

The sun is oppressive and mornings are freezing. The day before yesterday I went to see the Prussmen in Vouziers, a prefecture of 10,000 souls, seven km from here. It cheered me up.

I'm in an abominable situation. Not a book, not a tavern within reach, nothing doing in the streets. This here French country life is a real horror! My fate depends on this book for which a half-dozen atrocious stories are yet to be invented. How can you invent atrocities here? I won't send you any stories, even though I already have three, *it costs too much*! Anyway, there you have it!

So long, you'll see them at some point.

RIMB.

Soon I'll send you some stamps so you can buy and send me Goethe's *Faust*, Biblioth[èque] Populaire edition. Postage should cost a sou.

Let me know if there are any trans. of Shakespeare on that pub's list of new titles.

In fact, if you can send me their latest catalogue, do.

R.

To Paul Verlaine

London, Friday p.m. [July 4, 1873]

Come back, come back, my dearest friend, my only friend, come back. I promise to be good. I know I was short with you, but it was just a joke that dragged on too long, and I regret it more than words can say. Come back and we'll forget the whole thing. How sad you thought I was being serious. I haven't stopped crying in two days. Come back. Be brave, dearest friend. Nothing is lost. You've only got to retrace your steps. We'll keep living here, bravely and patiently. Ah, I beg you. Anyway, it's for your own good. Come back, you'll find all your belongings. I hope you now know there was no substance to our argument, that horrible moment! But you, when I waved for you to get off the boat, why didn't you come? We've lived together for two years, only to end up where we are now! What will you do? If you don't want to come back here, shall I come to where you are?

Yes it was all my fault.

Oh you won't forget me, will you?

No you can't forget me.

But I'm still here.

Talk to me, answer your friend, shouldn't we keep living together?

Be brave. Answer me quickly.

I can't stay here much longer.

Listen only to your kind heart.

Quick, tell me if I should come join you.

Yours forever.

RIMBAUD

Answer me, quick, I can't stay here any later than Monday evening. I don't have a penny left, I can't mail this. I left your books and papers with *Vermersch*.

If I'm never to see you again, I'll enlist in the navy or army.

O come back, I start crying at the drop of a hat. Tell me to come find you, I'll do it, just tell me, send me a telegram— I have to leave by Monday night, where are you going, what do you want to do?

To Paul Verlaine

[London, July 5, 1873]

Dear friend, I received your later dated "At sea." You're wrong this time, you're very wrong. First, nothing definitive in your letter: your wife will or won't come in three months, three years, who knows? As for doing yourself in, I know you. So while waiting for your wife and your death, you're going to kick and scream, gad about, make a pain of yourself. Haven't you realized yet that our anger was just as fake on both sides! But in the final account, it's you who'll be wrong, since even after I called you back, you still clung to your fake feelings. Do you really believe your life will be better with someone else: *Think about it!*—Ah! certainly not!—

Only with me can you be free, and since I promise to be much nicer from now on, since I deplore my share of wrongs, and my mind is finally clear, and since I love you, if you don't come back, or let me come to you, you're committing a crime, and *you'll regret it for* MANY LONG YEARS, *by losing all your freedom, and by much more horrible troubles* perhaps than you've ever experienced. And besides, remember what you were like before you met me.

As for me, I'm not going back to my mother's: I'm going to Paris, I'll try to be gone by Monday night. You're forcing me to sell all your clothes, I have no choice. They haven't been sold yet: they won't be taken away until Monday morning. If you want to send me letters in Paris, write c/o L. Forain, 289 rue St. Jacques, for A. Rimbaud. He'll know my address.

Of course, if your wife comes, I won't compromise you by writing,—I'll never write.

The only true words are: come back, I want to be with you, I love you, if you listen to me, you'll show courage and sincerity.

Otherwise, I pity you.

But I love you, I hold you in my arms and we'll see each other again.

RIMBAUD

8 Great Colle[ge Street] etc....until Monday evening, or Tuesday noon, if you call.

Statement to the Police Commissioner, Brussels

July 10, 1873 (around 8 p.m.)
For the past year, I have been living with Mr. Verlaine in London. We wrote articles for the newspapers and gave French lessons. Life with him had become unbearable, so I expressed a wish to return to Paris.

Four days ago, he left me to come to Brussels and sent me a telegram to join him here. I arrived two days ago, and went to lodge with him and his mother at 1 rue des Brasseurs. I still expressed the wish to return to Paris. He replied:

"Go ahead, leave, see what happens!"

This morning, he went to buy a pistol at a gun shop in the Galeries Saint-Hubert, which he showed me when he returned, at around noon. We then went to the Maison des Brasseurs on the Grand'Place, where we talked further about my departure. Back at our lodgings at about two o'clock, he locked the door and sat in front of it; then, after loading his pistol, he fired two rounds, saying:

"Take that! This'll teach you to try to leave!"

These shots were fired from a distance of three meters; the first one wounded me in the left wrist, the second missed. His mother was present and gave me first aid. Then I went to Saint-Jean Hospital, where they dressed my wound. I was accompanied by Verlaine and his mother. After I'd been bandaged, the three of us went home. Verlaine was still saying not to leave and to stay with him; but I didn't want to give in and left at around seven that evening, accompanied by Verlaine and his mother. When we had almost reached Place Rouppe, Verlaine walked ahead several steps, then turned around to face me: I saw him put his hand in his pocket to grab his gun; I turned and ran the other way. I came upon the police officer and explained what had happened, and he asked Verlaine to go with him to the police station.

If the aforesaid had just allowed me to leave, I would not have filed charges against him for the injury he inflicted on me.

A. RIMBAUD

To Jules Andrieu

London, 16 April 74 [*dateline in English*]
Sir,

—With all apologies for the form of what follows,—

I'm looking to undertake a literary work in installments, to be titled: Splendid History. I reserve rights to: format; translation (English first and foremost), as the style should be negative, and the strangeness of the details and (magnificent) perversion of the overall work should be couched in phrasings that do not hamper easy translation:—In addition to this cursory pitch: I appreciate that a publisher can only commit upon submission of two or three well chosen passages. For such an undertaking, do I need to prepare something of a bibliographic nature, or, I *don't know*, some other thing?— In any case: This could be speculations about our present ignorance of history, (the only moral marketplace not being exploited these days)—and here in particular (so they tell me (?)) they know nothing about history—and for such speculations this type of form seems fairly compatible with their literary tastes—In short: I know how to pose as a double-visionary for the masses, who were never concerned with seeing, who perhaps don't need to see.

In just a few words (!) an as yet undetermined number of historical showpieces, beginning with some ancient annals or fables or recollections. The real starting point of this noble endeavor is a striking advertisement: the pedagogical continuation of these *pieces* can also be fostered by ads at the head of each installment, or a separate insert.—For descriptions, remember the procedures used in *Salammbô*: for mystical connections and explanations, *Quinet* and *Michelet: better:* Then an ultraromantic archaeology following the drama of history; the mysticism of *style*, touching on every controversy; the prose poem as practiced in this country; storytelling skills for obscure points.—I should mention that I don't have in mind any more panoramas, or any more historical *curiosities* than a college graduate would—I want to make a deal here.

Sir, I know what you know and how you know it: so I'm addressing these questions to you, (this looks like an impossible equation), what work, by whom, can be considered the earliest (*latest*) beginning? At a certain date (this must be in the series) what universal chronology?—I think I should only plan for the ancient part, leaving aside the Middle Ages and modern period; I don't dare plan anything further—can you advise which older annals of science or fables I might consult? After that, what general or partial archaeological works or chronicles? Finally, I'll ask what date you'd give for peace in Greece Rome Africa taken together. Let's see: there will be illustrated prose à la *Doré*, the decor of religions, the *features* of the law, the *enharmony* of popular inevitabilities shown with costumes and landscapes,—everything captured and unspooled at mostly horrible moments: battles, migrations, revolutionary scenes: often a little exotic, and so far shapeless, in classrooms or fanciful accounts. Besides, once the matter is settled, I'll be free to go in a mystical, or popular, or scholarly direction. But we need a plan.

Although this is completely mechanical and the hours spent preparing this work seem negligible, its composition strikes me as rather difficult. As such, I won't send my requests for information in writing, which would make it cumbersome to reply; I'm asking only for a half hour of conversation, at a time and place of your choosing, *certain*

that you have grasped the plan and that we can lay it out
quickly—for an innovative and English form—

Kindly reply.

Respectfully yours.

RIMBAUD

30 Argyle square, Euston Rd. W.C.

To Ernest Delahaye

[Stuttgart,] February [*sic* for March] 5, 75

Verlaine came by the other day, a rosary in his mitt... Three hours later he had renounced his god and caused all 98 wounds of J.C. to bleed. He stayed for two and a half days, very well-behaved, and at my insistence returned to Paris, after which he'll go finish his studies *over yonder in the [British] Isles*.

I have only a week left at Wagner and I regret all that money paying for hate, all the time pissed away for nothing. On the 15th I'll have Ein freundliches Zimmer somewhere, and I'm blowing through the language in a frenzy, at this rate I'll be done in two months max.

Everything here's subpar—with one excepshun: Riessling, of vhich I trink ein glass to your imperpetuous health, facing der zlopes from vhich it kommt. It's sunshining and freezing. And dull as dust.

(After the 15th, *General Delivery Stuttgart.*)

Yours.
RIMB.

To his family

[Stuttgart,] March 17, 1875

Dear family,

I decided not to write until I'd found a new address. Today I received your latest money order, for 50 francs. This is how you address the envelope to send me letters:

```
Wurtemberg,
    Mr. Arthur Rimbaud
    2, Marien Strasse, 3 tr.

                              STUTTGART
```

"3 tr." means 3rd floor.

I have a very large room here, nicely furnished, in the center of town, for ten florins, or about 21 francs 50 c., including service charges; and they've offered me board for 60 francs a month: in any case, I don't need it: these little schemes are always just tricks and constraints, however economical they might appear. So I'm going to do my best to make it to April 15th with what I've got left (50 francs), since at that point I'll need another advance: for, either I'll have to stay here another month to really get things moving, or I'll place want ads for employment, and following up on them (travel, for ex.) will require cash. I hope you find all of this frugal and reasonable. I'm trying to absorb the ways of this place by every possible means, learn as much as I can; though the people here can really be unbearable. Greetings to the army, I hope Vitalie and Isabelle are doing well, and

please let me know if there is anything you'd like from here.
Yours faithfully,

A. RIMBAUD

To Ernest Delahaye

[Charleville] 14 8ber [October] 75

Dear friend,

Got the Postcard and V.'s letter a week ago. To make life easier, I told the mailman to send the gen'l. deliv. letters to my house, so you can write me here if you still can't get anything through gen. deliv. I won't comment on Loyola's latest vulgarities, and anyway I've got nothing more to do with all that: it seems the second "portion" of the "contingent" of the "class" of 74 is going to be called up on November 3 or just after: in the barracks at night:

DREAM

We're hungry in the barracks at night—
    Too right...
Emanations, explosions. An engineer:
    "I'm the gruyere!"—
Lefêbvre: "All clear!"
The engineer: "I'm the Brie!"—
The soldiers hack at their bread:
    "That's life, see?"
The engineer:—"I'm the Bleu!"
    —"It'll be the death of you."
    —I'm the gruyere
    And the Brie!...etc.

WALTZ

They've paired us up, Lefêbvre and I, etc.

You can get totally wrapt up in such thoughts. Still, it would be good if you could send along any "Loyolas" that might turn up, when you have the chance.

One favor: can you tell me clearly and concisely—what are the current requirements for a science degree: classics, math, etc....—Tell me what grade you've got to get for each part: math, phys., chem., etc., and then what books (and how to get them) they use in your school, for ex. for the degree exam, unless it changes with the different universities: in any case try to find out what I've asked from some well-informed professor or student. I need to know as precisely as possible, since I'll have to buy the books soon. As you see, I've got two or three pleasant seasons in store, what with military instruct. and this degree business! Anyway, to hell with that "noble labor." Only, be kind enough to let me know the best way to get started.

Nothing doing around here.

—I like to think the Pharthounds and stinkpots full of patriotic beans (or not) aren't distracting you any more than you need. At least it doesn't snow in dumps, the way it does here.

Yours "to the best of my humble abilities."

You write:

A. RIMBAUD
31, rue St-Barthélémy,
Charleville (Ardennes), goes without saying.

PS: The "uniformed" mail has gotten to the point where friend "Némery" had a *policeman* deliver Loyola's newspapers to me!

NOTES

INTERPRETING RIMBAUD'S POETRY can be a hazardous affair, and these notes are not intended to "explain" it. There have been many exegeses of his work; readers wishing to learn more can read the available studies or, better yet, puzzle out his writing in their own way. What I have tried to do is highlight references that a French reader of the time would have grasped, illuminate a few obscurities that the fact of translation threatens to make even more so, signal points of convergence with other writings, and provide biographical sidebars when they help set the poems in a useful context.

For the information contained here and in the introduction, I have leaned especially on the 1972 Pléiade edition of Rimbaud's *Œuvres complètes*, edited by Antoine Adam; Suzanne Bernard's critical edition in the Classiques Garnier series (1960); Graham Robb's biography *Rimbaud* (2000); Charles Nicholl's partial biography *Somebody Else: Arthur Rimbaud in Africa* (1997); Edmund White's monograph *Rimbaud: The Double Life of a Rebel* (2008); as well as various other sources, cited when possible. For those wishing to dive deep, a real rabbit hole of information and critical commentary is Alain Bardel's French-language website *Arthur Rimbaud le poète*, http://abardel.free.fr/index.htm, which has helped me find my way through some of Rimbaud's thornier phrasings, and on which I discovered the little-known and previously untranslated letter to Jules Andrieu from 1874. I'm grateful to all of them.

Poems

THE ORPHANS' GIFTS

The earliest known French verse by Rimbaud, written when he had just turned fifteen, this was one of only three poems published at his own instigation (the other two being "First Evening" in 1870 and "The Crows," a work inspired by the Paris Commune, in 1872); apart from the volume *A Season in Hell*, everything else was published through someone else's efforts—mainly Paul Verlaine's—and much of it posthumously.

"The Orphans' Gifts" was calculated to appeal to the family periodical *La Revue pour tous*, a kind of French *Saturday Evening Post*, which printed the poem in its January 2, 1870, issue. The lilting rhythms and tearjerker subject reflect both the magazine's standard fare and Rimbaud's readings, sometimes in fairly direct borrowings: Victor Hugo, Charles Baudelaire, the Parnassian poet Théodore de Banville (to whom he would soon send work), and the popular playwright and poet François Coppée (whom he would later satirize mercilessly). Still, the cruel twist in the final lines, and the underlying coldness with which it's conveyed, suggest a kind of Clement Clarke Moore with fangs. The author of "The Hanged Man's Ball" and "Sleeper in the Valley" was not far behind.

"two little boys": The original simply says "children," but I've taken the liberty of specifying boys, not only for the rhythm but because it's hard not to picture little Arthur and his older brother, Frédéric—just as it's difficult not to see the ghost of Captain Rimbaud in the "long gone" father and the dead mother as a (wishful thinking?) projection of Vitalie *mère*, who in fact outlived her son.

SENSATION

One of the poems Rimbaud submitted with his letter of May 24, 1870, to Théodore de Banville, to no effect. Although dated March on the manuscript, Rimbaud dated it April 20 in the letter.

Another poem transcribed in the letter to Banville. Rimbaud's likely inspirations include not only Shakespeare (several lines, such as "and spreads wide / Her clothes so limply borne by the waves" derive closely from *Hamlet*) but also literary treatments of Ophelia's drowning by Banville himself, as well as visual depictions by John Everett Millais and Eugène Delacroix. The partial repetition of the first stanza at the end, also seen in poems like "The Hanged Man's Ball" and "First Evening," was a favorite device of Banville's, and indicates that Rimbaud was keenly aware of his audience.

"Norway": Rimbaud seems to be taking poetic license in relocating Elsinore from Denmark, possibly for the purpose of maintaining rhyme (*neige* / *Norwège* in French)—a rhyme he seems to have copped from his elder contemporaries Banville and Théophile Gautier.

THE HANGED MAN'S BALL

Likely written in the spring of 1870, this variation on the popular theme of the danse macabre reflects Rimbaud's intense interest in the Parnassian school, which he had just discovered through his teacher Georges Izambard. (Rimbaud's letter of May 24 to Banville, asking to be published in the next volume of the group's periodical *Le Parnasse contemporain*, probably coincides with the writing of "The Hanged Man's Ball.") The other influence is, of course, François Villon, whose work Rimbaud was reading fervently at the time.

DEAD OF '92

As broadcast in the dateline, this poem *appears* to have been written while Rimbaud was in Mazas prison for having hopped a train to Paris without adequate train fare (see his letter of September 5, 1870, to Izambard). Given this, we might be tempted to think that the poem expresses a mix of revolutionary fervor and rage against

Rimbaud's own sense of being unfairly persecuted by the authorities. More likely, however, the poem was written the previous July, in response to the outbreak of the Franco-Prussian War. The Cassagnacs name-checked in the last line, father and son, published the patriotic newspaper *Le Pays*, in which they drew parallels between the "grand, noble" response to the Prussian invasion of the Lorraine in 1792 and the current conflict. Given Rimbaud's disdainful attitude toward the recently declared war, as his letters of the time attest ("my nation is rising up!...Personally, I'd rather it stay seated," he wrote to Izambard on August 25), the tone of this exhortation becomes more complex than it might first appear. In fact, what has roused his ire is that chauvinists like the Cassagnacs, boosters of the conservative Napoleon III, are disturbing the "Republican peace" of those "millions of Christs" and putting their memory in the service of a derisory cause.

FIRST EVENING

Published in the satirical newspaper *La Charge*, on August 13, 1870, as "Three Kisses," and possibly written as early as May. A manuscript version is titled "Comedy in Three Kisses."

ROMANCE

One of Rimbaud's most celebrated early verses. Its French title ("Roman") can be translated either as "Romance" or (as it conventionally is) "Novel"; I've opted for "Romance" because it encapsulates both the literary form hinted at and the subject matter, and because it sharpens the irony. The manuscript date of September 29 could refer to the date on which the poem was copied out rather than composed, which might have been in June or July. As Adam notes, "Romance" is one of a cluster of poems (along with "First Evening" and "Dream for Winter"), written close together, that explore the doubts and pitfalls of novice love.

"No one's serious at seventeen": A projection, as he was still sixteen.

"Crazy heart Crusoes": Rimbaud's coinage *robinsonne* makes a verb of the famous castaway's name, whose story Rimbaud would certainly have known.

"Held up till August": The French adjective is *loué*, meaning both "rented out" (therefore unavailable) and "lauded"; "held up" similarly attempts to do double-duty.

EVIL

Some commentators have interpreted this poem as a defense of God, an ally of the poor, versus the organized religion that upholds the interests of wealth. However, Adam and others argue much more convincingly that Rimbaud is merely illustrating the principles of thinkers like Pierre-Joseph Proudhon, the "father of anarchism" and an early influence on Marx, who famously equated property with theft and God with evil.

"red or green legions": The warring armies' uniforms were scarlet (French) and green (Prussian), here jumbled in egalitarian slaughter.

DREAM FOR WINTER

If indeed this poem was written "in a train compartment" on October 7, as the manuscript indicates, then it was during Rimbaud's escape to Belgium, between his departure from Charleville on October 2 and his impromptu arrival at the home of Izambard's putative aunts, the Gindre sisters, on October 11; the journey is referenced in the letter to Izambard of November 2. Rimbaud had already enjoyed the hospitality of the kindly dowagers the previous month, after his liberation from Mazas prison; their ministrations are perhaps reflected in the poem "The Lice-Pickers." The October escapade, which took Rimbaud through Douai, Charleroi, and Brussels, also inspired a clutch of "road poems" written in close succession, among them "At the Green Tavern," "Cunning," and "My Bohemia."

The dedication, which on the manuscript takes the form "for * * *
Her," is thought to have been originally simply "for * * *," with the
asterisks substituting for a specific name. As to who "Her" is, there
is speculation that she was a young woman Rimbaud fell for in
Charleville. But one scholar has also pointed out a number of simi-
larities with a poem by Banville, "À une muse folle," and it's pos-
sible that Rimbaud is re-creating a purely literary experience in his
own terms.

SLEEPER IN THE VALLEY

Another of Rimbaud's anthology pieces, this antiwar poem was
most likely inspired by literary models—mainly George Sand,
Leconte de Lisle, and Victor Hugo—rather than an actual sighting.
Despite the play of colors surrounding the solider, Rimbaud takes
care not to specify that of his uniform.

AT THE GREEN TAVERN

It appears there never was a Cabaret-Vert in Charleroi. There was,
however, a Maison-Verte at the time of Rimbaud's visit, which
boasted green walls and furniture, and even employed a buxom
server named Mia. Regardless of how factual the setting, the sense
of pure contentment in this poem is palpable, and rare for its au-
thor. One of Rimbaud's most Englished poems, it was notably
turned into a model of concision by Ezra Pound, who began: "Wear-
ing out my shoes, 8th day / On the bad roads..."

CUNNING

Another poem reflecting Rimbaud's getaway to Belgium. In 2020,
the French blues singer Charlélie Couture recorded a version of the
poem set to music, with an accompanying video that "updates" the
episode in hipster terms.

"*catched* a cold": In the original, the server says her cheek has
caught "*une* froid" instead of the more usual "un froid." Whether

this is a Belgian regionalism or a grammatical mistake depends on who you ask.

MY BOHEMIA

One of Rimbaud's best known "songs of the open road."

"fists in pockets": See Rimbaud's letter to Izambard of November 2, 1870, around when this poem was written: "Off we go, hat, coat, fists in pockets, and out."

"Big Dipper Inn": That is, in the rough.

EVENING PRAYER

Apart from serving as a prime example of Rimbaud's anticlericalism—this was the period when he went around scrawling "Shit on God!" on the walls of Charleville—the poem is notable for its slambang juxtapositions of learned terminology ("hypogastrium," or lower abdomen; the botanical "hyssop") with earthier vocabulary.

SEVEN-YEAR-OLD POETS

Izambard claimed that Rimbaud wrote this poem while staying with him in Douai in September 1870, after he received a letter from Mme Rimbaud ordering her son, the "little scoundrel," home. (See notes to "Sideshow" in *Illuminations*.) Others consider it more likely composed closer to May 1871, the date on the manuscript. In either case, feelings of rage against the woman he nicknamed "La Mother" and "the Mouth of Darkness" are plainly in evidence. The poem seems to draw upon the years 1860 to 1862 (between ages six and eight), when the Rimbauds lived on rue Bourbon in a poor area of Charleville, before moving to more middle-class lodgings.

"exercise tome": Some see this as a reference to the Bible, others to homework. Not that one necessarily precludes the other.

"blue eyes": Both Rimbaud and his mother had strikingly blue eyes, remarked upon by many; his friend Ernest Delahaye said they were the color of "forget-me-nots and periwinkles." Even witnesses such as Verlaine's estranged wife, Mathilde, who had few reasons to compliment the young home-wrecker, recalled being struck by his "rather beautiful blue eyes," which nonetheless had "a shifty expression that, in our benevolence, we mistook for shyness." Later in the poem, Rimbaud underscores the resemblance by describing his mother's "pale blue eyes,—that lie!"

"In summer": See Rimbaud's letter to Delahaye of "Junphe" 1872: "I hate summer, which kills me when it even begins to show its face."

TORTURED HEART

Enid Starkie, in her 1938 biography of Rimbaud, claims that this poem relates his rape at the hands of Communard irregulars while staying in the rue de Babylone barracks during one of his flights to Paris. Most scholars today doubt this interpretation, seeing the work instead as a reflection of Rimbaud's more general disillusionment with his ideals, transposed onto a squalid garrison or ship's hold (the imagery plays on both). Regardless of its inspiration or its intent, the sense of sexual betrayal is heavy, in its double entendres as well as in its tone of desperation—a desperation whose very exaggeration provides an undercurrent of ironic humor. And in fact, when sending the poem to his friend Paul Demeny in June 1871, as "Le Cœur du pitre" (Heart of a Clown), Rimbaud described it as "an intentionally humorous sketch" (un motif à dessins drôles). The previous month, he had sent it under the present title to Izambard, in the first "Seer letter," calling it "just fancy," but with the admonition: "It doesn't mean just nothing." (The poem is also known by a third title, "Le Cœur volé": The Stolen Heart.) Izambard's reaction, incomprehension mixed with sarcasm—he sent back a parody version of his own devising—as well as disapproval of its "scatological images," effectively ended the friendship.

"Ithyphallic": Another use of technical language to describe something much less lofty, in this case a hard-on.

"soldieresque": Rimbaud's coinage *pioupiouesque*, based on the slang term *pioupiou* ("soldier boy"), comically deflates the grandiosity of "ithyphallic."

"At nightfall they act out": Alongside a number of other variants in the three drafts, one version of this line reads "At the helm one sees," furthering the nautical imagery.

"O waves abracadabrantesque": According to one scholar cited by Adam, little Arthur imagined the magic formula "abracadabra" to be an effective cure for illness.

PARIS REPOPULATES (PARISIAN ORGY)

This poem is usually said to translate Rimbaud's fervent response to the Paris Commune and to its violent suppression by government troops. In that reading, Rimbaud's exhortations, shot through with exclamation points and enflamed rhetoric, mix sarcasm for the so-called right-thinking citizens with rage at the crushing of his and so many others' brief dream. The critic Marcel Ruff (cited by Adam), however, has made a convincing case that the poem was written *before* the start of the Commune in mid-March 1871, and instead describes the quick resurgence of the old order after Prussia's defeat of France in January: Rimbaud, who was in Paris between February 25 and March 10, might well have seen German troops parading victoriously down the Champs-Élysées on March 1 ("The boulevards that one night the Barbarians thronged"). The target of his wrath, however, is not the Prussians—France's military defeat meant little to him—but rather the Parisians themselves, orgiastically celebrating in a city still smoldering from bombardments as if the humiliating armistice were a victory, heedless of the hardships the war had visited on the city's poor, and eager to reestablish the kind of conservative order that Rimbaud despised.

More specifically, Rimbaud likely had in mind "Parisian Ballad," an editorial by Eugène Vermersch in the radical newspaper *Le Cri du people* on March 6 (one of the "admirable fancies" mentioned in his letter to Demeny of April 17) that excoriated the Paris bourgeoisie for merely getting back to business while the poorer populations seethed and suffered—and soon after erupted in revolt.

JEANNE-MARIE'S HANDS

Unlike "Paris Repopulates," this poem *was* inspired by the Paris Commune and its brutal suppression, and unlike the other poem, Rimbaud was not on hand to witness it. The Commune, which began on March 18 and ended when government troops entered Paris on May 21, pitted a large segment of the Paris population against the conservative National Assembly formed after the armistice. At the outbreak of civil revolt, which was fueled by the hardships of the recent war and France's defeat, the Assembly retreated to Versailles; independent elections in the capital set up a parallel regime of Commune representatives in late March. Over the next two months, the army in Versailles waged war on its own citizens, bombing Paris and its working-class suburbs, until the downfall of the Commune as a whole in late May. It's possible, though unproven, that Rimbaud was in Paris for part of the Commune, perhaps from late April through early May, and even that he took part in it; but he had definitely returned to Charleville before the "Bloody Week" (May 21–28) in which thousands of militants were slaughtered or summarily executed by French government forces.

Regardless of what he actually witnessed, Rimbaud's fervor for the ideals and energy of the Commune, and his despair at its overthrow, clearly inform the imagery and almost martial rhythm of "Jeanne-Marie's Hands." Its heroine, most likely a composite of the militant women who fought on the barricades, was directly inspired by the *pétroleuses* who tossed gasoline bombs. Rimbaud, who absorbed accounts of the Commune in the revolutionary press, saw these women as the antithesis of the idle bourgeoise who wishes only "for security" and enters into marriage with "cold disdain" (*A Season in Hell*)—whereas these martyrs, as one article put it, were "strong, devoted, tragic, knowing how to love and how to die." A romantic young man's dream companion and, in passing, the polar opposite of Mother Rimbaud.

"Juana's idle hands": The opposite of Jeanne-Marie's tanned, useful hands, and possibly a reference to Alfred de Musset's popular tale in verse "Don Paez," featuring the pale-handed Countess Juana d'Orvado.

"belladonnas' blackened blood": With this line, Rimbaud briefly switches from describing the hands of kept women of luxury to Jeanne-Marie's hands, before setting up a parallel dichotomy between the revolutionary and the ordinary worker (whose hands swat away flies, wash infants' diapers, and slave away in factories, but do not advance the cause). Only with the line "These are hands that fracture spines" does the poem firmly settle on Jeanne-Marie.

"a cousin's hands": One reading is that *cousine* was nineteenth-century slang for a sex worker.

"links of chain": The arrest and torture of Communards during the "Bloody Week."

THE SISTERS OF MERCY

The French title, "Les Sœurs de charité," literally means "Sisters of Charity," but I've opted for the more colloquial rendering.

Though the manuscript is dated June 1871, Rimbaud's remarks to Demeny in his letter of April 17 about "miserable wretches who will never find the Sister of Mercy, wife or ideal"—remarks that closely echo several lines of the poem—suggest that it might have been written earlier. It's also thought that the poem, a litany of disappointments ranging from love and women ("heap of entrails") to the "Green Muse" (absinth), justice, science, and religion, reflects a recent amorous failure, as attested by the bitter misogyny of stanzas 4 through 6. If the poem *was* written in June, it would also encompass the political disappointment of the fall of the Commune the previous month, the "impassioned Justice" that has equally let down the "young man" with "lithe body of twenty years" (Rimbaud was actually sixteen). In the end, the only Sister of Mercy who doesn't disappoint is Death.

VOWELS

This poem, among Rimbaud's most famous, has given rise to a multitude of interpretations—synesthesia, printed colored alphabets, letter forms, Baudelairean correspondence, hashish dream, absinth delirium, description of a woman's body—which it would be tediously long, and ultimately pointless, to rehearse here. Instead, I'll note that the poem was probably written soon after Rimbaud had given his recipe for becoming a "seer" to Izambard and Demeny in May 1871, and that around the same time, he told Delahaye that he wanted to create a poetics of "pure sensation." Two years later, in "Alchemy of the Word," he credited himself with having "invented the color of vowels." The images, whether derived scientifically, instinctively, or chemically, are their own justification, but let's give the final word to Verlaine: "I knew Rimbaud, and I know he didn't give a fuck whether A was red or green. That's how he saw it, end of story."

"Mizzing about": The French *bombiner*, a rare term Rimbaud also used in "Jeanne-Marie's Hands," seems to have been taken from Rabelais.

"Your Eyes": The original says "*Ses Yeux*," which could mean *his* or *her* eyes. Several scholars, cited by Adam, maintain that the sonnet was written for a young woman, possibly the same one who had recently broken the poet's heart (see the note to "The Sisters of Mercy"). However, other interpretations—in which God is a frequent contender—make this less certain, and I've preferred to give the English the same ambiguity as the French. One person it almost certainly does not refer to, though this, too, has been advanced, is Verlaine, whom Rimbaud had not met when he wrote the poem.

THE LICE-PICKERS

This poem might or might not have been inspired by Rimbaud's stay with Izambard's relatives the Gindre sisters in the fall of 1870 (see the note to "Dream for Winter"). Izambard firmly believed it was, and though the poem was more likely written in 1871 or 1872 (several critics relate it stylistically to "Seven-Year-Old Poets"), Rimbaud could nonetheless be describing their mothering kindness after the fact—but, as with so many of his works, it's impossible to know.

"Harmonica sighs": The glass harmonica played with a wet finger on tumblers, not a mouth organ.

THE DRUNKEN BOAT

Rimbaud carried this poem with him when he went to Paris in September 1871 at Verlaine's invitation. It was written over the course of the summer, and he considered it his most important work to date, the one that would bring him fame and fortune. He had reason to think so: The poem's opening gambit of plunging the reader, directly and with no warning, into the "mind" of a boat, though perhaps less remarkable today, was a striking innovation. And its torrent of images—inspired by sources as diverse as James Fenimore Cooper, Edgar Allan Poe, Jules Verne (especially *Twenty Thousand Leagues Under the Sea*), Leconte de Lisle, the Parnassian poets, picture magazines, and children's adventure novels, among many others—and the energetic rush of its rhythms make it a work of great excitement and verve. It is also a work of great despair: Delahaye, to whom Rimbaud read "The Drunken Boat" shortly before leaving for Paris, recalled him reciting it "convulsively, like a child telling of some great grief."

"impassive Rivers": "*Fleuves impassibles*" suggests (as I have tried to do with "impassive") both "unemotional" and "unnavigable."

"The green water entered": The image of water as a cleansing agent was also used in "Tortured Heart."

"Virgins' luminous feet": According to Adam, a reminiscence of Hugo's *The Man Who Laughs*, in which a figurehead depicting the Virgin Mary is lit at night and used as a beacon to light the waves.

"fabulous Floridas": When he wrote "The Drunken Boat," Rimbaud had never seen the sea, let alone Florida.

"dorados": Also known as mahi-mahi or dolphinfish. The singing fish referenced in the next line had become a craze at the time, after being revealed in a popular travel magazine.

"Hanseatic ships or clad Monitors": The Hanseatic League was a merchant guild that dominated, among other things, sea trade. The *Monitor* was an armored warship, first used in the 1860s, which gave its name to a class of armored vessels.

"haunted eyes of prison rafts": These were decommissioned ships used in wartime to hold enemy prisoners. At the time Rimbaud wrote this, as he was all too aware, they were being used to hold arrested Communards, many awaiting execution.

"WHAT'S IT TO US, HEART OF MINE..."

Paterne Berrichon, the husband of Rimbaud's sister Isabelle and one of his first chroniclers (though not always a reliable one), claimed that this poem was "written in Paris, in a café in the presence of friends, in early 1872 or rather the end of 1871." It translates the anger, bitterness, despair, and persistent hope that Rimbaud and his new Paris acquaintances, most of them ex-Communards, felt over the crushing of their hopes earlier that year. These stanzas might be part of a longer poem, the rest now lost.

"Never will we work": See, in *A Season in Hell*, "I loathe every trade" and the Infernal Bridegroom's vow "Never shall I work," as well as numerous complaints in Rimbaud's letters about Vitalie's attempts to make her boy get a job.

THE CASSIS RIVER

According to Delahaye, the imagery of this poem derives from the Ardennes landscape, possibly in the vicinity of Charleville. The "Cassis River" is most likely the Semois, a tributary of the Meuse, whose waters turn purplish-black (the color of cassis syrup) at dusk.

"Dear crows so delicious": Rimbaud used the same phrase (*"Chers corbeaux délicieux"*) in his poem "The Crows," most likely written around the same time.

SHAME

This poem, written in the thick of Rimbaud's relationship with Verlaine, has been variously interpreted as reflecting a lovers' quarrel between the two men (of which there were many), Vitalie's reproaches toward her son (of which there were many), or Rimbaud's own stock-taking and ultimate acceptance of his troublesome wild-cat nature. The "he" throughout is almost certainly the poet himself.

"wonder of wonders": Verlaine, who nicknamed Rimbaud "the man with soles of wind," noted how his legs were made for extended journeys, such as the hundreds of miles he covered between Charleville and Paris or Belgium. See also Delahaye's description of the inveterate walker: "His long legs calmly took formidable strides; his long, swinging arms marked the very regular movements; his back was straight, his head erect, his eyes stared straight into the distance. His face wore an expression of resigned defiance."

This work, one of the most hermetic and autobiographical of Rimbaud's verse poems, was likely written (as was "Shame") in the spring of 1872, during a temporary return to the family home at Verlaine's insistence, so that the latter could attend to his troubled marriage. The river imagery of the first two parts, and the implied merger of water and sky, suggest both the bucolic surroundings of the Ardennes and the failed union of Rimbaud's parents—the latter coming into clearer focus in the next two sections, which more explicitly evoke family memories.

"Madam stands too erect": Mother Rimbaud was known to stand rigidly upright, to the locals' mirth.

"parasol / between her fingers rolled": In the French as well, Rimbaud plays for exaggerated effect on internal rhymes: *ombrelle, ombelle, pour elle.*

"after the man is gone": Quite possibly Captain Rimbaud, who abandoned his family for the last time when Arthur was not quite six years old. Without reading too much into it, the memory might have been stirred by Verlaine's "banishment" of Rimbaud from Paris, given Rimbaud's tendency to imbue male friendships with a fatherly quality (to Izambard on September 5 he wrote, "I love you like a brother, I will love you like a father").

"to what muck": In what sludge of family history is his little boat mired? Compare in "Bad Blood" (*A Season in Hell*): "We're not leaving."

A Season in Hell

Along with the three verse poems cited above, *A Season in Hell* was the only literary writing that Rimbaud intentionally published. It was likely begun in the spring of 1873 in the village of Roche where Vitalie had inherited a farm, continued in London, and completed that summer, again in Roche, after the incident of the gunshot wound inflicted by Verlaine in Brussels in July (though some scholars have disputed the dateline April to August, claiming that the entire text was written either before or after Brussels). The book was published in October at the author's expense by the Belgian printer Poot & Co. (mainly known for legal journals) in an edition of five hundred copies; legend has it that Rimbaud's mother paid for the printing, but some feel it was more likely Verlaine, who by then was in prison and feeling penitent. Rimbaud retrieved only several copies from the printer's, which he distributed to friends (including Verlaine), leaving the bulk of the first edition to rot undisturbed until the stock was rediscovered by chance in 1901.

Edmund White, in his brief biography of Rimbaud, points out that the entire text is built on a dialectic of contradiction, of assertion and denial, a rhetorical strategy more suited to "polemics or other forms of prose argumentation" than to poetry. And indeed, the reader constantly feels buffeted by the conflicting currents of the author's thought, first hectored into bending to a vehement assertion, then seeing it undercut a few lines later. As for the themes Rimbaud debates with himself, several stand out in particular: the "inferiority" of his ancestry, the problematic relations between the sexes, and the inner struggle between ambition and inaction, including the dubious utility of work—this latter, as White mentions, likely being an ongoing concern as Rimbaud's mother and sisters "labored in the fields while he stayed alone in the attic muttering to himself." But as Rimbaud says early on, "lying and laziness" are his heritage, and "the writer's hand is worth the plowman's" (that is, not much).

Graham Robb, for his part, pegs *Season* as "one of first modern works of literature to show that experiments with language are also investigations into the self...Fifty years before *Ulysses* and *The Waste Land*, Rimbaud, at the age of eighteen, had invented a linguistic world that can be happily explored for years like the scrapyard of a civilization."

"my last *croak*": Largely on the basis of this remark, many scholars have dated the composition of this preamble as later than most of the text, or in any case following the Brussels shooting; it's also possible, however, that it refers to a bout of congestion that landed Rimbaud in the hospital while still in London earlier that spring. More suggestive of its retrospective character is its recap of the spiritual journey that follows.

"'You'll always be a hyena'": An echo of Rimbaud's acceptance of his status as a "silly little beast" and treacherous wildcat in the poem "Shame" (written perhaps the previous year, perhaps more or less contemporaneously with *A Season in Hell*), as well as his boast in the next section of having "every vice."

"some last cowardly turpitudes": *Lâchetés* can mean both "cowardice" and "vileness"—in other words, further writings to come.

BAD BLOOD

By most accounts, this was the first part of *Season* that Rimbaud composed, initially in vastly different form (as shown by the existing rough drafts), and even before having decided what shape to give the overall work. In his letter to Delahaye of June 1873, he speaks of "writing little tales in prose . . . It's stupid and innocent."

"The writer's hand is worth the plowman's hand": The French ("*la main à plume vaut la main à charrue*") presents a fine ambiguity: the writer's hand is *just as valid* as the plowman's, but also *no better than*—depending on whether Rimbaud is trying to validate the act of writing or disparage it.

"Solyma": Another name for Jerusalem. Rimbaud also uses it in "Ordinary Nocturne" (*Illuminations*), possibly written around the same time.

"I'll return with limbs of steel": As many have commented, this could be read as a remarkably prescient, if caricaturish, description of Rimbaud's later life.

"appeared red and black": Compare with "Childhood" in *Illuminations*: "The mud is red or black."

"I'm a beast, a nigger": Rimbaud's initial titles for *Season* were *Pagan Book*, or *Negro Book* (to Delahaye in May 1873). His insistent use of the word *nègre* here is deliberately offensive, and meant to mark his rejection, like the criminal at the beginning of this section and the descendants of Ham soon after, of the "white men's" stultifying civilization. In "What's it to us, heart of mine...," he invokes his solidarity with his "brothers": "Black strangers, let us go on!" Which does not entirely absolve Rimbaud from racist attitudes, as suggested by some of his letters during his tenure as a trader in Africa. But as Edmund White points out, "his misanthropy was general."

"Enough! here is punishment": In this schematic last stanza, it's hard not to see another reminiscence of the "Bloody Week."

A NIGHT OF HELL

The original title of this section was "False Conversion." The references to conversion, damnation, salvation, heaven, hell, and the Christian God, as well as the fleeting glimpse of "peace and strength," suggest that these pages were written upon Rimbaud's return to his turbulent life with Verlaine in London, following his retreat to Roche in April and May—the rough draft contains the lines: "I've resumed my furious existence with rage in my blood, bestial life, senselessness..." This was also the time when Verlaine, unable to choose between Rimbaud and his wife, experienced a short-lived (or false) conversion to Christianity, which would become more rooted during his imprisonment several months later.

"Satan, Ferdinand": According to Delahaye, "Ferdinand" was a local nickname for the Devil in Rimbaud's native region.

DELIRIA I: THE FOOLISH VIRGIN

The imagery of the "divine Bridegroom" and the "foolish virgin" comes from Matthew 25:1-13, continuing Rimbaud's dialogue with Christianity that echoes throughout his season in hell. This section is almost universally considered to have been inspired by his relations with Verlaine in their final months together (much like the roughly contemporary poem "Vagabonds" in *Illuminations*), making it a kind of *Autobiography of Alice B. Toklas* sixty years *avant la lettre*, with Rimbaud as seen by Verlaine as written by Rimbaud. Still, as with all things Rimbaud, there are dissenters. Adam, for instance, tortuously following the lead of Ruff, sees both protagonists as the two warring sides of Rimbaud's own psyche, one striving after wisdom and innocence, the other besotted with evil and sensual "disordering." Whatever the case, the bridegroom as described here bears more than a passing resemblance to Rimbaud, who was "little more than a child," and whose pronouncements throughout this section—"I am of a distant race," "Never shall I work," etc.—echo many of the sentiments expressed on his own behalf. As to the virgin, her dependence and weak will ("I followed him; I had no choice!") make it hard not to see this, at least in part, as the unflattering depiction of a Verlaine who was rapidly taxing his lover's admiration and patience. On top of which, nothing says both interpretations can't coexist.

"He claimed to know": Compare to "A Night of Hell": "I possess every talent!" as well as the poet's enumeration of his attempted triumphs in "Alchemy of the Word."

DELIRIA II: ALCHEMY OF THE WORD

This is both Rimbaud's ars poetica and a history of renunciation, "one of his follies." As Adam writes, it describes his "ambition to create a language that directly elicits sensations, rather than ideas and feelings, as in earlier forms of poetry." After a brief review of his influences and affinities, including specific references to the poem "Vowels" and the "Seci letters," Rimbaud moves into an annotated anthology of his most recent (and among his last) verse poems, which had been written the year before. Brief, enigmatic, simpler, and more jagged than the verses of 1870 and 1871, these poems bear traces of what Rimbaud described as a "gentle fatalism," a retrenchment after what he considered the failure of his time in Paris and, perhaps, a discouragement with poetry such as he had conceived it up until that point: to Delahaye, he downplayed these "various romances" as "songs...childish, rustic, naïve, and sweet." The differences between the initial versions and the ones reproduced in *Season* bear out the contention that Rimbaud was quoting his own verse from memory, often imperfectly.

"I captured whirlwinds": This enigmatic phrase (*"Je fixais des vertiges"*) can be, and has been, translated any number of ways. Literally, it means "I pinned down giddinesses."

"General, if there remains": Early drafts of the text specify that the "General" is the sun.

LIGHTNING

"In my hospital bed": This could refer to Rimbaud's hospitalization in London in the spring, or in Brussels in July for an infection resulting from his gunshot wound—or to neither. The "odor of incense," on the other hand, bears a direct connection to his "shitty childhood" and its enforced religious observances.

FAREWELL

"I tried to invent new flowers": Looping back to the litany of accomplishments in "Alchemy of the Word."

"the hell of women": See the Infernal Bridegroom's reflections on the conditions imposed on women by marriage and society, as well as Rimbaud's letter to Demeny (May 15, 1871): "When the endless serfdom of woman is toppled..."

Illuminations

The tortuous history and highly uncertain dating of the poems that compose *Illuminations* have added to the aura of mystery surrounding the work. For a long time, based on early testimony and the valedictory nature of *A Season in Hell*, scholars were convinced that these prose poems had all been written prior to *Season* and to Rimbaud and Verlaine's breakup in Brussels in July 1873. Later researchers made the contradictory assertion that the poems were all written after *Season*. It is now considered most likely that these texts straddle the composition of *A Season in Hell*, in other words, that Rimbaud had already begun experimenting with prose poems as early as 1871, and that he continued to write them ("some last cowardly turpitudes") through 1875, the year he supposedly abandoned literary production, or even perhaps as late as 1878.

The manuscript—actually a sheaf of loose pages in no specified order—was apparently given in 1875 by Rimbaud to Verlaine with instructions to hand it on to Germain Nouveau, a young poet with whom he had briefly lived in London the year before, so that Nouveau might see to their publication. Whether or not this happened, by 1878 the pages were with Verlaine's ex-brother-in-law, Charles de Sivry, who resisted Verlaine's entreaties to return the manuscript (possibly at the behest of his sister, Verlaine's ex-wife, Mathilde), delaying their publication. Finally, in 1886, the editor Gustave Kahn managed to retrieve the manuscript and published *Illuminations* (apart from five additional pieces that resurfaced later) in the May and June issues of his periodical *La Vogue*, followed by a book edition that same year with a preface by Verlaine. The order of texts—established for the magazine by the critic and editor Félix Fénéon, then reworked for the book edition—differed substantially from the one adopted by all current editions, as well as the present translation, though in fact we have little idea what arrangement Rimbaud might have given the work, nor in which order the pieces were written. The fact that the manuscript pages are a hodgepodge of different papers, inks, and even handwritings (some of the poems were transcribed by Nouveau, perhaps when he and Rimbaud were in London) further obscures the tracks.

According to Delahaye, Rimbaud had been fascinated by Baudelaire's volume of prose poems, *Paris Spleen* (published in 1869), and immediately tried his hand at them. The Paris literary circles that he began frequenting in the fall of 1871, including Verlaine and Charles Cros, also wrote prose poems, which by then had become something of a fashion. It is not certain that any of the poems Rimbaud composed during this period ended up in *Illuminations*, nor is it certain that the "fragments" Verlaine alludes to in a letter to Rimbaud of May 1873 are among the forty-two poems that make up the entire collection; that said, it's not unlikely that some of them do.

As for the title *Illuminations*, supposedly Rimbaud intended it, based on a slightly shaky knowledge of English, in the sense of illumined manuscripts rather than enlightenment, and even added the English phrase "Painted Plates" as a subtitle. But since our only source for this claim is the not always trustworthy Verlaine, both Rimbaud's intent and the title itself remain forever unverified.

AFTER THE FLOOD

This poem has been interpreted in various ways, most often in relation to the recent experience of the Franco-Prussian War and the Paris Commune, and to the bourgeois trappings that quickly reemerged in the wake of these upheavals as if nothing had happened. In this reading—but of course there are others—the blood that "flowed in Bluebeard's castle" would be the "Bloody Week" that suppressed the Commune, the "house of windows" a school (which "the child"—Rimbaud—refuses to attend), and the Floods petitioned at the end of the poem, an avatar of the "healthful" wind that sweeps away all these horrors. (See the notes for "Paris Repopulated" and "Jeanne-Marie's Hands.")

"Madam *** installed a piano": Possibly a reference to Mme Rimbaud's rental, at her son's demand, of a piano during his short-lived intent to become a musician. The hoisting of the piano up a narrow staircase to the Rimbauds' apartment must have made it seem like Alpinism. If this is the case, the fact that this event occurred in late 1875 might date "After the Flood" among the last poems written for *Illuminations*, though it has consistently been placed at the head of the collection. Rimbaud had crossed the Alps in April 1875 en route to Milan.

"bucolics in clogs": Rimbaud's peculiar use of the term *églogue* (eclogue or pastoral poem, something not normally shod) reflects his distrustful attitude toward all things bucolic, from these "grumbling" rustics to the peasant "with aged claw malicious" in "The Cassis River."

"the Sorceress": The figure of the witch or sorceress, who reappears numerous times in Rimbaud's work, was most likely adopted from Jules Michelet's *La Sorcière*, in which the Sorceress is a figure of refusal (of civilization and its constraints), divination, and secret knowledge—which she will not deign to reveal.

CHILDHOOD

While the first four sections of this complex poem seem to draw on flashes—real or fantasized—from Rimbaud's childhood, the fifth seems to be located in the nightmarish present, and possibly reflects his time in "monstrous" London. As such, the "tomb...way deep underground" could be a basement apartment, or perhaps the tunnel beneath the Thames through which he took his mother and sister when they visited him in July 1874.

"he's in India": Although this is hardly a definitive connection, Rimbaud was in the Dutch East Indies (present-day Indonesia) in July and August 1876, as a member of the Dutch Foreign Legion, from which he then deserted. If the line was inspired by this incident, it would put the composition of this poem, or at least of some final touches, a good year after Rimbaud is generally thought to have stopped writing literature. Similarly, the "little dead girl" at the beginning of the paragraph might refer to his sister Vitalie, who died of a tumor on the knee—diagnosed at the time as "tubercular synovitis," but possibly cancer (as with her brother a decade and a half later)—in December 1875, aged seventeen.

"The mud is red or black": See the notes to "Bad Blood" (*A Season in Hell*).

"a seeming aperture": Perhaps a basement window looking out on a London sidewalk, or the semblance of a window owing to the chalk white of the walls.

TALE

"astounding revolutions of love": See, once again, the Infernal Bridegroom's damning reflections in *A Season in Hell* about women and marriage, as well as his pronouncement that "love has to be reinvented." It's more than possible that this poem was written around the same time.

SIDESHOW

A number of similarities have been raised between this text and a passage by the Swiss author and cartoonist Rodolphe Töpffer (the "father of the comic strip") in his 1844 travel memoir *Voyages en zigzag*. Recounting a visit to the Duomo in Milan, Töpffer describes a group of "undignified minor priests or novice priests" in terms much like the ones Rimbaud uses in this apparent description of an itinerant and somewhat unsavory theatrical troupe. Perhaps not coincidentally, Rimbaud lived in Piazza del Duomo for a few weeks in April and May 1875, which might have given him "the key" to this scene.

"Solidly built scoundrels": The French *drôles* (which can also be translated as "hoodlums," "rowdies," or "jokers") also figures in Töpffer's description. However, Rimbaud might have had a more personal reference in mind, as his mother had used the same term for him (see the note to "Seven-Year-Old Poets").

"endowed with terrifying voices": That is, the voices of castrati, who would indeed have had a difficult time relating to the horny page Cherubino from Mozart's *The Marriage of Figaro*.

"'family-friendly' ditties": "*Chansons bonnes filles*," literally, songs suitable for proper young ladies.

"this savage parade": The phrase *parade sauvage* (also "savage sideshow," in echo of the title) was reprised as the title of one of the primary journals of Rimbaud studies.

BEING BEAUTEOUS

The title, in English in the original, most likely came from Longfellow's poem "Footsteps of Angels," possibly discovered during Rimbaud's stays in London. While there have been various interpretations of the imagery, Adam maintains that it's all about sex, with the "scarlet-and-black wounds" representing a woman's nipples and vagina, the "fur badge" her pubic hair, and the "cannon" the organ by which the poet satisfies his literary-erotic fantasy.

LIVES

This poem, a kind of projected autobiographical novel, stages a character who resembles and doesn't resemble the author—and, needless to say, seems to anticipate his "vast labors" and hoped-for "retirement" in the East. The poem is peppered with shards of read or lived imagery, though little of it can be directly related to known incidents in Rimbaud's life. The third section, which seems to mark a thematic break with the first two, was in fact written on a different sheet and in different handwriting, suggesting that it might have been added at another time.

"an old passageway in Paris": Unlike many of the references, this one is probably a specific nod to Passage Choiseul, where the Parnassian poets held their gatherings.

DEPARTURE

This gnomic farewell, halfway between prose and verse, is distinguished in French by the internal rhyme of the three initial verb forms: *vu / eu / connu* (literally, "seen," "had," "known"). I've tried to replicate this sonority in English, while retaining the basic sense.

MORNING INTOXICATION

This poem is one of the few on which virtually all scholars agree, to wit, that it was inspired by Rimbaud's experiments with hashish, probably his first experiences in Paris in late 1871 (though whether the poem itself dates from then or later is unknown). The exalted tone and the aggressiveness of the last line indeed seem to reflect the enthusiasm of the recent convert, as does the attentiveness to such physiological sensations while under the influence as nausea and icy cold. While a certain pessimism regarding the drug's spiritual enlightenment, such as the inevitable return to a "former disharmony," undercuts the giddiness promised by the title, the poet is willing to maintain his "faith in the poison" and his devotion.

"O my Beauty": The French "O mon Beau!," with its use of an adjective in place of a noun (literally, "O my Handsome!"), gives the phrase a specifically male character, heralding the erotic undercurrent that also runs through this poem ("our most pure love"): this sleepless night of intoxication is shared.

"the hour of the *Assassins*": As is well known, the word "assassin" derives from the Arabic *hashishin*, referring to a group of Ismaili

Muslims who carried out political killings in the twelfth and thirteenth centuries, purportedly under the influence. Henry Miller used the line as the title of his idiosyncratic memoir of Rimbaud, *The Time of the Assassins*.

PHRASES

This is actually two separate poems, sometimes (as here) grouped together. The first, titled "Phrases" and comprising the first three sections, was written on the same sheet as "Morning Intoxication" and seems to be related to it. According to Adam, it contains a barbed parody of various themes in Verlaine's poetry, including the "black wood" and faithful "children" (all just "phrases" in Rimbaud's estimation, verbiage). Its dour meditation on sexual dependence might also reflect the two poets' relationship.

The second poem (beginning "An overcast morning"), written on a different sheet and using different punctuation, moves from the black wood to a cold, rainy July day, and from codependence to masturbatory solitude.

BRIDGES

Generally considered to be an allusive description of an etching, perhaps of London.

CITY

Here again, while many commentators have read this poem as depicting London, there is no certainty that Rimbaud was thinking specifically of that city, or any city; nor that the various impressions translate personal experience; nor that the "I" of the poem is Rimbaud. That said, while the lack of "any monument to superstition" (churches) hardly squares with St. Paul's, Westminster, and many others besides, "eternal soot" could well apply to a metropolis that at the time was nicknamed the Big Smoke.

For once, there is almost universal agreement that this vignette describes Rimbaud's tortured relations with Verlaine, the "pitiful brother." In condensed form, the poem shares many thematic features with the "Foolish Virgin" chapter of *A Season in Hell*, and might have been written at a similar time.

"satanic doctor": The expression, all the while mirroring the Virgin's characterization of the Bridegroom (Rimbaud) as "a Demon," was recognized by Verlaine as applying to himself. In a letter to Charles de Sivry of August 1878, he noted that he had "reread *Illuminations* (Painted Plates) by the gentleman you know full well, as well as his *Season in Hell* in which [*sic*] I figure as a Satanic Doctor (which isn't true)." The poet Léon Valade, a familiar figure in Verlaine's circle, described Rimbaud soon after his Paris advent as "Satan in the midst of the doctors."

"Child of the Sun": See Rimbaud's letter to Verlaine of July 5, 1873, in which he exhorts Verlaine to "remember what you were like before you met me"—shackled by convention, trapped in a bourgeois marriage, unworthy of his own talent.

"Adam's ale": *Vin des cavernes*, in the regional dialect of the Ardennes, is spring water.

MYSTIC

Like "Bridges," this is generally thought to be the description of a visual work, though what work is the subject of many divergent views. One of the more convincing explanations is that it evokes a scene of the Last Judgment, in which the damned are those, to the left, who practice violence, and the chosen those who follow "the line of progress." But the condensed imagery leaves the door open to many other interpretations.

"the eastern line": The progressive nature of eastern orientation is developed in the "Impossibility" chapter of *A Season in Hell*.

DAWN

Several scholars have noted the shared imagery between this poem and "After the Flood"—"gemstones watched" and "precious stones that hid"; anthropomorphized flowers; arms "flailing" and windmilling; "spires and domes" versus "steeple cocks" and "cathedral"—suggesting that the two were written in close proximity, which is further supported by similarities in structure and tone. The sense of adventure and discovery also harks back to such early road poems as "Sensation" and "My Bohemia."

"blond wasserfall": A possible reference or reminiscence of Rimbaud's stay in Stuttgart in early 1875. In his letter to Delahaye of March 5, he uses several German or faux-German expressions.

"Dawn and the child": Rimbaud refers to himself as "the child" in several works—among them, "After the Flood."

ORDINARY NOCTURNE

The French title, "Nocturne vulgaire," can also be translated as "common," "average," or "vulgar." According to Adam, Rimbaud wrote the poem under the influence of both hashish and Baudelaire's *Artificial Paradises*, which describes similar effects of rooms transforming and chimerical figures appearing.

"Solymas": Jerusalem, also used in "Bad Blood."

ANGUISH

Whether "She" and "the Vampire" refer to a specific woman, women in general, or Rimbaud's inner struggle between ambition and indolence, this poem presents a number of analogies with the final sections of *A Season in Hell*—and, as with many of the *Illuminations*, might have been written in the same period.

METROPOLITAN

While at first blush taking the form of a long hallucination, this poem contains a number of possible reminiscences, especially if it was written during or after Rimbaud's stint in the Dutch Foreign Legion in 1876 (see the note to "Childhood"). It also reflects the intellectual and physical restlessness of a young man who both read widely and found it hard to stay long in one place.

"blooms you might call plumes or wombs": Like "Damas damning in doom" immediately following, this self-conscious "artistry" seems a swipe at the "poety" poets of Rimbaud's former Paris circle, no doubt including Verlaine. The rhyming French phrase (*"fleurs qu'on appellerait cœurs et sœurs"*) literally translates as "flowers that one might call hearts and sisters."

"you and She wrestled": Perhaps a sister of the "She" in "Anguish."

YOUTH

As with the other *Illuminations* with multiple parts and autobiographical titles ("Childhood," "Lives"), this one offers a smattering of possible memories, disparate images, and hermetic phrasings. It was not included in the original *Vogue* publication. The part title "At Twenty" recalls the "Lithe body of twenty years" in "The Sisters of Mercy" and the determination to "make it to twenty" in the "Lightning" chapter of *A Season in Hell*. (Rimbaud turned twenty in October 1874.) In the fourth part, the exhortations to an unknown interlocutor—Rimbaud himself?—echo the wrestling with frustrated ambition, past follies, and persistent hope that inform poems such as "Anguish" and "Lives."

BOTTOM

The key to the title lies in the reference to "an ass" in the last paragraph, relating it to the self-important, donkey-headed weaver in *A Midsummer Night's Dream*. Although it's often imprudent to link these poems to specific events, it is also worth noting that in April and May 1875, Rimbaud spent several weeks in Italy, where he was taken in by an older widow; he left around June.

"brilliant aquarium": A possible reference to the huge marine aquarium built at London's Crystal Palace in 1872, which Rimbaud apparently saw during his time in the city.

H

Among quite a few fanciful attempts to elucidate this poem is one that proposes the reader "find" Hortense to be an anagram for the English phrase "then eros."

DEVOTION

The religious terminology in this poem, as in much of *A Season in Hell*, allowed readers such as the Catholic poet Paul Claudel (egged on by Rimbaud's devout, devoted younger sister Isabelle) to consider "poor Arthur" a Christian mystic in pagan's clothing—an interpretation that other admirers, such as the staunchly anticlerical surrealists, resisted like hellfire.

"Louise Vanaen of Voringhem": The "de" in the French names de Voringhem and d'Ashby could be either a nobiliary particle or simply mean "of" or "from." While both readings are possible (and while many translations retain the "de" as if it were part of a compound name: Aubois d'Ashby), mine is that these are place-names— as Ashby indeed is—like stations of Rimbaud's devotional cross. According to one critic, Louise Vanaen might have been a sister of mercy at Saint-Jean Hospital in Brussels, near the North Sea, where Rimbaud was treated for his gunshot wound in July 1873.

"Baou": This word, which doesn't exist in French or English, has puzzled many a scholarly head and bedeviled Rimbaud's readers for more than a century. Some see it as a French transcription of the

English "bow": either the bark of a dog in the "summer grasses" or, perhaps more likely, a devotional inclination.

"Circeto": No one knows who this name refers to, other than to a woman, real or imagined.

"glacial heights": Compare in "After the Flood" the Splendide Hotel "built in a tumult of glaciers."

"spunk": In English in the original.

GENIUS

This poem, not included in the original 1886 publication, is another whose overt religious tonalities emboldened Catholic interpreters of Rimbaud to consider him one of their own. While there are clear parallels between the "Genius" and Christ, this is a terrestrial Christ, a "Christ for the new age" (Adam), a figure of illumination without the attendant religiosity, who "will not leave us, will not come down from some heaven." As with his invocations of witches, Rimbaud's inspiration here was most likely Michelet, specifically his 1860 book *La Femme*, which contains several phrasings similar to ones in this poem.

Depending on context, the word *génie* can also be, and at other places in this volume has been, translated as "genie" (see "Tale") or "engineer" (see letter of October 14, 1875, to Delahaye)—and indeed, some translators, such as John Ashbery, have used the title "Genie" for the present poem. I've preferred "Genius" in the sense of (per Webster's) "a personification or embodiment especially of a quality or condition," akin to the *genius loci*.

"His light": *Son jour* is literally "his day."

"lost charities": See the ruminations on charity in *A Season in Hell*.

Selected Letters, 1870–1875

Although the vast majority of Rimbaud's known letters are from af-
ter 1878 and provide crucial insights into his final decade, I've lim-
ited this selection to the years when he was actively writing poetry,
as a running commentary on the works included in this volume.

TO THÉODORE DE BANVILLE, MAY 24, 1870

The poet and impresario Théodore de Banville was one of the
founders of the Parnassian school, which prized technique and for-
mal perfection over the freer expressions of feeling characteristic of
Romanticism. More important to Rimbaud, he was an editor of the
literary periodical *Le Parnasse contemporain*, to which the aspiring
poet had recently been introduced by Georges Izambard (see note to
next letter). Along with the flattery, Rimbaud enclosed three po-
ems: a slightly different version of "Sensation," "Ophelia," and the
long poem "Credo in unam" (later retitled "Sun and Flesh"). Al-
though they did not meet with the same success as had "The Or-
phans' Gift" with *La Revue pour tous*, Banville apparently sent an
encouraging reply that has now been lost.

"Honored Sir": Rimbaud's greeting, *"Cher Maître"* ("Dear Mas-
ter"), is a standard honorific in French, but it doesn't play in Eng-
lish. In the first sentence, he lies about his age: he was fifteen and a
half at the time.

TO GEORGES IZAMBARD, AUGUST 25, 1870

Barely older than his protégé, Izambard was briefly a professor of
rhetoric at the Collège de Charleville, where Rimbaud was enrolled.
Rimbaud soon latched on to him as one of his earliest brothers/
fathers, and Izambard, recognizing the boy's precociousness, sup-
plied him with books outside the school syllabus—such as *Les Mi-
sérables*, which earned him a stiffly worded rebuke about "unsuit-
able" reading from Mme Rimbaud. When Izambard left Charleville

and the *collège* for Douai, Belgium, Rimbaud, who keenly felt the loss, wrote him a series of letters that detail his adventures over the fall and following spring. The friendship seems to have sputtered out around July 1871, possibly over Izambard's disappointing reaction to the first "Seer letter" in May and to "Tortured Heart" (see note to "Tortured Heart").

"patridiotism": Rimbaud's portmanteau *patrouillotisme* combines the words for "patriotism" and "patrol," but also enfolds *trouille*, slang for "fear"—the operative note being ridicule.

TO GEORGES IZAMBARD, SEPTEMBER 5, 1870

"I was arrested": Because the ongoing Franco-Prussian War had interrupted train service between Charleville and Paris, Rimbaud took an indirect route via Charleroi, Belgium; lacking sufficient fare, he was detained when he arrived in Paris at the Gare du Nord and taken to Mazas prison, near the Gare de Lyon. It was while he was awaiting release that Napoleon III surrendered to Germany (see notes for "Dead of '92" and the next letter).

"you'll take me to Douai": Having paid Rimbaud's fine, Izambard indeed took him back to Douai, where Rimbaud was cared for by his relatives, the Gindre sisters (see notes to "Dream for Winter" and "The Lice-Pickers"). Rimbaud returned to Charleville on September 27, accompanied by Izambard, who delivered the prodigal son to Vitalie *mère* and had the door slammed in his face. The prodigal ran away again to Belgium less than a week later.

TO GEORGES IZAMBARD, NOVEMBER 2, 1870

This sullen account immediately follows Rimbaud's return to Charleville after an escapade that took him through various Belgian towns, including Charleroi and Brussels, and included a second stay with the Gindre sisters. His monthlong adventure is reflected in poems such as "Dream for Winter," "At the Green Tavern," and "My Bohemia."

"no siege yet in Mézières": Napoleon III's surrender entailed the fall of the Second Empire but not the end of the Franco-Prussian War; the Third Republic, established on September 4 after a popular uprising in Paris, refused to capitulate, and Germany pursued its attacks, leading to the Siege of Paris beginning September 19. Meanwhile, the eastern part of France, including the Ardennes, was subject to bombardments and occupation by German troops. Rimbaud's remark suggests that Mézières, the community next to Charleville and (as he'd put it) "a town you can barely find," was hardly worth occupying. Charleville and Mézières merged in the 1960s.

TO PAUL DEMENY, APRIL 17, 1871

Paul Demeny, a friend of Izambard and the Gindre sisters, had recently published his first book of poems, *Les Glaneuses*. Although Rimbaud apparently had little use for Demeny's verses, the two men struck up a friendship during Rimbaud's first stay in Douai—in which Demeny assumed the role of another brother/father—that would engender several important letters, most notably the second "Seer letter" the following month. How much of the friendship was genuine and how much opportunism is open to interpretation.

"I've been sorting mail": Having refused to return to school, Rimbaud, at his mother's insistence (the "Mouth of Darkness"), found a job with the newspaper *Le Progrès des Ardennes*, which had been established the previous November as a counter to the region's other paper, the conservative *Courrier des Ardennes* (see Rimbaud's letter to Izambard of August 25). Rimbaud had originally hoped the paper would publish his poems, but he settled for a menial job instead—which in any case did not last long, as the newspaper offices had been damaged by a German bomb the previous December and its publication suspended.

"never find the Sister of Mercy": See note to "The Sisters of Mercy."

"these verses from Ecclesiastes": There seems to be no such verse in Ecclesiastes.

"admirable fancies by Vallès and Vermersch": See note to "Paris Repopulates."

"February 25 to March 10": During those two weeks in Paris, Rimbaud would have witnessed the German occupation, the aftermath of the siege, and the accommodations by the Paris bourgeoisie that he excoriated in poems such as "Paris Repopulates."

"the lances of the rain": Demeny no doubt recognized this line as borrowed from Paul Verlaine's *Poèmes saturniens*.

TO GEORGES IZAMBARD, MAY 13, 1871

Rimbaud had applauded Izambard's relinquishing of his teaching post in July 1870 (even as he deplored his friend's departure), and his sour reaction to Izambard's return to the profession no doubt helped determine the aggressive tone of this letter—not only his critique of "subjective" poetry but even more so his promotion of the "disordering" required of the seer. Apart from a letter in July asking for books he could sell for cash, this appears to be Rimbaud's last communication with his former teacher (see notes to "Tortured Heart" and to letter of August 25, 1870).

"beers and bottles": *"En bocks et en filles"*: a bock is a strong dark beer; according to Adam, *filles* refers here not to girls but, in local dialect, to half bottles of wine—though Rimbaud, playing to Izambard as much as to the yokels, was no doubt perfectly aware of the double entendre.

"Stat mater dolorosa": Although Rimbaud excelled at Latin in school, he makes a few slips here. The correct quote is *"Stabat Mater dolorosa iuxta crucem lacrimosa dum pendebat Filius"* ("The grieving mother stood [weeping near the cross] where her Son was hanging"). Rimbaud's partial quote might have been suggested by the near-homonyms *filles* and *Filius*.

"the fighting in Paris": An allusion to the Paris Commune, which began on March 18 and would be crushed a week after Rimbaud wrote this letter (see notes to "Jeanne-Marie's Hands").

"becoming a *seer*": The word *voyant* can also be translated as "visionary"; however, "seer," though less resonant in English, has become so established in literary culture that it seemed pointless to change it now. The notion itself is not original to Rimbaud; an almost identical phrase ("The true poet is a seer") had appeared in the progressive magazine *Le Mouvement* in 1862, in an article by Henri du Cleuziou, who ascribed it to the German Romantics.

"I is an Other": This pronouncement, one of the most quoted in all of French literature, is often translated "I is somebody else." But Rimbaud's visionary is not only other people but other *things* as well—the "copper [that] wakes up as a clarion," as he wrote to Demeny two days later—so I've preferred this slightly less anthropocentric, and syntactically closer, version. See Baudelaire's statement in *Artificial Paradises*, a key reference for Rimbaud's disordering, that when intoxicated, our "contemplation of external objects makes us forget our own existence," and our "I" becomes "Other."

"Tortured Heart": For the various titles Rimbaud gave this poem, see the note to "Tortured Heart."

TO PAUL DEMENY, MAY 15, 1871

This second, more extensive "Seer letter" gives a much fuller development of Rimbaud's thoughts about the uses, mission, and demands of poetry, suggesting that he had spent the two days between his letter to Izambard and this one ruminating what he might initially have dashed off as a matter of pique, and turning it into a veritable manifesto. The ellipses between brackets indicate places where Rimbaud inserted poems, specifically "Chant de guerre parisien" (Parisian War Cry), a long poem inspired by the bombardments of the Paris suburbs during the Commune; "Mes petites amoureuses" (My Little Lovelies), a crassly misogynistic diatribe against real or imagined former girlfriends; and "a pious hymn," the anticlerical "Accroupissements" (Squattings).

"Hugo's Comprachicos": A Spanish neologism meaning "child-buyers." In Victor Hugo's novel *The Man Who Laughs*, the Comprachicos mutilate the kidnapped hero in childhood and give him his eternal rictus. As an aside, Conrad Veidt, in the film adaptation of *The Man Who Laughs*, was the model for Batman's perpetual antagonist the Joker.

"long, massive, and reasoned *disordering*": The other common translation for this, "derangement," strikes me as too chaotic. The French *dérangement* suggests disruption, dysfunction, something "out of order" in both senses of the term. As many have noted, the addition in this second letter of the word "reasoned" (more appropriately active than the other frequent translation, "rational") makes clear that this was no surrender to madness but rather a clear-eyed, controlled experiment: making yourself a seer is a process. By nature a scientist and explorer as well as a poet, Rimbaud was rarely one to let his emotions run away with him.

"Rollesque declamation": Rimbaud's target is Alfred de Musset's hugely popular poem *Rolla*, about the ruinous passion of a young bourgeois for a courtesan. In 1878, the painter Henri Gervex would have a succès de scandale with his painting based on the story.

TO PAUL DEMENY, JUNE 10, 1871

The letter begins with transcriptions of "Seven-Year-Old Poets" and another anticlerical poem, "Les Pauvres à l'église" (Poor People in Church).

"Heart of a Clown": As in the letter to Izambard of May 13, the poem here bears a draft title.

"burn *all the poems*": As noted above, Rimbaud stayed in Douai twice in the fall of 1870. The twenty-two poems he was "dumb enough" to leave with Demeny—the so-called "Demeny collection" or "Douai dossier"—were most of the known verses he had written between March and October of that year. Needless to say, Demeny did not heed this request.

TO THÉODORE DE BANVILLE, AUGUST 15, 1871

As in his earlier letter to Banville, Rimbaud exaggerates his age by more than a year. The poem that prefaces the letter is a long piece entitled "Ce qu'on dit au poète à propos de fleurs" (What to Tell a Poet About Flowers), which subtly satirizes Parnassian poetry, including the addressee's. Several scholars have also pointed out that the self-deprecating nickname "Alcide Bava" (roughly, "Acid Drool") is not dissimilar in sound to "Banville." No doubt recognizing that he'd get nowhere with Banville, Rimbaud made his first outreach to Paul Verlaine, a more promising contact, the following month.

TO PAUL DEMENY, AUGUST 28, 1871

This familiar litany of complaints about his mother and his lot is Rimbaud's last known letter to Demeny, shortly before his definitive escape to Paris.

"the *Family Buffon*": *Le Buffon des familles*, subtitled "History and Description of Animals," was one of many popularizations by Nicolas-Auguste Dubois (who made a veritable industry of it) of works by the eighteenth-century naturalist Georges-Louis Leclerc, Comte de Buffon.

TO PAUL VERLAINE [FRAGMENTS], [SEPTEMBER 1871]

This letter to Verlaine was preceded by at least two others in the same month, both lost, that mixed flattery for the older poet's work with copies of Rimbaud's recent poems, among them "Tortured Heart," "My Little Lovelies," and "Paris Repopulated." The snippets given here of this and the following entry are all that remain of these two subsequent letters, preserved in memoirs by Verlaine and his ex-wife, Mathilde. (The originals were apparently destroyed during or after Mathilde's separation from her husband, possibly by her father.) Verlaine's oft-quoted reply to these solicitations was, "Come, dear great soul, we're calling you, we're waiting for you"— an invitation that Rimbaud wasted no time in accepting.

"Zanetto": The wandering minstrel in François Coppée's play *Le Passant*. The role of Zanetto, a fetching youth, was played by Sarah Bernhardt in drag; in writing to Verlaine, Rimbaud knew his audience.

TO PAUL VERLAINE [FRAGMENTS], [APRIL 1872]

Jump-cut from initial overtures to the end of the first act of a tumultuous relationship. By the spring of 1872, Rimbaud had been welcomed by and had alienated virtually the entire group of bohemian poets around Verlaine, whose marriage and reputation were buckling under the strain of the two men's relationship. A gossip column the previous fall by one of their circle, Edmond Lepelletier, had described Verlaine at the theater with "a charming young lady, Mlle Rimbaut" on his arm, which had resulted in Rimbaud coming after Lepelletier with a steak knife. Many others in the group had quickly decided that, genius or not, the disruptive kid ("that troublesome brat," Rimbaud said of himself; or, in someone else's estimation, "a vile, vicious, disgusting, smutty little schoolboy") was not worth the bother. Verlaine, pressed by his wife to get rid of Rimbaud after several episodes of aggravated spousal abuse, finally ceded to family pressure and sent Rimbaud home to his family in early March (see notes to "Shame" and "Memory"). Rimbaud's irritation at his lover's betrayal is clear in the surviving passages of the present letter. In any case, peace in the Verlaine household was short-lived, as a note from Verlaine to Rimbaud that same April hints at plans for a trip the two men would take together, and Rimbaud is known to have returned to Paris, and the havoc, by early May.

This sardonic account of Rimbaud's daily routine in Paris ("*Par-merde*") was written against the backdrop of an increasingly tense relationship with Verlaine, whose violent abuses toward his wife and infant son had grown worse as he waffled between bourgeois security and the walk on the wild side represented by his young lover. The following month, Rimbaud would drag Verlaine to Brussels, disrupting a final attempt at marital reconciliation, and by September the two men were living in London.

Rimbaud's correspondent Delahaye had been a friend since early adolescence, and the two would continue to see each other sporadically until Rimbaud's departure for Africa. Although this is the first surviving letter between them, many details of Rimbaud's early life come to us via Delahaye, who wrote memoirs not only of Rimbaud but also of Verlaine and Germain Nouveau. A talented caricaturist, Delahaye produced a number of affectionately satirical drawings of his friend in various settings. For the next three years, he would be a frequent sounding board for Rimbaud's reports and musings.

"Carolopolishit": A play on "Carolopolis," that is, Charleville.

TO ERNEST DELAHAYE, MAY 1873

There are apparently no surviving letters from Rimbaud between the last one of "Junphe 72" and this one, nearly a year later—and therefore, no account by him of his life in London with Verlaine over the winter, during which time he likely began drafting the prose poems of *Illuminations*, nor of his six-week return to Charleville in December 1872. What is known is that Rimbaud and Verlaine left London in early April 1873, and Rimbaud took refuge at the family farm in the "sorry shithole" of Roche (misspelled "Roches"), where he worked on *A Season in Hell*. This was his first visit to the property. By the end of the month, he was back with Verlaine, first in Belgium, then again in London—the final act in the melodrama that would soon culminate in Verlaine shooting Rimbaud.

"Laïtou": What Rimbaud meant by this word has been mystifying scholars since the letter was first published in 1914. A marginal doodle showing a clutch of houses is captioned "Laitou, My Village." It might be worth noting that the expression "Tra-la-*la-itou*" is a common indication of yodeling, akin to the English "Yodelay-hee-hoo."

"O my mother!": The referenced watercolor, a self-portrait of Rimbaud hiking through the woods, also includes the lines "o nature o my sister!" (spoken by a local yokel) and "o nature o my aunt" (spoken by a goose).

"the *Nôress*": The Charleville newspaper *Le Nord-Est*, where Rimbaud had once worked.

"My fate depends on this book": *A Season in Hell*, earlier referred to as the "*Pagan Book*, or *Negro Book*."

TO PAUL VERLAINE, [JULY 4, 1873]

Toward the end of May, Rimbaud and Verlaine took a lodging at 8 Great College Street in Camden Town (today Royal College Street), living on occasional allowances from Verlaine's mother. Newspaper want ads from June show that they also tried to find work giving French lessons, to little avail, and their renewed proximity and penurious living conditions soon led to frequent spats (see "Vagabonds" and note). On July 3, in a famous incident, Rimbaud shouted through the window at Verlaine that he "looked like a cunt," at which Verlaine stalked off to the docks and hopped a departing steamer to Antwerp. Rimbaud, left on his own, sent this plea the following day, a jumble of teary mea culpas and possible separation trauma (did Verlaine's departure revive memories of Captain Rimbaud's abandonment?), with no doubt a portion of self-interested manipulation.

TO PAUL VERLAINE, [JULY 5, 1873]

On July 3, while "at sea," Verlaine sent Rimbaud a "very urgent" letter arguing that "this violent life full of meaningless *scenes* due to your whims was more than I could fucking take." In the same breath, he both threatened suicide and mentioned having asked his wife to meet him in Brussels—prompting this rather more acerbic response from Rimbaud. (A third letter, dated July 7, tries to dissuade Verlaine from returning to London and lists some items of his that Rimbaud had sold off.) Ultimately, it wasn't Mathilde who showed up in Brussels but Rimbaud, who arrived on July 8. Two days later, as he attempted to leave for Paris, Verlaine shot him in the wrist, as detailed in Rimbaud's police deposition that same evening.

STATEMENT TO THE POLICE COMMISSIONER, BRUSSELS, JULY 10, 1873

This is the first of two depositions Rimbaud made to the Brussels legal system (the second, dated July 12 while he was being treated at Saint-Jean Hospital for an infection of his wound, is a much longer account of the same events). Although he ultimately declined to press charges, and although he corroborated Verlaine's claim of drunkenness at the time of the shooting, the court—having first lengthily examined Verlaine's anus for signs of sodomy—sentenced Verlaine to two years in prison, where to his former lover's disgust he underwent a religious conversion. Rimbaud left Saint-Jean on July 20 and went to recuperate in Roche, where he completed *A Season in Hell*.

TO JULES ANDRIEU, APRIL 16, 1874

First discovered in 2018 and, as of this writing, not yet included in any volumes of Rimbaud's work or translated into English, this letter was found in the Andrieu family archives and first appeared in a biography of Andrieu by his great-grandson Alain Rochereau, *C'était Jules: Jules Louis Andrieu (1838–1884), Un homme de son temps* (free download at http://renaissance.carnot.pagesperso-orange.fr/ Andrieu/index.html). A full account of the discovery, by Frédéric Thomas, was published by one of the main journals of Rimbaud studies, *Parade Sauvage* ("Découverte d'une lettre d'Arthur Rimbaud," September 2018, https://sites.dartmouth.edu/paradesauvage/ decouverte-dune-lettre-de-rimbaud-frederic-thomas/#_ftnref2), with a further "clarification" by Rochereau ("L'Histoire Splendide, ou La Splendide histoire d'une succession ordinaire," February 24, 2019, https://sites.dartmouth.edu/paradesauvage/alain-rochereau-la-splendide-histoire-dune-succession-ordinaire-sur-la-lettre-du-16-avril-1874/). *Parade Sauvage* has also made available a facsimile and transcription of the letter at https://sites.dartmouth.edu/pa-radesauvage/fac-simile-de-la-lettre-du-16-avril-1874-arthur-rim-baud-a-jules-andrieu/. While the document's authenticity has not been indisputably verified, many of the leading Rimbaud scholars have accepted it as genuine and, with these reservations in mind, I judged it worth including here.

A journalist, poet, historian, and polymath, Jules Andrieu was a prominent member of the radical community living in exile in London after the fall of the Paris Commune, and one of Verlaine's and Rimbaud's closest contacts as of their first stay in England. Rimbaud mentions him anxiously in his letter of July 7, 1873, to Verlaine, who was already proposing an about-face to London after their blowup: "You have no idea how badly you'd be received by everyone! And the looks I'd get from Andrieu and the others, if they saw me with you again."

As for the project outlined in the present letter, Delahaye in his 1923 memoir of Rimbaud recalled his friend telling him "of a new project—that brings him back to the prose poems he tried out the year before, wants to make something grander, livelier, more visual than Michelet, that great painter of crowds and collective actions, has found a title for it: *Magnificent History*, starting with a series he's calling *Photographs of Times Past*." Granted, none of this in itself is proof positive.

Assuming it is genuine, this letter is the only correspondence we have from Rimbaud from the year 1874; otherwise, a gap stretches between the July 7 dispatch to Verlaine mentioned above, just before their ill-fated reunion in Brussels, and the letter to Delahaye from March 1875.

What we do know is that, following the publication of *A Season in Hell* in October 1873 and its disappointing reception in Paris, Rimbaud returned to London in March 1874 in the company of his recent acquaintance and fellow poet Germain Nouveau. In early April, both men took out memberships to the British Museum library, where Rimbaud worked on the poems of *Illuminations* (several of which were copied over by Nouveau) and read widely, possibly with the "Splendid History" project in mind. Nouveau returned to France later that spring, and in early July, Rimbaud's mother and sister (both named Vitalie) visited Arthur in London; a letter of July 7, 1874, from the younger Vitalie to her sister Isabelle excitedly describes all the sites her brother has taken them to see. Having made various attempts to find work as either a French tutor or a traveling companion, Rimbaud left London in late July for other parts of England (possibly Scarborough and Reading), before repatriating to Charleville at the end of the year.

"the earliest (*latest*)": The word "latest," underlined and in English, is Rimbaud's faulty translation of "*le plus ancien*," which in fact means "oldest" or "earliest."

TO ERNEST DELAHAYE, FEBRUARY [*sic* FOR MARCH] 5, 1875

For several months in the spring of 1875, Rimbaud lived in Germany, "blowing through" his study of the language, supporting himself on meager earnings from French lessons and a monthly allowance from his mother. The described reunion with Verlaine, then *fresh out* of prison, has sometimes been mythologized as ending with a final, *brutal* beating in the Black Forest. While this was indeed the last time the two would meet, the affair seems in reality to have concluded not with a pugilistic bang but with a sexual whimper. It was also during this visit that Rimbaud entrusted Verlaine with the prose poems that would make up *Illuminations*, with instructions to turn them over to Nouveau for publication (see the note to *Illuminations*). The manuscript of the letter clearly says February 5, but the postmark on the envelope (March 6) indicates that this was almost certainly an oversight.

"week left at Wagner": Most commentators read this as a reference to Rimbaud's address—there is a Wagnerstrasse in Stuttgart—but Graham Robb, based on Rimbaud's marginal doodle of a hanged man with the heading "WAGNER VERDAMMT IN EWIGKEIT!" ("Wagner damned for all eternity!"), posits that Wagner, a policeman residing at 137 Neckarstrasse, was the poet's landlord. If so, both Rimbaud's comment and his doodle suggest that there was no love lost between them—and in fact, shortly after this, he did indeed find "a pleasant room" in a family boardinghouse on Marienstrasse.

"all that money paying for hate": Perhaps a reference to his landlord, but possibly also a commentary on the general attitude in Germany toward Frenchmen (especially young, impecunious ones) in the years following France's defeat. In late April, Rimbaud left for Italy.

TO HIS FAMILY, MARCH 17, 1875

This is the first surviving letter from Rimbaud to his family, which after 1878 would compose the bulk of his correspondence and provide much of what we know of his life in Africa. Five years before he embarked on his career as a trader, this account (clearly addressed to his mother) already shows the dry practicality, penny-pinching, and general distrust that would strongly mark the letters of his final decade.

"Greetings to the army": Rimbaud's older brother Frédéric, then in the service. The reference to his sister Vitalie in the next sentence is poignant, as Vitalie would die nine months later. Funeral-goers noted that, seemingly overnight, Rimbaud had changed from the "plump, fresh, baby-faced" boy of Verlaine's description to a young man of sober mien and sunken cheeks—who, moreover, had shaved his skull, perhaps as a sign of mourning, or because he suspected his thick hair was the cause of frequent headaches.

TO ERNEST DELAHAYE, OCTOBER 14, 1875

The two fragmentary poems included in this letter are Rimbaud's last known verse poems—such as they are—and, with two exceptions over the next ten years, his last letter to Delahaye. As with the letter from March, it drips with scorn over Verlaine's ("Loyola's") religious conversion, especially since Verlaine was then petitioning Rimbaud to follow suit. The inquiries about a science degree might be seen as the prelude to five peripatetic years, during which Rimbaud would travel extensively and try out a wide variety of occupations before embarking in March 1880 for Alexandria and the next phase of his life.